THE REACTIONARIES

John Harrison, born in 1937, is a graduate of Sheffield University, where he won the Moore Smith English Prize. At present, he is Lecturer in English at Bradford University.

THE REACTIONARIES

YEATS · LEWIS · POUND
ELIOT · LAWRENCE

A Study of the Anti-Democratic Intelligentsia

by

JOHN R. HARRISON

Introduction by
WILLIAM EMPSON

SCHOCKEN BOOKS
NEW YORK

Published in the U.S.A. in 1967
by Schocken Books Inc.
67 Park Avenue, New York, N.Y. 10016

Copyright © John R. Harrison, 1966

Library of Congress Catalog Card No. 67-10648

Printed in Great Britain

To the memory of
my Mother

"Convinced that the strength of the State depends on authority, they defend autocratic systems, arbitrary government, the reason of state, the religions which teach blind submission to authority, and they cannot sufficiently denounce all institutions based on liberty and discussion. This denunciation of liberalism, notably by the vast majority of contemporary men of letters, will be one of the things in this age most astonishing to history."

JULIEN BENDA

CONTENTS

INTRODUCTION

by William Empson

"OH, IT'S A wild life in the Near West, between one revelation and another", said Wyndham Lewis, describing the intellectual scene around him as a fun fair; that was in *Time and Western Man* (1928), and I felt the exhilaration of it, even then. Now that everything is so dismal we should look back with reverence on that great age of poets and fundamental thinkers, who were so ready to consider heroic remedies. Perhaps their gloomy prophecies have simply come true. But may it not be that their curses are still operating, or their confusions adding to the fog, in some preventable way? Mr. Harrison feels that the political scandal of their weakness for Fascism is what most needs to be faced; and the great merit of his book is to present the evidence about that aspect of them coolly, with justice and understanding.

It is well worth doing, but one may doubt whether that question is the central one; and Mr. Harrison himself judges in terms of breadth of sympathy rather than political technique. An early stage in the revolt against Parliamentary democracy can be seen in the comic novels of Belloc, written around 1910, largely inspired by the Marconi Scandal. Anti-semitism is already prominent, perhaps mainly as a device for smearing capitalists. Parliament is attacked as a pretence behind which an oligarchy of capital rules as it chooses; being a Distributist, Belloc is putting forward a mild form of Anarchism. His objections to the existing system are practically those of a Communist, and the split between Communism and Anarchism strikes him as fairly recent. His own sentiments are presented as vigorously democratic; the joke of the story is regularly that the voting system is used to cheat the voter. One needs to realise that these squibs sold very widely, and were a welcome expression of what honest men felt needed saying. Looking back, the line of talk seems plainly dangerous; a modern type of state needs a secret ballot and a broad electorate more than a previous one did, instead of having grown out of the need as Belloc somehow suggests; precisely because it is otherwise too strong, too convenient for a vested interest or a mad dictator. But that the electorate are liable to be deluded we ought not to deny; nor even that a patriot (whether under a fossilised old constitution or a rawly new one) may sometimes rightly thrust aside a technicality to meet an urgent need. At any rate, for a poet to think so is not proof of a bad heart. I cannot help feeling that Lewis was tiresomely silly to be taken in by Hitler, but by the end of the war he was almost willing to say that himself; and maybe if Yeats had lived another ten years we would be thinking of him as rather like Smuts.

The cult of Unnaturalism, I think, is the real trouble with the whole school, and it is still very much with us, at any rate in academic literary criticism. Almost anyone who writes in literary journals about these great Reactionaries would agree that they have had a good intellectual effect, for example, in making people deny that man is the measure of all things, or deny that he should aim at the greatest happiness of the greatest number. There are logical fallacies here, and one of them may be observed in the Sammael of Wyndham Lewis. It is pleasant to find the author expressing tender admiration, for the first time, in his old age, even though he knows it is for a devil. He assumes that his mind can realise that Sammael is greater than mankind, and that the minds of his readers can too; apparently he also meant them to realise that Sammael's policy was wrong. But at both stages they are to "measure" him. Very likely there are states of being too high for us to conceive, but then we had better not pretend to talk about them. The result of pretending, as one can see in T. E. Hulme as well as Lewis, is to imply: "Because all men are infinitely below God, some men ought to be free to bully others—the ones who are on God's side, like I am." As to Bentham, the idea of a false claim to calculate is no doubt offensive, but I have never found an opponent giving a telling example to prove that a man ought not to attempt the estimate which Bentham recommends. No doubt he should look after his immediate dependants unless prevented by a clear public duty; but a citizen must be ready to act on such a duty, or democracy becomes impossible. Most people who deny the Benthamite position do not realise, I think, how far a preference for transcendental modes of judgement can go: "I shot the President because God told me to, in a dream; it was not for me to calculate, after God had spoken." No state can carry on if it produces many of these citizens, whatever voting technique it has. The same line of talk sounds harmless about our preferences in literature and the arts, where sensibility needs to act ahead of theory; but to put a

premium on being capricious encourages bluff, and we have had
plenty of that.

James Joyce is the test case here, proving that an original and
rigorous author of the time could avoid these political and
religiose fashions. He remarked in a letter of 1934: "I am afraid
poor Mr. Hitler will soon have few friends in Europe apart from
my nephews, Masters W. Lewis and E. Pound", and in a more
fretful mood wondered why he was thought a member of their
clique. He was untempted, no doubt, because he had actually
escaped from a theocracy such as many of the authors examined
in this book were recommending. Lewis is the most theoretical
and fanatical, at least on this quasi-religious side; and I share
Mr. Harrison's disgust for his descriptions of the fiery tortures
imposed on mankind by Sammael. The books which ought to be
banned for obscenity are those which pander to sadism, but what
can you expect from a state religion whose symbol is a torture?
These descriptions in Lewis are no worse than the sermon which
made the young Joyce vomit in the *Portrait of the Artist*. Joyce
meant to satirise his teachers there; he expected life to be normal,
and found this abnormal; but he treated it as so usual that Mr.
Hugh Kenner could regard him as in favour of priests and
intending only some merry paradox. Lewis on the other hand,
judging from his *Letters* (1963), held a heretical view but did
not know it. He explains that "Sammael's idea was to combine
the best of the Human spirit with his Angel's nature", and on
August 29th, 1955, Mr. Hugh Kenner, who had written a book
on Lewis and was writing a further article, received a fuller
statement:

> "In the last book of all, the hero, Pullman, is at last in Divine
> Society. He favours the Divine. I favour the Divine. There is a
> gigantic debate, in which Sammael's purpose to combine the
> Human and the Angelic is discussed, the Celestial spokesman
> naturally attacking Sammael's big idea. . . . Pullman is, of course,
> an adherent of the Divine, not of the Diabolic."

Naturally the spokesman of God had to attack the idea, because
T. E. Hulme had said that one must keep the divine and the
human absolutely separate, boasting about seducing shopgirls
and then boasting about revelation. But the Athanasian Creed
calls the Incarnation "the taking of the manhood into God".
Lewis evidently felt he needed to hustle Mr. Kenner into accepting the orthodoxy of his lay-out, but I don't believe he realised

that his theology was completely upside-down. He did not live to write this final debate.

There is some hope of a lifting of this fog. The Cambridge theologians who took part in the symposium *Objections to Christian Belief* (1963), at any rate, reject the entire position of the aesthetes discussed by Mr. Harrison. The Dean of King's says that an ethic of sacrifice leads to a great deal of cruelty, and "we need fresh air blown upon these discussions by a sane ethic of utility"—thus recalling the Utilitarianism of Bentham. The Dean of St. John's says that:

> "nothing can be true *for any mind* except as that mind can be brought to perceive its reasonableness ... alleged revelation is of no use except as it enables man to attain his own insights."

So he rejects any dichotomy such as that of Hulme. I am afraid that nothing can purge Christianity of the Father who was satisfied by the Crucifixion; an impersonal Divine Ground, as in Aldous Huxley's *Perennial Philosophy*, is the only Supreme Being that can be worshipped without moral shame. But it is comforting to find the Divinity School at Cambridge nowadays talking with the clearheadedness and generosity of H. G. Wells, however much the English Literature School still regards the basic Christian tradition as enshrined in the textbooks of Unnaturalism, *Les Fleurs du Mal*, *A Rebours*, and *The Portrait of Dorian Gray*. I notice too that Mr. Harrison cannot help looking at his authors with a kind of social surprise, all the more because he is trying to be charitable. They have come to seem rather odd, in the eyes of the young, whether it is the fault of the modern world or not.

INTRODUCTORY

The Anti-Democratic Intelligentsia

THE ANTI-DEMOCRATIC INTELLIGENTSIA

I

THE TWENTIETH CENTURY has produced extreme forms of society and political philosophies. In Germany and Italy in the 1920s and thirties, a society was created which was authoritarian in the extreme, the antithesis of democratic society. It is unnecessary here to describe the fascist society created by the Nazis; the atrocities that were committed, and the fear and hatred they aroused, are common knowledge, although no less horrible for that. It is a strange and disturbing phenomenon, however, that five of the greatest literary figures of this century, Yeats, Lewis, Pound, Eliot and Lawrence, were attracted by Italian and German fascism before the Second World War; and in Pound's case, during and after the war. Why is it that great creative artists can totally reject a liberal, democratic, humanitarian society, and prefer a cruel, authoritarian, bellicose society? The question is important for the student of literature, for these writers' views are bound to affect their creative work, and unless the reader is himself lacking in human sympathy, his judgement of this work will be clouded. Literature cannot be judged simply on what the writer says, but neither can it be judged satisfactorily if we ignore what the writer says. The writer's views may, as in the case of Yeats, help to work some wonderful transformation in technique; but the reader's enjoyment is almost certainly reduced by his antipathy to the content of what he is reading. It might also be argued that the writer's achievement is lessened. Menon, referring to Yeats, writes, "I think a measure of the greatness of a writer is how significant his interpretation of the present is for future generations."[1] The conclusions which these five writers reached regarding authoritarianism are difficult to accept; so are their views on democracy and its effect on literature, which are even more important for us today.

Only since the end of the last century has there been any separation between the artist's activities and the study of society. The idea still persists to some extent that a man must choose between poetry, for example, and sociology; that he cannot pursue both. The common conception of the poet is still of a languid, "sensitive" person, who is baffled by the world of affairs and at a loss in any activity not connected with poetry. Any radio play or popular novel shows this, if it includes a poet. The image is that of Wilfred Desart, a fugitive from twentieth-century society, dying as a result of some unknown, and presumably "romantic", activity in Siam. This conception would have surprised the Romantic poets. Wordsworth wrote political pamphlets, Blake was tried for sedition, Coleridge and Shelley wrote social philosophy, and Byron died fighting for a political cause. The refusal to take notice of what a poet says about the society in which he lives is good neither for literature nor for criticism. To say that a poet ought not to meddle in politics, and that if he does we ought to ignore that part of his work, is bound to produce a one-sided view and likely to lead to misinterpretations of the poetry itself. In *Culture and Society*, Raymond Williams writes, "nearly all theoretical discussions of art since the Industrial Revolution have been crippled by the assumed opposition between art and the actual organisation of society, which is important as [a] historical phenomenon . . . but which can hardly be taken as an absolute".[2]

Professor Wind, in the 1960 Reith Lectures, says that it is important to the aesthetic appreciation of a work of art to know exactly what the artist means, what is his "message". He gives as an example Raphael's painting of the Renaissance metaphysical idea that any proposition in Plato can be found to have its counterpart in Aristotle, if we take into account the difference in mode of expression between Plato's poetic, imaginative language and Aristotle's more rational, scientific language. Professor Wind believes that a knowledge of the theory makes a difference to one's visual impression of the painting. The relationship of the forms is fully appreciated only if we know what the painting means. That is, aesthetic appreciation of a work of art is heightened by understanding of its intellectual content. Since the Industrial Revolution, much of the intellectual content of literature has been concerned with social problems. It is only possible, therefore, to appreciate this literature fully if we study what the writers have to say about politics and society.

Moreover, Yeats, Pound, Lewis, Lawrence and Eliot all saw themselves as leaders of society, and they put forward their recommendations as practical policies. It is in this light that their views should be examined, not as the mildly interesting or amusing ramblings of eccentric genius. This latter approach presupposes a rejection of the poet's social function. F. R. Leavis, for example, writes of Lawrence's social criticism, "[These conclusions] were Lawrence's and Lawrence was an artist of genius: that is why they are to be considered."[3] This presumably means that the conclusions are of no real importance in themselves, and that Leavis is discussing them only because he thinks Lawrence wrote good novels. Lawrence would not have been very pleased with this attitude to his work. Moreover, how on earth can anyone appreciate Lawrence's novels without taking his social criticism seriously? One has not only to understand Lawrence's ideas but to make some attempt to sympathise with them, before one can begin to appreciate a novel such as *The Rainbow*.

Much of what Lewis and Pound wrote about democracy and fascism is likely to arouse anger and contempt; but it is important to know why they rejected democracy and were attracted to fascism. It is easy to be wise after the event and say that these writers ought to have recognised the dangers of fascism. As I shall show later, the fascist system attracted a great number of European intellectuals; Chesterton, for example, was especially pro-Mussolini, as a Catholic and Distributist. It is useless to condemn these writers simply because they supported fascism, and because fascists were largely responsible for terrible atrocities and the Second World War. In that case, we must condemn Auden and Spender and their associates for supporting communism. The question whether or not Yeats, Eliot and Lawrence, for example, were fascists seems to me unimportant. People who writer letters to the *Times Literary Supplement* saying that Eliot said such and such a thing, *therefore* he is a fascist, *therefore* he is a bad man, are wasting their time. What is important is to find out why they held such views. This leads one to examine not only their social and political principles but their artistic principles. In the very close connection between those two sets of principles, and their very deep concern for the arts, lies the answer to this question.

George Orwell, in *Critical Essays* (1946), wrote, "The relationship between fascism and the literary intelligentsia badly needs investigating, and Yeats might well be the starting-point. He is best studied by someone like Mr. Menon ... who knows that a writer's political and religious beliefs are not excrescences to be laughed away, but something that will leave their mark even on the smallest detail of his work."[4] First, however, a certain amount of background needs to be filled in.

II

Nazism was made possible not only by the economic and political situation in Germany between the wars, but also by a long tradition of German thought and political action,[5] a tradition which made whatever ideology the Nazis professed acceptable to many people both inside and outside Germany, especially writers and intellectuals who were familiar with, and impressed by, German culture. A lot has been written about Nietzsche's contribution to this tradition; in fact it has sometimes been exaggerated.[6] It need only be noted here that his emphasis on aristocracy, power and war, and his rejection of happiness as the goal of mankind, belong to the main trend of German thought. He epitomises the anti-humanitarian, anti-democratic bias of the tradition and provides a direct contrast to the predominant thought of Western Europe, particularly Benthamite utilitarianism. Many earlier conservatives and reactionaries, Schlegel, Schleiermacher and Adam Müller, for example, revered a patriarchal order of society in which they looked to princely thrones and noble houses to provide a benevolent despotism. Fichte, who showed a romantic tendency to idealise the Middle Ages, a characteristic of much nineteenth-century and twentieth-century extreme conservative thought, advocated a rigidly planned economy in which all uncontrolled individual enterprise would be impossible. His was an embryonic national socialism.

The stress on the all-powerful state and on force as the chief instrument of the state has been traced as far back as Luther, and can be found in Hegel, Bismarck and the tradition of Machtstaat. It was Hegel and his followers who developed the concept that the state is the divine will which is not only present in the world but determines its form and organisation. Hegel argued that it was wrong to stand by the form of religion in opposition to the state, that in practice there must be a transfer of authority from the divine to the secular in the form of the state. He summed up his political teaching in this way: "We must hence honour the state as the divine upon earth."[7] Man must worship the state and not judge its actions by any recognised standard of morality. The vocation of the Germanic peoples was to provide "bearers of the Christian principle". What he meant by "the Christian principle" is clarified by the following statement: "Frederick comprehended the protestant principle from the temporal side and, while discountenancing the religious controversies ... he possessed the consciousness of universality which constitutes the uttermost depth of the spirit and the self-conscious power of thought." In other words, he adapted the principles of religious authoritarianism to politics, and attached as little importance to the individual when set against the state as an authoritarian church does when its authority is challenged : "Special attention must be devoted to Frederick in that he has grasped intellectually the general purpose of the state, and that he was the first among the rulers who adhered to the general in the state, and did not allow the particular further validity if it was opposed to the purpose of the state."

Hegel's stress on the state corresponded to Prussian tradition, but he also lent support to the idea that whatever is is right by his identification of the real with the rational, with world-historical right. This again is a parallel with the religious attitude that whatever is is right because it must be God's will, manifested in Victorian England in the optimistic belief that God's in his Heaven, all's right with the world. Hegel's doctrine almost ranked as the official doctrine of the German intelligentsia. It was taken up by Haller, who rejected the contractual basis of the power of rulers, and restated the doctrine of divine right and applied it to the state. Even Ranke, who refused to allow his historical method to be affected by Hegelianism or any form of theoretical folk historicism, echoes Hegel in implying that state authority derives from, and is a particular form of, religious authority. In his *Political Conversation* between Carl, who maintains that the state is no doctrine, and Friederich, who believes that the state has the force of a spiritual being, Carl is a state counsellor, a politician, while Friederich is a Benedictine monk.

Nationalism, which became increasingly dominant in nineteeth-century German thought, had its basis in Herder, who put forward the idea of the "Volk" as the basis of a hierarchic but classless national body. His was a cultural nationalism, however, and he warned against the extremes to which his folk theory could be carried. With Fichte, the Germans became *the* people, the "Urvolk", and cultural nationalism became dependent on political nationalism. Darwin's *Origin of Species*, with its doctrine of the survival of the fittest, gave impetus to the belief in the vigour of the folk in the power-political struggle, while Gobineau's *Essai sur l'inégalité des races humaines*, 1853–5, had an even greater influence in Germany, asserting that the last remnants of true life in a world of degenerating mankind were to be found only in the Aryan race, including the British. This racial doctrine found its practical expression in anti-semitism, a prejudice which was traditional in Germany, the Junker party erecting anti-semitism into a political principle. Gobineau's racial doctrine, which provided a spurious, pseudo-scientific basis for the prejudice against Jews, was reiterated by Wagner, Houston Stewart Chamberlain and Eugen Dühring. Nationalism and racialism, in conjunction with Prussian military tradition, resulted in the kind of idolatry of war found in Von Treitschke and Von Bernhardi, whose book, *Germany and the Next War*, published in 1911, had run into six editions by 1913.

The growth of Nazism coincided with an upsurge of neo-romanticism in the arts. The rallying of literary romantics to the cause of reaction in the early nineteenth century was perhaps more striking in Germany than anywhere else. Romantic poets like Arnim and Kleist harnessed romanticism to reaction in practical politics and were active supporters of the Prussian Junkers. Neo-romanticism was given an impetus by men like Rathenau, who detested the growth of mechanisation and equated it with arid intellectualism. This attitude was widespread not only in Germany but in other countries; it is obvious in the work of Yeats and Lawrence. Rathenau argued that people could no longer distinguish what was genuine from what was false because they did not feel, they only reasoned. It was necessary, therefore, to go back to the irrational springs of the true German spirit. Keyserling also scorned logic and rational thought and said that any sort of human advance would be achieved only through non-intellectual, irrational forces. He described fascism as a new aristocratic order which was emerging everywhere because the democratic idea had triumphed in the First World War. In the post-war years there was a trend towards the mystical and occult, and the growth of a powerful neo-romanticism which revived the theories of the older romanticists of the early nineteenth century and refashioned them for an attack on rationalist and liberal humanitarian democracy.

A specific link between the two periods is provided by Thomas Mann, who described himself as fighting a rearguard action in the grand manner, the last of a romantic German middle-class outlook. He stressed the part played by nineteenth-century German writers in creating the *Weltanschauung* of twentieth-century Germany, and gave a warning to those whose attitude

towards Germany was determined largely by admiration for
German culture: "The sculptors and educators of German
humanity, Luther, Goethe, Schopenhauer, Nietzsche, George and
the like were no democrats—oh, no. If people abroad honour
them, let them reflect upon what they are doing. It was they
who created the idea of Kultur with a big K, who formed the
centre of power of the German war-ideology."[8] His belief that
the cultural discipline of the aristocratic community contrasted
favourably with the social sluggishness of democratic society was
shared by many others. Moeller van den Bruck, for example,
said that the "lurch to the right" came from a realisation that life
should consist in cohesion, not disintegration, identified, of
course, with authoritarianism and democracy respectively.

Mann thought the "superficial democratisation" of Germany,
the result of defeat in 1918, was bitter to the German people not
because it involved ruin or a fall from power, but because it was
the destruction of German belief and ideals, the collapse of
ideology, and particularly of the centre of power of this ideology,
the idea of culture. Spengler shared his belief. He hated the
"dirty revolution" of 1918 from the first day, but also thought
the constitution of the Weimar Republic was accidentally the
most advanced of the age, because in a naïve way it made possible a dictatorship of the party machines. He wanted what he
called a new spirit of caesarism and said the constitution embodied the caesarism of organisations. With a few small altera-
tions it would give unlimited power to individuals. Spengler, with
his praise of irrationalism, obedience to the state, and strict discipline, was extremely influential, and not only in his own country.
The writings of men like Spengler, Junger and van den Bruck
attracted to Nazism, when it appeared, intelligent, cultured
people who otherwise would never have suppported it.[9] Many
German university professors in the 1920s also prepared people's
minds for the Nazis, and swallowed Nazism's absurdest theories.
The faculties of social science and law were particularly anti-
liberal and anti-democratic, preaching nationalism and anti-
semitism, prejudices which were spread by those who became
judges, administrative officials and lawyers. The theory of the
anti-liberal, total state was developed by academics like Smend
in Berlin, Carl Schmitt in Bonn, Othmar Spann and Werner
Sombart. Hans Freyer and Eduard Spranger explained how the
"charismatic Führer" emerges as an emanation from the will of

the people, and Gerhart Hauptmann was intoxicated by his meeting with Hitler.

This politico-literary tradition was particularly influential among the educated classes. It may not have caused the development of the conservative-reactionary state culminating in the Third Reich, but it does partially account for the "lurch to the right" among many of the intelligentsia of Europe between the wars, particularly when it is seen as only one current in a much wider stream of thought.

III

Many elements of this political outlook were only variations of general ideas which were influencing Europe as a whole. Montesquieu and Burke were forerunners of the historical view of politics, and the rise of romanticism was an international phenomenon. Nationalism was a widespread force, the cult of Nordic and Teutonic superiority being known in Victorian England as well as in Bismarck's Germany. Great Britain led the way in imperialism and talked of the white man's burden while the Germans were stressing Nordic superiority and Germany's supernational mission. As I shall show later, the syndicalist Sorel and the Action Française challenged liberal democracy, while French thinkers from de Maistre to Bergson challenged the rule of reason. In Italy, as elsewhere, the revival of nationalism was in large measure a literary phenomenon.[10] Its spokesman was Gabriele D'Annunzio who was extolling the model of imperial Venice at the time when Kipling was writing about the mission of imperial Britain. The fact that he was not a systematic thinker made him the more suitable as the representative of a new nationalism which was a confusion of vague, undigested yearnings. On behalf of the Italian fascists, De Vecchi organised research to discover eminent forerunners of fascism. They went as far back as Julius Caesar; Dante was upheld as a premature nationalist, and Mussolini wrote a short disquisition on Machiavelli's *The Prince* for his honorary doctoral degree at Bologna. There was, however, a genuine Hegelian influence in Italy, and the idea that true liberty can exist only in a strong state made it possible for a man like Giovanni Gentile to rationalise his acceptance of fascism.

English Methodism, even more clearly than German pietism, was a revolt against the deism, scepticism and democratic thought of the eighteenth century. It created a highly emotion-alised outlook and a preoccupation with problems of personal salvation, stressing the need to preserve order in society and for loyalty to public authorities. The Statutes of the Wesleyan Body of 1792 demanded loyalty and obedience to the government, and Wesley himself was an extreme conservative and opposed to democracy. By supporting the existing social and political powers and diverting attention from the problems of contemporary society to those of personal salvation, Methodism not only held up reform but created an intellectual opposition to democratic ideas.

In some ways romanticism as a current of opinion is com-parable to pietism and Methodism.[11] Once the current of the French Revolution had begun to flow, few of the romantic writers who experienced the Revolution were not converted to reaction. Chateaubriand, who had been deeply influenced by the writers of the Enlightenment, became one of the founders of the aesthetic, neo-medieval Catholicism which attracted many devout people in the nineteenth century. Joseph de Maistre and de Bonald, advocates of absolute order and authority, became the theorists of this movement, and before 1830 Lamartine and Hugo followed Chateaubriand in their political and religious beliefs. Restoration France, disgusted with the timid foreign policy of the Bourbons after the position France had held during the Revolution, readily accepted Herder's concept of "nation" which spread across Europe in the early nineteenth century. Quinet's translation of Herder had an important effect on Michelet, one of the most influential French historical writers of the nineteenth century. Like Fichte, Michelet used Herder's ideas to justify a proud and intolerant sense of racial superiority.

English romantic writers never succumbed to the creed of political reaction as completely as did the French and Germans, although Scott's novels provided a romantic view of the past, an imaginative medieval setting, and Wordsworth and Southey, eager supporters of the French Revolution at the start, later changed their minds. Realising that the doctrines of the Enlight-enment had not made men good, they assumed that they had made men evil, and rejected them. Later romantics embraced the liberal cause. Shelley enshrined the old Jacobin doctrines in *Prometheus Unbound*, and Byron preached a gospel of boundless liberty and hatred of all existing governments. The forces of classicism and later romanticism clashed most violently in France, as classicism had there reached its highest pitch. This conflict had political overtones. Young writers gradually identified their romantic literary aspirations with the political ideas of democracy —Hugo said that romanticism was liberalism in literature. The romantic attitude which existed throughout Europe was strongly nationalistic, and although it was initially a cultural nationalism, it helped to create an atmosphere favourable to the development of an exaggerated political nationalism which was characteristic of the later nineteenth century, and which became so much a part of political reaction.

In Britain the growth of democracy proceeded relatively smoothly, when compared with the continual bitter crises which occurred on the Continent. Nevertheless, there existed a powerful anti-democratic trend of thought, and not only among those with a vested interest in reaction, but among the best writers and thinkers. Burke, deeply influenced by the French Revolution, was appalled by the prospect of a proletariat growing in numbers and increasing in consciousness and power, and put forward the idea of the state as the necessary agent of human perfection. His thinking had a profound influence not only in Britain but on the Continent.[12] Carlyle also was an ardent opponent of democracy, and has been described as a forerunner of fascism. He adopted Goethe's essentially aesthetic attitude of withdrawal from an increasingly scientific and industrial age. It should be remembered that Goethe was seventy-five years of age when he and Carlyle began to correspond, and that Goethe had lived for most of his life in a small town, had never seen London or Paris, and had little knowledge of, or interest in, the complexities of the Victorian era.[13] Although Carlyle was very much concerned with the contemporary scene, his attitude to it was bound to be retrospective. In his later work Carlyle's leading principle is that of the "hero", the strong leader possessed of personal power. In 1853 he published *The History of Frederick II of Prussia* in which he admired Frederick as the ideal kind of hero. He deplored the emptiness of the social and personal relationships of his time, which were based, he said, almost solely on cash payment. He wanted to replace them with a relationship based on the recognition of personal power in the individual.[14]

Critics like Carlyle and Ruskin were forced to look to the past to find the ordered, stable society they wanted, which accounts for their "medievalism". This kind of thinking about an organic society resulted, in Ruskin's work, in the idea of the paternal state, with a rigid class structure based on the different functions of individuals. This tradition acquired a future reference rather than a backward look with Morris and the rise of socialism, but particularly in the case of Ruskin, the social criticism would not have taken the form it did if it had not arisen from his views about art. His art criticism and his social criticism are closely related because they are applications in different directions of the same principles. Ruskin believed that good art is impossible in a corrupt society, and his social criticism is directed towards the cause of great art. Ruskin's attitude, reinforced by the aesthetic movement in the nineties, has been reflected in the social criticism of many twentieth-century writers, particularly Yeats, Lewis, Pound and Eliot.

IV

The aesthetic movement, ostensibly the least political of all literary "movements", nevertheless had a profound effect on the political beliefs of many writers and artists. Shelley, although a passionate democrat, stressed the autonomy of the artist and of poetry in particular; public opinion was no longer to be the ultimate criterion of literary worth. Poets in the early nineteenth century tended to retire to a private world where they cultivated the belief in their superiority to practical life. This belief in the superiority of the artist, in the autonomy of his work, together with an idealisation of the past, became the accepted belief of a literary movement which spread throughout Europe. Inevitably it implied a dislike of the growth and spread of democracy, socialism and science. Contempt for the taste and judgement of the public can easily become contempt for the public itself, particularly when that public is becoming more numerous and self-assertive. Baudelaire, for instance, actively disliked democracy, and the aristocratic aestheticism of German writers like Goethe, Kant and Schiller helped to strengthen anti-democratic trends. The German aesthetic movement around Stefan George, which was part of a general reaction to the industrialisation and mechanisation of life, came later, but it illustrates the connection between literary aestheticism and political reaction. It was Oscar Wilde who developed the idea that the beautiful contains a higher morality in itself, thus enabling the creative artist to assert his own moral superiority. When the aesthete enters the sphere of politics, he tends, as did Barrès, to reject democracy and prefer a hierarchic system where the opinion and judgement

of the mass should have no effect on the rulers, whom, by virtue
of their moral superiority, he would prefer to be creative artists.
Thus is produced the concept of the artist-hero in modern
politics.

One of the most important causes of anti-democratic feeling
among the intelligentsia has been the fear that democracy
destroys all cultural standards. William James in 1908 wrote,
"Democracy is on its trial and no one knows how it will stand
the ordeal. Fickleness and violence used to be, but are no longer,
the vices which they charge to democracy. What its critics now
affirm is that its preferences are inveterately for the inferior. . . .
Vulgarity enthroned and institutionalised, elbowing everything
superior from the highway; this, they tell us, is our irremedial
destiny." The critics of democracy believed that the privileged
aristocracies of old, despite their iniquities, did preserve a taste
for higher human quality and forms of refinement by their
traditions. Ortega y Gasset's *Revolt of the Masses* epitomises the
fear and hatred aroused by the developing mass society. This
attitude was widespread among the literary intelligentsia who
gave it its most articulate expression. In an essay entitled *The
Younger Generation*,[15] Henry James said he detected the influence of democratic ideals on the work of H. G. Wells, and
provided an early statement of the belief that political tendency
can directly affect literary style. James equated democracy with
formlessness in the novel. Form was to him of paramount
importance, particularly in controlling the kind of interest, the
choice of material, and the technique of presentation in the
novels he was discussing—what he called "slice of life" novels.
He thought that order must be imposed on these anarchic tendencies, which he believed resulted from the democratic principle
in politics, or there would be a continuing decline in literary and
artistic standards, a decline he had already detected. Fifteen
years later J. C. Powys was voicing the same view rather more
stridently. *The Meaning of Culture*, published in 1930, is an
extended diatribe against the destruction of cultural standards
occasioned by the spread of democracy : "outworn, misused, mis-
applied for so long, the aristocratic ideal is now quite dead. There
is no escape from machinery and modern inventions; no escape
from city vulgarity and money power, no escape from the
dictatorship of the uncultured."[16] The only solution for him was
to withdraw completely from the world : "An individual man or
woman, carrying to a comfortless job through clanging streets

the cheapest editions of some immortal book, can mount the stairs of his secret psychic watch-tower and think the whole antheap into invisibility." This indicates the problem which faced men like Powys, and also Yeats and the others; baffled by the complexity of the modern world, they could only withdraw, yearn for some idealised past, or adopt an anti-democratic political ideology. Powys and Yeats astonishingly looked forward to Spengler's prophecy of the destruction of modern civilisation by powerful warring leaders, producing chaos and out of this a great new "Platonic year".

v

A very powerful influence on the whole system of anti-democratic thought has been the development of the idea, and later the theory, of "élites".[17] The word itself was not widely used in social and political writing until the late nineteenth century in Europe, and the 1930s in Britain and America, when it was diffused through the sociological theories of élites, especially in the work of Vilfredo Pareto and Gaetano Mosca. The idea that the community should be ruled by a group of superior individuals is prominent in Plato and even more in the Brahminical caste-doctrines which regulated ancient Indian society. Many religious creeds have expressed the notion of an élite in terms of the "elect of God". The modern social and political conception of élites may perhaps be traced back to Saint-Simon's advocacy of the rule of scientists and industrialists. In the positivist philosophy of Comte, the élitist and authoritarian elements in Saint-Simon's thought were restored to prominence, allied with the ideas of de Bonald, and thus directly influenced the creators of the modern theory of élites, Mosca and Pareto. The concept of a political élite formed part of the political doctrine opposed to modern democracy, and even more to socialism. The nineteenth-century European doctrines of rule by an élite of superior individuals, Carlyle's hero and Nietzsche's superman, for example, as well as the more prosaic studies of Mosca, Pareto and Burckhardt, are attempts to revive ancient ideas of social hierarchy and erect obstacles to the spread of democratic ideas.

Pareto always emphasised the complete distinction between the governing élite and the masses, and attacked modern notions of democracy, humanitarianism, and progress, and this hostility was even more marked in the case of those, such as Carlyle and

Nietzsche, who presented social myths rather than scientific theories of politics. They saw democracy as a stage in the "revolt of the masses", leading inevitably to socialism or anarchy. Men like Mosca, Pareto, Weber and Michels tried to demolish what they called the optimistic and metaphysical methods which they saw as the basis of socialist thinking. They tried to show that a classless society is impossible since in every society there is, and must be, a minority which actually rules, and for the idea of a class that rules by virtue of economic or military power, they substituted the notion of an élite which rules because of the superior quality of its members. It has been suggested that the problem of political leadership was raised by sociologists in those countries which had not established a genuine bourgeois democracy, that is, in countries where feudal elements were still strong; for instance, Max Weber's concept of charisma in Germany, and Pareto's theory of élites in Italy.[18]

VI

Between 1885 and 1914 in France, apart from the republican positivist school of Renouvier and Littré, there were no major thinkers who did not react in some way against the revolutionary or democratic current stemming from the French Revolution. The most violent reaction came from Sorel, and from the movement known as the Action Française, especially Barrès and Maurras.[19] The need for a strong leader or a dictatorship, the stress on action, even purposeless action, the cult of energy, the concept of the élite, the denial of political equality, bitter antisemitism, even the idea of national socialism are all found in the works of these three. They illustrate, Sorel less than the others, the interconnection in France between politics and culture, the political importance of literature. It was an article by Barrès in *Le Figaro* in 1892, discussing the differences between poets supporting the classical French tradition and admirers of Tolstoy and Ibsen, that caused the transition from literary to political nationalism. Had it not been for his political preoccupations, Barrès might well have been a fin-de-siècle dilettante. His idea of active leadership was based on his image of Disraeli, whom he described as a poet, dandy and ambitious leader of men, an image which he tried to live up to himself, and on his notion of the romantic hero acquired in his childhood from Sir Walter Scott's novels. He and Maurras identified the growth of democratic ideas with developments in the arts, impressionism, naturalism and "all other forms of degenerate romanticism", and rejected them all. Maurras accepted de Bonald's idea of unity and continuity, shared de Maistre's belief in a political science and the need for a strong leader, and approved of Comte's positivism and his stress on social order.

Sorel, Barrès and Maurras all denied the assumptions underlying democracy, that political positions are occupied on the basis of competence or aptitude, that careers are open to talents and that these talents are widespread. They saw an élite as a reality of political life, and insisted that there was a minority naturally suited, and inevitably destined, to rule. Their view of the élite was more rigid and limited than Pareto's, being essentially an aristocratic one, and this concept of the outstanding individual, the "hero", when applied to politics tends to produce either a monarchy or a dictatorship. They believed that men are not equal, and therefore liberty must be the prerogative of the few, because to guarantee the liberty of each individual results in the servitude of all. They thought majority rule incompetent because it was the regime of those least qualified and least interested in national life, the most inert and the least human. Their movement was not merely a political opposition party, or a philosophical school to change ideas and manners, but a conspiracy to prepare a state of mind through which to destroy the then existing regime in France.

This attack on democracy was partly anti-semitic in motive. They insisted that the real rulers of a democracy were plutocrats, and that international finance, symbolised by the Rothschilds, was the worst social evil. As early as 1890, Barrès had anticipated the Nazis in asserting that the word Jew was only an adjective indicating monopolist and usurer, and he wanted Jews to be deprived of all political rights. The Dreyfus Affair, which caused the birth of the Action Française movement, was for Maurras the supreme example of Jewish dominance and treachery, and Republican incompetence. He was obsessed with this affair until the end of his life. On receiving his sentence in 1945, he shouted, "It is the revenge of Dreyfus."[20] Anti-semitism was widespread in France in the late nineteenth century; Drumont's anti-semitic *La France Juive* sold 100,000 copies within a year of publication in 1886, and a considerable number of aesthetes, left unemployed by the publishing crises at the end of the century, became anti-semites and joined the Action Française.

Maurras in particular stressed the distinction between romanticism and classicism, and developed the political reference of those terms. He attacked romanticism in politics as leading to liberalism and anarchy, democracy and Protestantism, and advocated the "classical" ideals of aristocracy and rigid discipline, hierarchy and Catholicism. Terms like "romanticism" and "classicism" are difficult, almost impossible, to define, and Maurras, like Hulme and Lewis after him, tended to describe as "romantic" anything he did not like, and to call what he did like "classical". He was the dominant figure in French neo-classicism and could claim writers like Hulme, Yeats, Pound, Lewis and Eliot among his intellectual disciples. His attitude was one of bewilderment before the problems of the modern world, in which the traditional authority of political groups, symbols or ideas, rules of form and style had lost its effect, destroyed by romanticism and democracy. The supporter of democracy believed in man's natural goodness, humanism, optimism, progress and challenge to external authority; against these the neo-classicists stressed the need for known and accepted rules, form in literature and authority in politics.

VII

The effect which Orwell believed a writer's political beliefs must have on even the smallest detail of his work has already been noted. In the same essay he speaks of a writer's "tendency", by which he means his political affinities, or the political philosophy which attracts him most. Yeats's "tendency", he says, was fascist, and he goes on : "No one has succeeded in tracing the connection between 'tendency' and literary style. Texture cannot seemingly be explained in sociological terms. But there must be some connection."[21] I shall attempt to show the relationship between the "tendency" of these five writers and their literary style, also their literary principles.

A look at the aesthetic and social criticism of T. E. Hulme will help to make this relation clear. It is likely that his was the seminal mind from which Lewis, Pound, Yeats and Eliot derived their ideas; at least, his thinking is typical of theirs. His reading was largely in German philosophy and art criticism, and he translated Sorel on violence. He welcomed the break-up of the humanist tradition which had existed since the Renaissance, and said all philosophies since the Renaissance were essentially the

same, in that they were what he called "satisfactory"—to someone, usually the writer himself—within the humanist tradition.
That is, philosophers formed a view of the world and mankind
which was as they wanted it to be, not as it is in reality. Hulme
said there are three facets of reality. First, the inorganic world of
physical science. Second, the organic world of biology, history
and their allied studies. Third, the world of ethics and religion.
The first and third are alike in that they are absolutes, while the
second is a muddy world where nothing is definite. The humanist
tradition places too much emphasis on the second and not enough
on the others. The distinction is the same as that he makes
between the two elements of philosophy: *Weltanschauung*,
which is the expression of an attitude to life, and pure philosophy, which he classifies with science and logic. Hulme holds
that *Weltanschauung* has nothing to do with true philosophy,
and that humanist philosophers are doing nothing more than
expressing their *Weltanschauung*. (Yet Hulme himself was only
expressing his attitude to life.)

The humanist's belief in the perfectibility of man is wrong, he
says, and the reason for this is a failure to recognise original sin.
Life is essentially tragic and futile, and the old analogy of the
wheel is correct; all thought and action repeats itself. He criticises Goethe's idea of human existence as a spiral, a concept
similar to that of "progress", which is a false principle, but one
which has replaced religion in the modern mind. He makes a
direct contrast between the humanistic attitude and what he calls
the religious attitude. The latter says that man cannot achieve
perfection even if he sometimes reaches it in particular actions.
Ethical values are not relative to human life, but absolute and
objective. Maurras made the passion of men to found or
strengthen the state an object of religious adoration; Julien
Benda called this the "divinising of politics", or the "secularising
of the divine". This latter description is more applicable to
Hulme, for whereas the two processes are similar, Maurras substituted the state for God as an object of religious adoration,
while Hulme saw God as the ultimate object of worship, but
advocated that strict religious discipline and obedience to God
should have their counterpart in political discipline and obedience to the state. Man can only accomplish anything by discipline,
ethical and political. The humanist belief, on the other hand, is that
human life is the source and measure of all values, and that what
we should aim at is the spontaneous growth of the personality.

This, he says, distorts the nature of ethical values by deriving them from subjective things, for example, human desires and feelings. Such an attitude, Hulme thinks, leads to the conception of the "personality", and in literature to romanticism. This is the extreme development of humanism, and he wants a transformation both of literature and society according to principles which he calls "classical". In literature and the fine arts, this opposition of "romanticism" and "classicism" can be explained better by Hulme's contrast between "geometric art" and "vital art". Geometric art, he says, reflects a world attitude in which a separation of the human from the natural world is felt. Permanence is sought in fixity and rigidity, and there is a tendency towards abstraction. This is the "classical". Vital art is produced when man is at one with nature. Natural forms are preferred, and there is a tendency towards humanism and romanticism, and towards pantheism.

In the twentieth century, Hulme says, there is a desire for mechanical precision, austerity and bareness in literature and the fine arts, as opposed to the naturalism and vitality of post-Renaissance art. Modern art, he gives Gauguin as an example, returned to more primitive styles, and at first this seemed to be nostalgia and a romantic desire for the past. In fact, it was an impulse towards more austere, more direct forms. This explains the enthusiasm of Lewis, Pound, Gaudier-Brzeska and Yeats for Byzantine mosaics, Egyptian and Indian art, and West African sculpture.

It has been said, but it is not true, that Lewis, Pound, Yeats and Eliot did not know of Hulme and his ideas while he was alive, but only learned of him later. There is a very close connection between the social and artistic criticism of Hulme and that of Lewis, Yeats, Eliot and Pound. How far these principles were formulated by Hulme and adopted by the others is difficult to say. But it is not true to say that they knew nothing about him until afterwards, even though it was much later that Eliot began to popularise his ideas. Lewis and Yeats could have known of Hulme's ideas before 1913. But even if they had not, it is certain that Pound would have known of them. In a letter to René Taupin, written in French in 1928 about Imagist poetry, Pound says: "En 1908–9 à Londres (avant le début de H. D.): cénacle T. E. Hulme, Flint, D. Fitzgerald, moi, etc. . . ." Perhaps the misconception that Pound and the others did not know about Hulme comes from wrongly interpreting these words from

another of Pound's letters : "Hulme wasn't hated and loathed by
the ole bastards, because they didn't know he was there. . . .
[They] knew that *The English Review* existed."[22] The "ole
bastards" are "the respectable and the middle generation, illustrious punks and messrs, fakes like Shaw, stew like Wells, nickel
cash-register Bennett. All degrading the values. Chesterton meaning also slosh, at least then, and to me." *The English Review* was
edited for the first two years by Ford Madox Hueffer, and
Pound says they knew of this, not of Hulme. But obviously
Pound and his associates knew of him. The above quotation in
French shows that Pound knew Hulme as early as 1908. During
the summer of 1913, he shared a cottage in Sussex with Yeats,
and he was associated with Lewis and Gaudier-Brzeska in the
College of Arts before 1914. It is certain, therefore, that Pound
was familiar with Hulme's ideas, and it is likely that he discussed
them with Yeats and Lewis. Richard Ellman, in his biography
of Joyce, writes : "He [Pound] was convinced then that the best
poet writing in English was Yeats, and had soon delighted the
older man by his vivacity and shrewdness. Their closest period of
friendship was during the summers of 1913 and 1914, when they
shared a cottage in Sussex and tried to remake each other. Pound
had been deep in the Imagist movement, under the influence of
T. E. Hulme, but was about ready to leave it for Vorticism, a
tougher objectivism in which Gaudier-Brzeska, the sculptor, and
Wyndham Lewis accompanied him."[23] This tougher objectivism
was putting into practice the ideas which Hulme put forward.
Ellman is here describing the beginnings of the "neo-classic"
movement in England, which reflected Hulme's ideas much more
closely than the Imagist movement did.

What Yeats, Pound, Lewis and Eliot wanted in literature was
bareness, a hard intellectual approach ruled by the authority of
strict literary principles. They rejected the humanist tradition in
literature, and in society, the democratic, humanitarian tradition.
The same principles governed their social criticism as their
literary criticism, and led them to support the fascist cause, either
directly, as Pound and Lewis did, or indirectly, as Yeats and
Eliot did.

VIII

Those who find it difficult to appreciate that these writers were
attracted to fascism would do well to note the widespread
support for it among intellectuals and influential people in

countries other than Italy and Germany, what has been called the "intellectual foreign legion" of fascism. John Buchan, writing in the *Morning Post* on December 31st, 1929, summed up the decade in these words: "But for the bold experiment of fascism the decade has not been fruitful in constructive statesmanship."[24] The Conservative press saw Mussolini as the energetic saviour of Italy from Communist revolution, a leader loyal to the monarchy. Travellers returning from Italy had enthusiastic praise for the new Italian spirit which had at last succeeded in making trains run to time. It was thought impossible that fascism would ever menace the British Empire. In 1922, while the *Spectator*, representing moderate Conservative opinion, was approving the Fascist march on Rome and the take-over of the government, the *Daily Mail* carried no leader on Italian events; it was too busy attacking the Labour party, particularly Arthur Henderson, as Bolshevist. In July 1934, *The Times* said that in the years ahead there was more reason to fear for Germany than to fear her, while the Conservative press thought the Germans sincere workers for world peace. Graves and Hodge describe Lord Knebworth as a representative figure of the time, a man who found refuge from the insecurity of the inter-war period in the orderliness of Italian fascism, the discipline of the Catholic church and the routine of the R.A.F., which was itself suspected of having fascist leanings. Lord Rothermere and the *Daily Mail* supported Mosley and the British Union of Fascists. Rothermere admired the apparent energy of the dictators and thought Mosley could infuse the same energy into the lethargic British, while Winston Churchill met Mussolini in 1927 and praised those who backed fascism against the Reds. The British Union of Fascists under Mosley boasted 20,000 members only two years after it was founded in 1932.[25] The Communist Party of Great Britain exceeded this figure only during and after the Second World War. Many others living in what they considered a sluggish democratic society admired the dynamism of autocracy. A new word, "fifth-columnist", came into the language, being applied to certain political groups which seemed to be trying to bring Britain into the fascist camp. The Cliveden set were suspected of such activities, and it was said that they were pro-Nazi and behind all fifth-column activities in England. Lady Astor denied this, but her denial did not stop the rumours, either then or later.[26] Lord Lothian regarded Anglo-German friendship as necessary to resist

Franco-Russian domination in Europe, while the slogan "Rather Hitler than Blum" was used widely.

The Spanish Civil War gave an indication of the extent of the support for fascism. Of the press, the *Morning Post*, the *Daily Mail*, the *Daily Sketch* and the *Observer* were pro-Franco and printed no news from Spain that did not discredit "the Reds". The *Daily Express* and *Daily Mirror* had republican sympathies but thought nothing should be done to provoke the Axis powers. The *Daily Telegraph* and *The Times* set out to be impartial, but *The Times* would not publish articles from their military corre-spondent which pointed out the danger to the British Empire of a Spain friendly to the Axis powers. English authors writing on the Nationalist side included Douglas Jerrold and Arnold Lunn, two leading Roman Catholics; Arthur Bryant, the conservative historian; Sir Henry Page Croft, a Tory protectionist; Francis Yeats-Brown; Sir Arnold Wilson, a Conservative M.P., who wrote the introduction to the Nationalists' official report on Communist atrocities. In answer to the question, "Are you for or against Franco and fascism?" authors who declared themselves neutral included Eliot, Pound, Sean O'Faolain, H. G. Wells, Victoria Sackville-West and Alec Waugh. Those who openly declared support for Franco were Edmund Blunden, Arthur Maclean, Geoffrey Moss, Eleanor Smith and Evelyn Waugh. Waugh sup-ported Italian action not only in Spain but in Abyssinia, and Wells in fact stated that the rise of fascism had vindicated his idea of the Samurai, a small élite of scientists which he had said, in *A Modern Utopia*, should have control of government. In *Looking Back on the Spanish War*, George Orwell listed people who were diverse in political attitudes but all of whom regarded fascism as the ultimate champion of their own kind.[27] This list included Pétain, Montague Norman, Pavelitch, William Ran-dolph Hearst, Streicher, Buchman, Pound, Juan March, Cocteau, Thyssen, Father Coughlin, the Mufti of Jerusalem, Antonescu, Spengler, Beverley Nichols, Lady Houston and Marinetti. The "intellectual foreign legion of fascism" was more widespread and numerous than many might think.

I

W. B. Yeats

I

W. B. YEATS

YEATS'S POETIC DEVELOPMENT is often described as a
search for a style, a search which took him from the Pre-
Raphaelite twilight of his youth to "a sense of something steel-
like and cold within the will, something passionate and cold",[1]
in old age. His description of Whitehead's style in a letter to
Olivia Shakespear could well be applied to his own later poems;
"his way of saying just enough and no more, his difficult scornful
lucidity".[2] But his was as much a search for a theme as for a
style. Reading about his youth and early manhood, one feels he
was convinced that he was going to be a poet before he even
knew whether or not he could write. Of course, in *Autobiographies* it is the successful poet who is looking back over his
childhood, and his impressions will no doubt have been affected
by experiences which came later. As for the themes of his early
poems, he chose the Ireland of the past, of the sagas, of
Cuchullain, Diarmuid and the rest. This was partly an attempt
to create a personal mythology which would, nevertheless, have
meaning for the people of Ireland, and partly to give himself
something to write about, a framework within which to do his
exercises. These heroes of the past were probably of some use to
Yeats in practising his poetic technique. But any attempt by an
English poet in the twentieth century to use Lancelot and
Guinevere as symbols could hardly have succeeded.

Neither did Yeats. He hoped to heighten the effect of his
poetry by introducing these figures; in fact, the effect is anything
but heightened. This might be because the reader who is not
Irish is unlikely to know the legends. Of course, he can find out
about them, but even so they are not likely to mean a great deal
to him. I doubt whether they meant much to the ordinary Irish-
man either.

Caught up in a circle which included Johnson and Dowson,
Yeats was walking about in a cloak and floppy tie, and wearing
an aesthetic philosophy to match. He was the enemy of what he
called "rhetoric", which, as Graham Hough says, "seems to be

extended to include propaganda of all kinds, everything to do with sociology and science, 'impurities' in poetry generally".[3] Writing to a school friend, Frederick Gregg, in 1887, Yeats says, "In literature nothing that is not beautiful has any right to exist." By this he means beauty of technique and not mere pictorial beauty, because he refers to the beauty which Hugo gives to the Hunchback. But he would not admit that politics, sociology, science or any affairs of the moment could be made beautiful, whatever treatment they received. He felt strongly about the antithesis between art and life, particularly life in modern society, right up to his death. In 1935 he wrote (untruly, of course): "I have lived in the midst of it, I have been always a propagandist though I have kept it out of my poems and it will embitter your soul with hatred as it has mine."[4] In the same letter he suggested that there is a more convincing reason why a poet should not admit propaganda into his life: "Goethe said we should renounce, and I think propaganda—I wish I had thought of this when I was young—is among the things they [artists] thus renounce." He is thinking of his middle age as young.

Yeats was attacked by the Young Ireland poets on this question. They reproached him for not finding subjects of moral significance in the world of his time, especially the First World War. But *The Leaders of the Crowd* is a poem written on an obscure Irish subject which also applies to Europe at war. Yeats is trying to avoid mention of specific modern problems; but many of his poems are general truths with recent applications, and they must often be interpreted in the light of these applications to make their meaning clear. Some indeed were prophecies; *The Leaders of the Crowd*, written about a specific event in Ireland, applies far more widely to modern mass-movements and mass-exploitation.

"So the crowd come they care not what may come."

In spite of his apparent unwillingness to say what he thinks about social problems, Yeats has what Narayana Menon calls an "uncanny awareness of the unsatisfactoriness of the European social organisation, of the nature of some of our struggles".[5]

In *The Trembling of the Veil*, dated 1922, Yeats has this to say of his relationship with the aesthetic movement in the nineties: "Our insistence on emotion which has no relation to any public interest gathered together overwrought, unstable men." The poet, then, should be the mouthpiece of a highly personal and subjective viewpoint. When this is combined with a complicated system of symbols and allusions, the results can be perplexing. Yeats was also looking for a system of thought. He thought he saw Maud Gonne and Ezra Pound misled by their faith in political programmes, and he found it impossible to accept any facile solutions supplied by revolutionary philosophers or economists. Yeats, however, was attracted by socialism for a while. He turned socialist through the influence of William Morris, and in the summer of 1887 he was reading Morris's socialist poems. (*Chants for Socialists* by Morris was published in 1885.) In June of 1891 he had to write a review for the *National Observer*, but found it almost impossible to review for so "ultra-Tory a paper". He said it would be easy if he were a Tory himself, or if he could descend to writing as a Tory who did not let political sympathies kill literary sympathies. But he could not put in the few saving clauses that would have made his review acceptable to the editor. Again, in *Autobiographies* he says he only gradually gave up thinking of, and planning for, a sudden change for the better. In 1919 he looked back at his early attempts to find a system of thought in socialism :

"We pieced our thoughts into philosophy,
And planned to bring the world under a rule,
Who are but weasels fighting in a hole."

The Civil War, he means, has had this effect. But such utopian dreams are futile :

"O but we dreamed to mend
Whatever mischief seemed
To afflict mankind, but now
That winds of winter blow
Learn that we were crack-pated when we dreamed."

It is strange that Yeats was ever attracted by socialism. He never seemed particularly concerned with the well-being of the masses, and he certainly had not the sympathy with ordinary humanity that one would expect a socialist to have. There are numerous references by people who knew him to his lack of human sympathy, his coldness and aloofness. Monk Gibbon thought there was "something cold about him : something in-human". After allowing for his studied playing of the part of the poet, "a sediment of real arrogance remained. He disliked and scorned average humanity, the common rut, whose lives seemed to him banal and submissive."[6] Yeats left Gibbon out of an anthology, but even so these are not the characteristics one would expect to find in a man attracted by socialism. He was probably attracted more by the idea of helping to cause some momentous change than by sympathy for the poor. He thought that he and his colleagues at the turn of the century were going to produce a book which would change the spiritual destiny of the world, and he said that *A Vision* would do it, some forty years later. Many sensitive people are attracted by socialistic ideas and ideals in youth; of these, few go as far in other directions as Yeats did in later life.

II

From the age of forty onwards, Yeats continually introduced themes of public interest into his poetry. In looking for a system of thought, Menon says, "he tried everything except Protestant Christianity and Marxian Dialectics"—the one because it was un-Irish, the other because it was scientific, mechanical and anti-imagination. When he started to formulate his system from his wife's automatic writing, he started on the most fruitful period of his poetic career. But it was not the system itself which revitalised his poetic technique. What it did was to provide a centre of intellectual interest, freeing his imagination and bringing intellectual vitality. He no longer needed to despise the affairs of the world as unfit for poetry. He began to say what he felt in the way most natural to him, instead of self-consciously writing in a deliberately "poetic" manner, producing a rather pale imitation of nineteenth-century "romantic" poetry. He did not produce his most characteristic work, or his best poetry, until he finally rejected the late nineteenth-century aesthetic view of the poet as a lone, sensitive, wilting being, flowering into words or gestures.

I have mentioned Yeats's belief in the antithesis between public life and action on the one hand, and private (artistic or contemplative) life and poetry on the other. In a song from *The Player Queen* which was included in his collected poems, he wishes he were

> "Anything else but a rhymer
> Without a thing in his head
> But rhymes for a beautiful lady
> He rhyming alone in his bed."

This means Yeats himself, and is partly a wish that he were

living the experience instead of writing about it. The poem appears in *A Full Moon in March*, published in 1935, and hints that he is dissatisfied with the theme of his earlier poems. But from middle age onwards Yeats was a man of action. He organised literary societies, helped to establish the Abbey Theatre, and was a member of the Irish Senate. In fact he was quite useful in public affairs. He took his duties seriously; later he became disillusioned and withdrew from public life, but he produced some of his best work out of his experiences in public affairs— poetry of impatience, arrogance and mockery.

Before he actually became involved in affairs of state, he was indifferent to politics. He thought that politics for a vision-seeking man can be only half-achievement. It was not politics or current affairs that constituted reality for Yeats, but the life of the imagination in artistic creation. Everything else is transient and trivial. It is not the poet's business in time of crisis to tell the statesmen what to do:

> "I think it better that at times like these
> We poets keep our mouths shut; for in truth
> We have no gift to set a statesman right."

This was written in 1915 about the First World War, or the Irish revolt which was still probable, and this seven-line poem was all he had written and all he was going to write about the war, which he dismissed as "bloody frivolity". Practical politics for him was "the dirty piece of orange peel in the corner of the stairs as one climbs to some newspaper office".[7]

In 1922 Yeats became a member of the Irish Senate and his connections with practical politicians were more direct. He did not feature prominently in debates; he kept quiet on most political issues, saving himself for things he "knew something about". However, he did make one impassioned speech, in favour of allowing Protestants divorce, as their consciences allowed it. His duties in the Senate, and his quarrels with officials about the staging of plays at the Abbey Theatre, increased his impatience with politics and politicians. In a letter to Dorothy Wellesley, dated 1937, he wrote, "You say that we must not hate. You are right, but we may, and sometimes must, be indignant and speak it. Hate is a kind of 'passive suffering', but indignation is a kind of joy."[8] His later poems are the passionate expression of this indignation—at old age, at the death of the noble and heroic past, at the evils of modern civilisation and at the suffering which

the Irish people had to endure. This magnificent passage from
the letter quoted above brings out the spirit of the later poems
better than any criticism could :

> "I am fighting in those ballads [Casement ballads] for what I have
> been fighting all my life, it is our Irish fight though it has nothing
> to do with this or that country. Bernard Shaw fights with the
> same object. When somebody talks of justice who knows that
> justice is accompanied by secret forgery, when an archbishop
> wants a man to go to the communion table when that man says
> he is not spiritually fit, then we remember our age-old quarrel
> against gold braid and ermine, and that our ancestor Swift has
> gone where 'fierce indignation can lacerate his heart no more',
> and we go stark staring mad."

In later life, Swift, Burke and Berkeley are his heroes, not the
figures of Irish legend. He praises the hard intellect, and it is
not true to say of the Yeats of the later poems what George
Moore said of the young Yeats, that "all he cares for is a piece
of literature".[9] Yet he would probably not have felt so strongly
about social and philosophical issues had he not seen them as
material for a poem.

By 1936 he had rejected politics altogether and had no faith
in any form of modern government. He said he would never
again be a politician, not even in Ireland. As his sense of reality
deepened, which it did as he grew older, he asserted that his
horror at the cruelty of governments grew greater. It was his
conviction that no government was less responsible than any
other : "Communist, Fascist, Nationalist, clerical, anti-clerical,
are all responsible according to the number of their victims. I
have not been silent : I have used the only vehicle I possess—
verse. If you have my poems by you, look up a poem called 'The
Second Coming'. It was written some sixteen or seventeen years
ago and foretold what is happening."[10] In the face of this, it is
useless to say that Yeats's poems have no political or sociological
content. This passage does not contradict other statements he
made. When he says he has not introduced propaganda into his
poems, it means (however untruly) that he has not taken sides
in a merely local quarrel, where neither side is entirely right.
Yeats's poems deal with the effects rather than the causes of
political upheavals, which is why he has written such good poetry
about Irish nationalism and the Irish rebellion.

In a letter to Ethel Mannin in 1937 he makes it clear that he

is writing poems about political events: "I have a horror of
modern politics—I see nothing but the manipulation of popular
enthusiasm by false news—a horror that has been deepened in
these last weeks by the Casement business. My ballad on that
subject has had success . . . I shall return to the matter again in
a new ballad. These ballads of mine though not supremely good
are not ephemeral." [11] The poem *Roger Casement* is a plea that
the stain should be removed from that man's name, but it is also
an indictment of modern political procedure:

> "He died upon the gallows,
> But that is nothing new."

Those who take part in political intrigues have always faced this
risk. But,

> "A perjurer stood ready
> To prove their forgery true;
> They gave it out to all the world,
> And that is something new."

Yeats implies that the wide diffusion of a perjury is what is new
and evil. This stems from his aristocratic attitude to society and
government. Perjury in affairs of state is not a recent phenomenon. What is new is that the spread of communications has
made people more aware of this kind of event, and governments
have to convince more people that what they are doing is right.
When government was in the hands of royal and noble families,
only those immediately concerned with the nation's affairs
needed to be reassured or hoodwinked. Alternatively, rulers did
not need to give any explanation for what they did. It was sufficient justification for an unethical policy if it proved successful
or appeared to be necessary. Consciences were salved by success,
or tongues quietened by fear. It is no use Yeats saying that if we
had such kings and nobles again these sordid affairs would not
happen. They are less likely to happen when the nation as a
whole has to have its conscience cleared. The excuses will have
to be more convincing at least. It is this false justification that
Yeats cannot stomach. If someone is attacking your interests,
Yeats admits that it might be necessary to get rid of him. But if
he is acting on his principles, bury him bravely and do not tell
lies about him.

The shuffling corruption of modern government is the subject
of *A Model for the Laureate*. In the past,

> "On thrones from China to Peru
> All sorts of kings have sat
> That men and women of all sorts
> Proclaimed both good and great;
> And what's the odds if such as these
> For reason of the state
> Should keep their lovers waiting,
> Keep their lovers waiting."

Even those "rascals black and white" who "rule because a strong right arm/Puts all men in a fright" can "keep their lovers waiting". Those who are best fitted to rule, by birth and wealth, and those who rule by strength and force, are contrasted with those who are elected to rule:

> "The muse is mute when public men
> Applaud a modern throne:
> Those cheers that can be bought or sold,
> That office fools have run,
> That waxen seal, that signature.
> For things like these what decent man
> Would keep his lover waiting?"

These are the words of a man who has been vitally interested in politics, but who has been completely disillusioned. They imply a total rejection of everything connected with politics:

> "A statesman is an easy man,
> He tells his lies by rote;
> A journalist makes up his lies
> And takes you by the throat;
> So stay at home and drink your beer
> And let the neighbours vote."
> (*The Old Stone Cross*)

Again there is the connection between politics and popular journalism. (It was implied when he described politics as "the dirty piece of orange peel in the corner of the stairs as one climbs to some newspaper office".) Yeats saw the increase of third-rate periodical writing as another symptom of the disease of democracy, pandering to the mob. His attitude to democratic government might be summed up as the election of those least able to govern by those least able to judge.

III

As a contrast with life in an industrial, scientific, democratic

society, he admired the aristocratic way of life. In his youth this
showed itself in his idealisation of noble, beautiful, cold and dignified women :

> "And ah, you proud maiden, you are not so fair when his oar
> Is heard on the water, as they were, the proud and apart,
> Who paced in the eve by the nets on the pebbly shore,
> When I was a boy with never a crack in my heart."

Yeats believed that the aristocracy in the old days fed the imagination by revealing a refined and ample ideal of life that was
impossible to a small chief or "Carle". Such a life drew them
away from the narrow world of "eating and sleeping, getting and
begetting", although there is plenty of this in his later poems. In
a letter he writes : "Thus do I, with my perhaps too literary
eyes, read history, and turn all into a kind of theatre where the
proud walk in a cloth of gold, and display their passionate hearts,
that the groundlings may feel their souls wax the greater."[12]

In *Autobiographies*, he describes his "dearest conviction : that
I love proud and lonely things";[13] he yearns to

> "seek alone to hear the strange things said
> By God to the brightest hearts of those long dead,
> And learn to chaunt a song men do not know."
>
> *(The Rose)*

Yeats frequently introduces a lament for "all the nobility of
earth", for "lost tradition", and asks, "How much of my own
verse has not been but the repetition of those words?" He implies
a connection between "the long-established life of the well-
born", and the artist's life. Permanence seems to be the common
factor; the well-born come from, and the artist creates, permanent things. Yeats believed that poets "carry in their heads that
form of society aristocracies create now and again at Versailles
and Urbino".[14] Like Carlyle and Ruskin, he idealised a previous
way of life and an earlier kind of society. Like them, he admired
the unity of art and life which he saw in medieval society. He
thought that Ireland might be the first in Europe to seek the
unity of the theologian, poet, sculptor and architect, which he
said existed from the eleventh to the thirteenth centuries.

He identified the aristocrat and the poet because he believed
that both are dignified, civilised, superior creatures—one by
means of wealth and breeding, the other because of his sensitivity and devotion to the arts. What fitted Lady Gregory for
her imaginative work was her family tradition—"semi-feudal

Roxborough, her inherited sense of caste, her knowledge of that top of the world where men and women are valued for their manhood and their charm, not for their opinions".[15] Keats, "the coarse-bred son of a livery stable keeper", was her antithesis in breeding and family, but Yeats believed that these two had a lot in common: "Is not all charm inherited, whether of intellect, manners, character or literature? A great lady is as simple as a good poet, neither possesses anything which is not ancient and their own."[16]

Yeats was fortunate in receiving the patronage of one so sympathetic to his own ideas as was Lady Gregory. The success with which these two worked together led Yeats to conclude that such a relationship was the ideal one. He thought that, with the passing of great houses and the system of patronage, the influence and intrinsic value of the arts had deteriorated:

> "The lovers and the dancers are beaten into the clay
> and the tall men and the swordsmen, and the horsemen
>   where are they?"

These have disappeared,

> "And we and all the Muses are things of no account.
> They have schooling of their own."

But he "passes their schooling by", and prefers to believe

> "That the swordsmen and the ladies can still keep company
> Can pay the poet for a verse and hear the fiddle sound,
> That I am still their servant though all are underground."
>   (*The Curse of Cromwell*)

Louis MacNeice said that these old houses contained no culture worth speaking of—nothing but obsolete bravado, insidious bonhomie and a way with horses. An example of Yeats's distortion of vision is his raising of the sporting exploits of one of Lady Gregory's brothers to heroic proportions.

Yeats is probably the last poet to receive the patronage of one of the noble houses, even though it was more of a working partnership. This taste of the leisured, sophisticated society enjoyed by noble families of the past made him thirst for more, and he was for a long time to believe that such a society is the one most beneficial to the arts.

> "I might have lived...
> Where every day my footfall might have lit
> In the green shadow of Ferrara wall;

> Or climbed among the images of the past—
> The unperturbed and courtly images—
> Evening and morning, the steep street of Urbino
> To where the Duchess and her people talked."
>   (*The People*)

In *The Green Helmet* he included a fine defence of the aristocratic tradition :

> "How should the world be luckier if this house,
> Where passion and precision have been one
> Time out of mind, became too ruinous
> To breed the lidless eye that loves the sun?"
> (*Upon a House Shaken by the Land Agitation*)

(It is significant that Yeats uses the words "passion" and "precision" in describing the aristocratic mind. The two most striking
features of Yeats's later poems are their passion and precision.)
The "Eagle Thoughts" and the "Lidless Eye" have been destroyed by the levelling action of democracy. *No Second Troy*
brings out the contrast between the noble men and women of the
past, with their aristocratic individuality, and the doctrine of
equality. They possessed

> ". . . a mind
> That nobleness made simple as a fire,
> With beauty like a tightened bow, a kind
> That is not natural in an age like this,
> Being high and solitary and most stern."

Although the subject of these lines, Maud Gonne, was not an
aristocrat by birth, she was a lady by birth and a leader of men.
Yeats thought that one of the greatest of Irish leaders, Parnell,
was the epitome of the aristocratic attitude—strong, stern and
aloof. He believed that intellectual freedom and social equality
are incompatible, and that no country could have a more natural
distaste for equality than Ireland; in fact the Irish people re-
spected a rule founded upon some visible supremacy. Yeats
probably learned his aristocratic nationalism from O'Leary. He
believed that leadership should be based on personal supremacy,
and that order, authority and hierarchy are necessary for stability and for a full life :

> "The soldier takes pride in saluting his captain,
> The devotee proffers a knee to his lord,
> Some back a mare thrown from a thoroughbred,
> Troy backed its Helen; Troy died and adored."

He implies here that Troy perished in a worthwhile, heroic
cause. But now,

> "When nations are empty up there at the top,
> When order has weakened or faction is strong,
> Time for us all to pick out a good tune,
> Take to the roads and go marching along."

When a nation has no great leaders it is bound to perish:

> "Where are the captains that govern mankind?
> What happens to a tree that has nothing within it?"

When the aristocratic families and the strong, stern leaders
disappear, a nation loses its greatness.

> "Great nations blossom above."

George Orwell said that Yeats's "tendency" was fascist, that
throughout his life his outlook was that of those who reach
fascism by the aristocratic route. We have seen that he believed
in a rigid hierarchy, concentration of great power in a few hands,
and unquestioning obedience to a leader by virtue of his personal supremacy. This is very close to the fascist ideal. In 1924,
two years after Mussolini came to power, he wrote this: "Generations to come will have for their task the recovery of liberty
from its errors—building up of authority, restoration of discipline, discovery of life sufficiently heroic to do without the opium
dream."[17]

IV

Yeats's defence of the traditional past is quite beautifully expressed in *Coole Park and Ballylee, 1931.* The tone is one of
calm, quiet acceptance and resignation. It is a personal tribute
to a friend who had encouraged him, and to an estate which
had sheltered and inspired him.

> "Upon the border of that Lake's a wood
> Now all dry sticks under a wintry sun,
> And in a copse of beeches there I stood."

Even if the reader thinks that privilege of birth and inherited
wealth is wrong, he must be moved by such sincere and personal
sentiment:

"We were the last romantics—chose for theme
Traditional sanctity and loveliness;
Whatever's written in what poet's name
The book of the people; whatever most can bless
The mind of man or elevate a rhyme;
But all is changed, that high horse riderless,
Though mounted in that saddle Homer rode
Where the swan drifts upon a darkening flood."

This poem was published in 1933, when the subject of most poetry was anything but "traditional sanctity and loveliness". The communist poets of the 1930s welcomed the declining influence of noble families and traditional values. They sought the destruction of wealth, privilege and hierarchy. But their attitude lacked depth and understanding. Their patronising and ill-conceived notion of the culture, or absence of culture, of the lower classes is theoretical and pale beside Yeats's belief in the traditional culture of noble families.

Yeats did not accept the idea that, however desirable an ideal hierarchic society might be, it can have no relevance to modern conditions. He said that Ireland was sterile because power had passed to those who lacked the kind of training which requires wealth to ensure continuity from generation to generation, and to free the mind from other tasks. He believed the ideal ruler to be the gentleman, who does not need to worry about his personal needs. As a result, he can be perfectly disinterested in his judgements and free from the temptation to accept bribes. Yeats thought it impossible to keep the idea of a nation alive where there are no national institutions to reverence, no national successes to admire, no model in the minds of the people; the Young Ireland poets were wrong in trying to create a mass of obvious images, images of immediate political or sociological interest, to fill the minds of the young with simple ethical ideas. He defended the movement of which he was part because it tried to do the same thing in a more enduring way, choosing as its theme "the old religion of the Irish with its magical view of nature, its unbounded sorrow at the universal victory of old age and decay, the ultimate rejection of nature by the lonely spirit of man".[18]

His admiration for aristocracy and wealth, however, sometimes becomes questionable, if not in motive, at least in sentiment. "We meet delightful people who appreciate all finer things and could not if some great-grandfather had not sold his country for gold.

We look at them affectionately from our garret windows." [19] This sounds strange coming from one who had advocated that the Laureateship should be freed from any necessity to praise prominent people. It sounds as bad as any of the dedications written when poets were obliged to rely on the patronage of the wealthy. If Yeats had ever spent any time in a garret he would not have said this kind of thing. George Moore ridiculed the idea which Yeats seemed to have that he had sacrificed his life for art. Yeats insisted that up to middle age his poetry never brought him more than two hundred pounds a year; but he was certainly never hungry, and his poetry was quite successful from the start. In fact his early poetry received recognition and praise in excess of its merits.

V

George Moore mentioned an attack Yeats made on the middle classes for not dipping into their pockets to keep the Lane pictures in Ireland, and said that Yeats had the strange idea that only "titled and carriage folk" can appreciate painting, that the middle classes have never done anything for the arts. Yeats thought that he himself was not from the middle class, and as he certainly did not come from the lower classes, thought that he belonged to the nobility. The claim was not too unreal. Mary Butler, who married Benjamin Yeats, inherited and brought into the family the lands of Thomastown in County Kildare, which remained in the family up to the poet's time. The Butlers, after the Fitzgeralds, were the most illustrious of the Anglo-Irish medieval families. John Butler Yeats, the poet's father, inherited a settled estate of 626 acres in County Kildare. The poet's uncle, Robert Corbet, owned Sandymount Castle, a well-known country house, and J. B. Yeats often spoke of Corbet and Sandymount to his children when they lived in London. To some extent this explains why Yeats, as George Moore said, thought he should have been the Duke of Ormonde. Nevertheless, it is an affectation, implying a defect of character, and this is reflected in his verse. O'Brien has pointed out that many people refuse to accept that Yeats could have been attracted to fascism because they believe that a great poet or novelist must be a "nice guy", even in politics. But there is evidence to indicate that in many ways Yeats was not a "nice guy". His preoccupation with aristocratic people or great leaders who are cold, aloof, stern and un-

approachable taught him to be unsympathetic. Moore said there
was a "lack of human sympathy in Yeats".[20] Narayana Menon
thinks that "outside his pet theories of determinist cycles, etc.,
the sphere of his human sympathy is very restricted".[21] He had
little concern for the mass of humanity in an era of increasing
violence.

This is particularly true towards the end of his life. Earlier, in
Easter 1916, for example, he lifts the ordinary people of Ireland
out of their "common rut", and gives them heroic proportions:

> "I have met them at the close of day
> Coming with vivid faces
> From counter or desk among grey
> Eighteenth-century houses."

He remembers,

> "A drunken, vain-glorious lout.
> He had done most bitter wrong
> To some who are near my heart,
> Yet I number him in my song
> He, too, has resigned his part
> In the casual comedy;
> He too has been changed in his turn,
> Transformed utterly:
> A terrible beauty is born."

These are Irishmen fighting for the freedom of the country Yeats
loved. On the other hand, Yeats's final verdict on the human
race seemed to be, "Let them fight it out until the only ones left
are the fittest, the strongest and the bravest. Their lives will then
be a lot better for not having the rabble dragging them down."
Yeats never identified himself with the Irish populace but always
with the leaders, the exceptional men, men like Parnell who
suffered at the hands of the mob:

> "When strangers murdered Emmet, Fitzgerald, Tone,
> We lived like men that watch a painted stage.
> What matter for the scene, the scene once gone:
> It had not touched our lives. But popular rage,
> Hysterica passio dragged this quarry down; nor did
>   we play a part
> Upon a painted stage when we devoured his heart."

He came to believe that the Irish people were to blame for the
failure of the Irish rebellion:

> "All that was sung,
> All that was said in Ireland was a lie
> Bred out of the contagion of the throng,
> Saving the rhyme rats hear before they die."

His own poetry has not been part of this lie. He also blamed the leaders, de Valera, Cosgrave and O'Duffy, who lacked Parnell's qualities and played to the gallery:

> "The Living men that I hate,
> The dead man that I loved,
> The craven man in his seat,
> The insolent unreproved,
> And no knave brought to book
> Who has won a drunken cheer,
> The witty man and his joke
> Aimed at the commonest ear,
> The clever man who cries
> The catch-cries of the clown,
> The beating down of the wise
> And great Art beaten down."

The difference between them and Parnell was that they had for

> "Their school a crowd, his master solitude;
> Through Jonathan Swift's dark grove he passed, and there
> Plucked bitter wisdom that enriched his blood."

If Parnell had lived, or if these other leaders had had more of his spirit, the result of the Irish revolt would have been nearer to Yeats's ideal—Grattan's Parliament of the late eighteenth century.

VI

In many ways Yeats embodies T. E. Hulme's ideas on art: both delight in the "aristocratic mind" with its "packed logic", in what Hulme calls geometric art. Yeats's ideal was a "Poem . . . as cold/And passionate as the dawn".

> "Once out of nature I shall never take
> My bodily form from any natural thing
> But such a form as Grecian goldsmiths make
> Of hammered gold and gold enamelling."

In this kind of art permanence is sought in fixity and rigidity. Hulme thought it had a tendency towards abstraction, while Yeats believed it to be the expression of a perfect unity of different aspects of life: "I think that in early Byzantium, maybe never before or since in recorded history, religious, aesthetic and practical life were one." The artist could take the forces acting within that society, fashion them to his own design, and use them as a theme for his art. This is what Yeats himself tried to do, but he saw himself thwarted by the intractable nature of the forces and of society itself. "I think if I could be given a month of antiquity and leave to spend it where I chose, I would spend it in Byzantium a little before Justinian opened St. Sophia and closed the Academy of Plato. I think I could find in some little wine shop some philosophical worker in mosaics who could answer all my questions, the supernatural descending nearer to him than to Plotinus even, for the pride of his delicate skill would make what was an instrument of power to princes and clerics, a murderous madness in the mob, show as a lovely flexible presence like that of a perfect human body."[22]

Hulme and Yeats are examples of what Eliot called the twentieth-century type of mind. It is not surprising, therefore, that Yeats, like Hulme, rejected the democratic ideals that pervaded nineteenth-century society. His poetry is the complete antithesis of that of Walt Whitman, prophet of democracy. Whitman wrote of the "new man", of a humane, tolerant form of government and society, in poetry that is half verse, half prose. Yeats despised the "new man" and the kind of society that was being created for him, and said so in poetry that is bare, compact and terse. Orwell, as we have seen, says there must be some connection between "texture" and "tendency". In these writers whose artistic principles are so closely connected with political principles this is probably true. Stefan George, who also held an aristocratic, hierarchic view of society, tried to achieve an effect of fixity and rigidity by careful use of verbs and nouns. He would write, for example, "Here stands the flag-waver", rather than, "He waves the flag", in order to produce a statuesque effect. Let us examine Yeats in this light.

His early poetry is characterised by what Menon calls an "un-English Celtic remoteness". He made an attempt to get out of the classical European tradition by using Irish legends and by trying to re-create the love of old Gaelic literature. His similes and metaphors created "that overcharged colour inherited from the Romantic Movement". Yeats deliberately sought to produce an impression of cold light and tumbling clouds. His early poetry has the "vagueness of a dream":

> "And it was bound with a pearl-pale shell
> That wavered like the summer streams
> As her soft bosom rose and fell."
> (*The Wanderings of Oisin*)

The poetry is characterised by "vagueness and inaction", melancholy, a concern with the past, fantasy, vague Celticism:

> "The Druid, grey, wood-nurtured, quiet-eyed,
> Who cast round Fergus dreams, and ruin untold."
> (*The Rose Upon the Rood of Time*)

The tone, the inversion of the noun and adjective, the separate components of the description—"quiet-eyed"—are symptomatic of the "romanticism" of his early verse. He frequently uses polysyllables, long lines and obvious rhythms:

> "I would that we were, my beloved, white birds on the foam of
>   the sea,
> We tire of the flame of the meteor, before it can fade and flee;
> And the flame of the blue star of twilight, hung low on the
>   rim of the sky,
> Has awaked in our hearts, my beloved, a sadness that may not
>   die."
> (*The White Birds*)

His early poems show his aristocratic bias, but it largely takes the form of a love of high-born, beautiful, regal women:

> "The dew-cold lilies ladies bore
> Through many a sacred corridor
> Where such grey clouds of incense rose
> That only God's eyes did not close."
> (*He Remembers Forgotten Beauty*)

His love of proud, remote beings, living in an imagined world of incensed splendour, is expressed in the kind of images used by the pre-Raphaelites: flowers, particularly roses and lilies; images taken from Christian rituals, without including Christian teaching or dogma; all in the language of traditional "romantic" poetry.

In 1916, however, he wrote this:

> "I have met them at the close of day,
> Coming with vivid faces
> From counter or desk among grey
> Eighteenth-century houses.
> I have passed with a nod of the head
> Or polite meaningless words."
> (*Easter 1916*)

The syntax is here natural, the tone conversational, the words
predominantly monosyllabic. The more concerned he became
with topics of sociological or political importance, the more
direct, hard and masculine became his poetry. Yeats said that
the new era in civilisation would be "harsh, surgical, masculine",
which is an exact description of his later poetry:

> "A bloody, arrogant power
> Rose out of the race
> Uttering, mastering it,
> Rose like these walls from these
> Storm-beaten cottages—
> In mockery I have set
> A powerful emblem up,
> And sing it rhyme upon rhyme
> In mockery of a time
> Half dead at the top."

As his "tendency" became more authoritarian, his verse in
general became monosyllabic, terse, the lines short, the rhythms
muscular. The symbols he used became more intellectual, less
poetic, symbols of hardness and authority: *The Tower, Lapis
Lazuli, A Bronze Head, The Old Stone Cross*. His similes and
metaphors are a complete reversal of those of his early poems:

> "And God-appointed Berkeley that proved all things a dream,
> That this pragmatical, preposterous pig of a world, its farrow
>   that so solid seem,
> Must vanish on the instant if the wind but change its theme."
> *(Blood and the Moon)*

In this part of *Blood and the Moon*, the lines are long, but the
rhythm is complicated and the words harsh, intellectual and dis-
cordant, just as the theme is intellectual and the attitude authoritarian:

> "I declare this Tower is my symbol; I declare
> This winding, gyring, spiring treadmill of a stair is my ancestral
>   stair
> That Goldsmith and the Dean, Berkeley and Burke have
>   travelled there."

The attitude, feeling, style, rhythm, metaphors all merge in
Yeats's later poetry to produce some of the most intellectual,
authoritarian, passionate and, as far as texture goes, the hardest
poetry ever written. It has what Hulme called a desire for precision, austerity and bareness in literature:

"When Pearse summoned Cuchulain to his side,
What stalked through the Post Office? What intellect,
What calculation, number, measurement, replied?
We Irish, born into that ancient sect
But thrown upon this filthy modern tide
And by its formless spawning fury wrecked,
Climb to our proper dark, that we may trace
The lineaments of a plummet-measured face."

(*The Statues*)

Just as later in his life he idealised the society which existed in
Byzantium at the time of Justinian, so he admired its art; and
he tried, as far as it is at all possible, to produce a type of poetry
that would be the literary counterpart of Byzantine mosaics. This
is difficult to achieve, and almost as difficult to describe. However, T. E. Hulme said of this kind of art that permanence is
sought in fixity and rigidity, and there is a tendency towards
abstraction. In his later verse, Yeats uses hard, predominantly
monosyllabic words, corresponding to the individual pieces of a
mosaic; he employs strong, heavily stressed rhythms to bind these
separate words into a unified whole, and yet the individual words
retain their identity, the stressed words standing out like the more
colourful pieces in a mosaic. The later poems, moreover, are
often highly intellectual, even baffling, precisely because of a
tendency towards abstraction :

"At midnight on the Emperor's pavement flit
Flames that no faggot feeds, nor steel has lit,
Nor storm disturbs, flames begotten of flame,
Where blood-begotten spirits come
And all complexities of fury leave,
Dying into a dance,
An agony of trance
An agony of flame that cannot singe a sleeve.

Astraddle on the dolphin's mire and blood,
Spirit after spirit! The smithies break the flood,
The golden smithies of the Emperor!
Marbles of the dancing floor
Break bitter furies of complexity,
Those images that yet
Fresh images beget,
That dolphin-torn, that gong-tormented sea."

(*Byzantium*)

There is clearly a definite correspondence in Yeats's later poetry between his "tendency" (that is the direction which his thinking followed on political and sociological matters, and the attitude he adopted) and his literary style.

VII

In a letter dated 1933 he wrote about his "anti-democratic philosophy". He did not believe that mankind in the mass is capable of choosing its own leaders, nor did he subscribe to the idea of "progress"—"The future of mankind will be much like its past, pretty mean." He despised democracy because he saw it as a standardising process. America and Germany had made the same mistake after the First World War, "the mistake of standardising life, the one in interest of monarchy, the other in interest of democracy, but both for the ultimate gain of a sterile devil. . . . Once both America and Germany had been abundant in variation from type and now all was type." [23] Yeats shared the contempt which many conservatives had for the Weimar Republic, and O'Brien has indicated that pro-fascist opinion was quite common in the Irish Protestant middle class to which Yeats belonged. The *Irish Times* welcomed Hitler as a bulwark against communism, and in Ireland as in Britain there was consistent admiration for Mussolini and condemnation of Soviet Russia.

Yeats had little hope of the future anywhere. He thought that all the systematic idealisms were dead, killed by "sheer mathematics". In 1921 he wrote, "Democracy is dead and force claims its ancient rights, and these men (Irregulars) having force, believe that they have the right to rule." [24] With the break-up of the democratic and humanist traditions he believed that the end of an era was approaching, the destruction of our civilisation. In the early 1920s he forecast a "reign of terror", but he did not know then what the new era would be like. At the moment of greatest stress the thirteenth phase—the incalculable—exerts its influence. He could not prophesy the new force or the new conditions:

> "And what rough beast, its hour come round at last,
> Slouches towards Bethlehem to be born?"

A change is inevitable, however. He asks,

> "Is every modern nation like the tower,
> Half dead at the top?"

Modern society is apparently unable to produce men like the

"... Laughter-headed Burke that proved the State a tree,
   That this unconquerable labyrinth of the birds, century after
      century,
   Cast but dead leaves to mathematical equality."

Yeats believed that democracy grew out of eighteenth-century
whig doctrines, or, at least, that democracy is what men have
made of eighteenth-century libertarian thought. He completely
rejected this kind of thinking:

   "Whence came our thought?
   From four great minds that hated Whiggery.
   Burke was a Whig.
                  Whether they knew it or not,
   Goldsmith and Burke, Swift and the Bishop of Cloyne
   All hated Whiggery; but what is Whiggery?
   A levelling, rancorous, rational sort of mind
   That never looked out of the eyes of a saint
   Or out of a drunkard's eye. All's Whiggery now,
   But we old men are massed against the world."
                                          (*The Seven Sages*)

Yeats made a contrast between the "rational mind" and the
intuitive mind of the saint or drunkard. Theirs is the real wisdom,
perhaps all the more if they lack formal education. Populism, a
belief in the creativity and superior worth of the uneducated and
the unintellectual, has much in common with German historical
and philological scholarship in the nineteenth century, imbued
with the Romantic hatred of the rational, the economic, the
analytic spirit, which it attacked as the source and product of
the revolutionary, rationalistic trend of Western European culture. The populistic element of Yeats's thought does not contradict his aristocratic attitude. Romanticism, with its distrust of the
rational and calculating elements in bourgeois society, shows a
populistic disposition, and Yeats's populism is the result of the
literary influence of romanticism rather than a sociological belief.
He saw a connection between the loss of individual minds,
rationalism, the spread of universal education and increasing
violence in society. He said that those who believe in the objective matter and space of popular science dominate the world and
make possible the stimulation and continuation of revolutionary
massacre and the multiplication of murderous weapons, "by
substituting for the old humanity—with its irreplaceable
individuals—something that can be chopped about".[25]

He did not want original minds stifled by formal education.

But the alternatives are poet or ignoramus. Yeats is prepared to let the majority remain illiterate as long as a few good poets are produced. The passionate, intuitive life which he said he wanted is apparently impossible if this kind of thing is allowed to happen :

> "The children learn to cipher and to sing,
> To study reading-books and histories,
> To cut and sew, be neat in everything
> In the best modern way."
> (*Among School Children*)

Yeats, to a certain extent, used the mask of the simple passionate person to escape from the painful or difficult problems of modern life. The "half-read wisdom of demonic ages" is made to take the place of a deeper realisation of the problems of modern society. Yeats's use of Romantic glamour implied a rejection of responsibility, at times at least. He took refuge from his despair in his poetry—in the end, sometimes a poetry of mockery :

> "In mockery I have set
> A powerful emblem up
> And sing it rhyme upon rhyme
> In mockery of a time
> Half dead at the top."
> (*Blood and the Moon*)

Towards the end of his life his pessimism concerning society was tempered only by his belief in historical cycles. He had no faith in the idea of progress, the belief that society is developing towards perfection. In fact, his only hope lay in a complete reversal of twentieth-century trends. He thought that something might come even out of hopelessness, and was convinced that some great change was imminent :

> "Because this age and the next age
> Engender in the ditch
> No man can know a happy man
> From any passing wretch."
> (*The Old Stone Cross*)

This idea that the future will be born out of confusion, suffering and violence is expressed in *The Second Coming*. With the destruction of tradition and authority, modern civilisation is mere chaos :

> "Turning and turning in a widening gyre
> The falcon cannot hear the falconer;
> Things fall apart; the centre cannot hold;
> Mere anarchy is loosed upon the world."

During his lifetime the First World War claimed its victims, and
the Black and Tans made an even greater impression on his
mind :

> "The blood-dimmed tide is loosed, and everywhere
> The ceremony of innocence is drowned."

In a letter to Ethel Mannin in 1936 he wrote, "I am not callous,
every nerve trembles with horror at what is happening in
Europe." In this letter he made it clear that he detested all
modern governments which are unconcerned at the suffering of
their peoples. He believed that violence is bound to follow "when
the sheep endeavour to lead the goats". It is one of the evidences
of the decay of democracy that

> "The best lack all conviction, while the worst
> Are full of passionate intensity."

There was no one to carry on Parnell's work in Ireland, no leader
with his principles or courage. Yeats thought this was disastrous
for Ireland :

> "Had de Valera eaten Parnell's heart,
> No loose-lipped demagogue had won the day,
> No civil rancour torn the land apart."
>   (*Parnell's Funeral*)

If de Valera had had Parnell's noble spirit he would have carried
the thing through by the force of his leadership, and would not
have let the modern tide run in again.

Images of violence and terror become more frequent; he felt
the catastrophe was approaching. In *Meditations in Time of
Civil War* he speaks of violence and confusion

> "We are closed in, and the key is turned
> On our uncertainty; somewhere
> A man is killed, or a house burned,
> Yet no clear fact to be discerned."

There is only the reality of suffering and death :

> "Last night they trundled down the road
> That dead young soldier in his blood."

Hatred breeds violence, which again breeds more violence, until
there is

"More substance in our enmities
Than in our love."

In verse which carries terrific power, he described the horror, the
confusion and the violence which he increasingly saw in public
life :

"Monstrous familiar images swim to the mind's eye.
'Vengeance upon the murderers,' the cry goes up,
'Vengeance for Jacques Molay.' In cloud-pale rags or in lace
The rage-driven, rage-tormented, and rage-hungry troop,
Trooper belabouring trooper, biting at arm or at face,
Plunges towards nothing, arms and fingers spreading wide
For the embrace of nothing."

He believed at the time that it was the indifference and apathy
to violence in the multitude which was the real evil. This inhuman indifference is described in the last section of *Meditations*.
For a generation or two before the First World War, it looked as
though we might be getting out of this indifference. But Yeats
saw its influence on society between the wars :

"The cloud-pale unicorns, the eyes of aquamarine,
The quivering half-closed eyelids, the rags of cloud or of lace
Or eyes that rage has brightened, arms it has made lean,
Give place to an indifferent multitude, give place
To brazen hawks. Nor self-delighting reverie,
Nor hate of what's to come, nor pity for what's gone,
Nothing but grip of claw, and the eye's complacency,
The innumerable clanging wings that have put out the moon."

The confusion and violence indicate to Yeats that our civilisation is nearing its end. Another one will come to replace it—"An
age is the reversal of an age"—and it will probably be the antithesis of our civilisation :

"Surely some revelation is at hand;
Surely the Second Coming is at hand."

Christian civilisation, he says, has placed importance on the
wrong values. Humanitarian ideals produced, in the long run,
cruelty and violence; democratic ideals produced "mere
anarchy". Now he knows

"That twenty centuries of stony sleep
Were vexed to nightmare by a rocking cradle."

Menon describes *The Second Coming* as a "faint hint of the coming of fascism". But it is more than this. It is the expression of Yeats's belief that a fundamental change is necessary in modes of thought and feeling. These are confused in modern society because there is no "Unity of Being". This, he says, can "only be achieved by arousing the full intensity of the will through contemplating the greatest possible obstacle without despair". It is doubtful whether Yeats achieved this unity himself; he seemed at the last to be able to avoid despair only by mocking everything he, or others, had held dear:

> "Come let us mock at the great...
> Come let us mock at the wise...
> Come let us mock at the good...
> Mock mockers after that."

VIII

Although Yeats found modern society so unsatisfactory, he rejected Russian communism from the very start of its existence. His main criticism of English policy was that its driving force was materialism. He thought this was also true of the Marxian criterion of values—"the spearhead of materialism". His faith in spiritualism and in the heroic spirit of the individual, as opposed to the doctrine of dialectical materialism and equality, was bound to make him reject communism: "What I want is that Ireland be kept from giving itself (under the influence of its lunatic faculty of going against everything which it believes England to affirm) to Marxian revolution or Marxian definitions of value in any form. I consider the Marxian criterion of values as in this age the spearhead of materialism and leading to inevitable murder." [26] In 1933 he was trying to work out a social philosophy which could be used to counteract communism in Ireland; "what looks like emerging is fascism modified by religion". [27] He wanted a period of authoritarian rule to destroy the influence of a century or more of liberalism and democracy, and he saw in fascism the nearest approach to what he wanted.

It is strange, however, that he should see the coming of violence and terror as early as 1921, when he wrote *The Second Coming*, and yet could not see, a few years later, that fascism had in itself the seeds of violence and bloodshed. He seemed confused about whether or not it would be permissible to use force to create a better society. He criticised Auden and Spender for looking for strength in Marxian socialism or in Major Douglas; he said they wanted marching feet, which was wrong: "The lasting expression of our time is not this obvious choice but in a sense of something steel-like and cold within the will."[28] Yet he himself advocated force and marching men to break the rule of the mob, and his own poetry sometimes reflects a taste for violence:

> "But good strong blows are delights to the mind,"
> "But a good strong cause and blows are delight."

The refrain of this poem, the first of *Three Songs to the Same Tune*, runs,

> "Those fanatics all that we do would undo;
> Down the fanatic, down the clown;
> Down, down, hammer them down,
> Down to the tune of O'Donnell Abu."

The stress on violence is even more marked in the second of these "songs". Here Yeats is insisting on carrying to the end the campaign for Irish independence:

> "Justify all those renowned generations,
> Justify all that have sunk in their blood,
> Justify all that have died on the scaffold,
> Justify all that have fled, that have stood."

The chorus to this poem is:

> " 'Drown all the dogs', said the fierce young woman,
> 'They killed my goose and a cat.
> Drown, drown in the water-butt,
> Drown all the dogs', said the fierce young woman."

It is impossible to say definitely that these are Yeats's own sentiments: but the attitude to violence, so strikingly expressed in these poems, is not the same as that in, for example, *Nineteen Hundred and Nineteen*, where it is one of horror. Here it is something like sympathy with foolishly violent persons, or even a violent urge for revenge born out of despair. These songs were written, presumably, to be sung. Yeats altered them later, and changed their title to *Three Marching Songs*.

In the second of these rewritten songs, Yeats himself shows a desire for marching feet. The "six feet marked in chalk" in the original version became marching feet in the rewritten one. He begins playing with the word:

> "A blast of the wind, O a marching wind,
>   March wind, and any old tune,
>   March, march, and how does it run?"

In 1933 he wrote this: "If I were a young man I would welcome four years of conflict, for it creates unity among the educated classes."[29] Menon says that Yeats did not see violence and tyranny as necessarily evil because the people, not knowing evil and good, would become perfectly acquiescent to tyranny.[30]

> "Constrained, arraigned, baffled, bent and unbent
>   By these wire-jointed jaws and limbs of wood,
>   Themselves obedient,
>   Knowing not evil and good;
>
>   Obedient to some hidden magical breath.
>   They do not even feel, so abstract are they,
>   So dead beyond our death,
>   Triumph that we obey."

This attitude to violence and suffering reaches its peak in *A Bronze Head*. Again he sees the "vision of terror" which he had seen many years before in *The Second Coming*. Now he looks

> "On this foul world in its decline and fall;
>   On gangling stocks grown great, great stocks run dry,
>   Ancestral pearls all pitched into a sty,
>   Heroic reverie mocked by clown and knave,
>   And wondered what was left for massacre to save."

With the world in the state it is in, with noble families gone —"great stocks run dry"—poetry ridiculed by those who cannot even begin to appreciate it, he seems inclined to welcome the coming catastrophe which will save whatever is left to save. He even wonders whether there is anything left worth saving at all. The old classes evaporate, "the mere multitude is everywhere with its empty, photographic eyes". When a civilisation ends, everything is turned upside down, Nietzsche's "transvaluation of values". In the above quotation, the word "save" implies that the massacre will be beneficial to some people at least. In *On the Boiler*, published in 1938, he said the danger was that there would be *no* war, but that European civilisation would accept decay. He also wrote, "love war because of the horror and because belief will be changed and civilisation renewed".[31] In his last poems he expressed complete pessimism concerning civilisation. Total war, which was once "bloody frivolity", seemed to

him in his last years the only way of achieving a transformation
of society great enough to destroy the existing evils. Yeats's belief
in historical cycles, the Great Wheel, the alternating of different
kinds of civilisations, and the need for authoritarianism, led him
to adopt this terrible view of the future. He had a total disregard
for the mass of humanity in his last years. Whether or not his
attitude would have changed had he lived through the Second
World War must be mere conjecture. To see his principles put
into practice, however, might well have had a chastening effect
on him. As we shall see later, this war aroused a degree of human
sympathy in Pound and Lewis which had not been apparent
before the war. On the other hand, Yeats had seen violence and
suffering in the Irish Rebellion; yet this did not prevent him
from looking forward to more violence with apparent relish.

Yeats would have us believe that his grasp of the evils contained in modern Western society was not the result of economic
or political analysis, but was based on his theory of historical
cycles and on his wife's automatic writings:

> "A livelong hour
> She seemed the learned man and I the child;
> Truths without father came, truths that no book
> Of all the uncounted books that I have read,
> Nor thought out of her mind or mine begot."

It is impossible to say how true this account is. Yeats was quite
capable of making the whole story up in his role of poet and
mystic. Menon said that Yeats's aversion to "progress" warped
his mind and led him into strange company and interests. It was
because he disliked analytical thinking that he expressed his conclusions about society in terms of historical cycles. The philosophy contained in *A Vision*, however, is extremely analytical,
but he tried to excuse this by saying it was purely intuitive. Still,
he had arrived at the conclusions through some kind of reaction
to the world spectacle, however "intuitive" he might make it out
to be.

His idea was roughly this: at the birth of Christ, religious life
became "primary" and secular life became "antithetical". In our
time an antithetical dispensation is approaching which will
reverse the present era. This great change is not going to happen
because "mere anarchy is loosed upon the world"; but violence
and terror and the destruction of order are symptoms of the end
of an age, and a sign that a new age is about to be born. To

some extent he attributed the violent and personal nature of his own verse to this approaching change:

> "It is very likely because I am a poet and not a painter that I feel so much more keenly that suffering of Villon ... in whom the human soul for the first time stands alone before a death ever present to imagination, without help from a Church that is fading away; or is it that I remember Aubrey Beardsley, a man of like phase though so different epoch, and so read into Villon's suffering our modern conscience which gathers intensity as we approach the close of an era? Intensity that has seemed to me pitiless self-judgement may have been but heroic gaiety." [32]

This implies that the vitality, the "tragic gaiety", of his own last poems was to some extent the result of social causes—because the era was coming to an end.

In *A Vision* Yeats was looking for a philosophy which would suffice even in the world of violence and suffering which he saw all around him:

> "I need some mind that, if the cannon sound
> From every corner of the world, can stay
> Wound in mind's pondering."
> (*All Souls' Night*)

He tried to give a semi-mystical justification to his scheme, but in spite of this, nothing could be more rigid and mechanical than his philosophy, in which all people belonging to the same phase have the same characteristics, with history repeating itself as the Great Wheel turns. His extreme dislike of modern civilisation, together with his concern for the future of civilisation, led him to accept authoritarianism as the only solution. He saw some kind of authoritarian rule as the only way to solve the problems facing modern society. Power should be invested in a few individuals, partly because chaos can only be organised by a strict authority, and partly because it is inevitable after an era of majority rule: "History is very simple—the rule of the many, then the rule of the few, day and night, night and day for ever." [33] The idea of eternal recurrence is also present in the writings of Vico and Nietzsche, two of the literary forerunners of fascism. As far as Ireland was concerned he was "constantly urging the despotic rule of the educated classes as the only end to our troubles".[33] Knights says it is only possible to speak of him as fascist or reactionary by ignoring the reasons why he stressed the aristocratic life. In *A Vision*, however, it is not the aristocratic life that Yeats admires, but the power invested in it. According to his theory of historical cycles, the new era would pay proper homage to this power. His "fascist and reactionary" tendencies are obvious in the following quotation:

"An antithetical dispensation obeys imminent power, is expressive, hierarchical, multiple, masculine, harsh, surgical. The approaching antithetical influx and that particular antithetical dispensation for which the intellectual preparation has begun will reach its complete systematisation at that moment when ... the Great Year comes to its intellectual climax." [34]

Although he fought against prejudice and the tyranny of religious and political societies, he looked forward to the new civilisation, which would be "an aristocratic civilisation in its completed form, every detail of life hierarchical, every great man's door crowded at dawn by petitioners, great wealth everywhere in few men's hands ... an inequality made law". [35]

The nearest approach to this kind of society in modern political terms is fascism. But Yeats hinted even more closely that he would prefer some kind of fascist system. In May 1922, he said that in Ireland the popular leaders represented a quite powerful minority who rejected an appeal to the vote, and might for some time prevent it. In October he called it a "revolt against democracy by a small section", and detected a drift towards conservatism, even autocracy. Then in November, he thought that Ireland was preparing to return to conservative politics, as elsewhere in Europe, or at least, "a substitution of the historical sense for logic". This was written in the year Mussolini came to power, and Yeats was obviously referring to fascist Italy: "Ireland is reacting from the present disorder and turning her eyes towards individualist Italy." [36] He was also obviously in favour of this trend. The "historical sense" in place of logic was just what he wanted. The fascist organiser of the Blueshirts brought his chosen leader, O'Duffy, to Yeats to hear his "anti-democratic philosophy". In July 1933, Yeats wrote, "Politics are growing heroic. . . . A fascist opposition is forming behind the scenes to be ready should some tragic situation develop. . . . There is so little in our stocking that we are ready at any moment to turn it inside out, and how can we not feel emulous when we see Hitler juggling with his sausage of stocking. Our chosen colour is blue, and blue shirts are marching about all over the country." [37]

If Yeats had, as O'Brien suggests, a profound and tragic,

intuitive and intelligent awareness of what the First World War
had let loose, and also of the imminence of the next war, nevertheless he welcomed violence as an agency of the transformation
of civilisation. The movement founded on Hobbes and popular-
ised by the Encyclopaedists and the French Revolution was
exhausted, he said, useless for centuries to come. The wheel was
coming round, the old autocratic principle reasserting itself, force
claiming its "ancient right". Viewed in terms of the suffering of
human beings, he sometimes expressed sympathy for the victims.
Seen as a historical event, the culmination of one historical cycle
and the beginning of another, it was welcomed by him. He
thought that out of some cataclysmic disaster a new form of
society would emerge, and only in this way would humanity be
saved. His views were not original or even uncommon. The stress
on violence as a regenerative force can be found in Sorel; the
idea that new values, a new civilisation, will follow a great
change, but that the values themselves do much to bring about
the change, is Nietzschean; while Spengler looked forward to the
destruction of modern civilisation by warfare and the creation
of a new "Platonic era". In political terms in the 1930s it was
the "values" of fascism which were driving Europe towards
disaster, and only if these triumphed would the new civilisation
be harsh, surgical, masculine, hierarchic—an "inequality made
law".

What really concerned Yeats in his definition of a satisfactory
society was whether or not that society would favour the growth
of the arts, and of literature in particular. He wanted George
Russell to write an essay laying down a cultural, economic and
political policy of national unity as practical advice, in simple
words, to some young man, and such advice should not be fitted
to any momentary crises but for the next fifty years. "This conception of unity and culture has become a cardinal principle in
all exposition of the future in my system."[38] In the same letter
he said, "We writers are not politicians, the present is not in our
charge but some part of the future is. Our speech will not make
it very happy, but it will be even less happy than it might be
perhaps if we are silent on vital points." One of these vital points
was the question of "intimacy" as the mark of fine literature; its
opposite, "generalisation", "creates rhetoric, wins immediate
popularity, organises the mass, gives political success, Kipling's
poetry, Macaulay's essays. . . . When you go from an Irish
country district, where there are good manners, old songs, old

stories and good talk, the folk mind, to an Irish country town. generalisation meets one in music-hall songs with their mechanical rhythm, or in thoughts taken from the newspapers." [39] Urbanisation and mass-communication destroy "unity of being", which produces fine literature, even at the folk level. Once again Yeats stressed the bad effect on literature of the break-up of traditional ways of life. One of the greatest struggles of his poetic career was to achieve a diction which had the dignity and simplicity of peasant speech. He believed that poetry must have its roots in ordinary life, while at the same time the poet should be able to choose his companions from the aristocracy. This led him from a passion for drama portraying ordinary peasant life, exemplified by Synge's plays, to the writing of stylised drawing-room plays for a select audience.

The advocate of democracy sees wealth, leisure, and privilege as having been the prerogative of a select few. He thinks, therefore, that privilege should be destroyed, and wealth and leisure shared more equally among the population. Yeats, however, believed that leisure and wealth were created as "soil for the most living". The following quotation implies his belief that imaginative literature depends on leisure and wealth : "The literature of suggestion belongs to a social order when life conquered by being itself, and the most living was the most powerful, and not to a social order founded on argument." [40] He saw modern civilisation as the product of such argument, and thought that the greatest danger to art and literature comes from the tyrannies and persuasions of revolutionary societies, and political and religious propaganda. These include the society produced by the Industrial Revolution, which has separated man from his true environment, from all that is "most living". He did not believe that the true imaginative man of letters can come to terms with the modern world. Throughout his life he stressed that such a man must keep free from its influences. His only hope lay in a reversal of our civilisation, and this he thought imminent. Without this, literature had little chance of survival; without literature, man's life is meaningless.

Many people, unwilling to accept that Yeats meant what he said about society, have insisted that he meant something else. Dorothy Wellesley, for instance, said that by "aristocracy" he meant simply "the proud, the heroic mind", which is clearly not true. This also applies to L. C. Knights when he tries to prove that Yeats was not a social reactionary because whatever he praised or advocated was done in the name of "the most living". Knights claims that this stress on the "fountain of life" provides the criterion by which Yeats makes his most significant judgement of human values, and quotes Blake: "Everything that lives is holy", with the stress on "lives". This is meant to be an explanation and justification of Yeats's hatred of all those who do not "live"—rationalists, democrats, scientists, journalists. Blake, however, meant that everything that has life is holy, and his statement does not, as Yeats's does, depend on an arbitrary definition of "lives". One is quite at liberty, of course, to accept Yeats's meaning as long as this meaning is clearly understood. A concern for the "most living", if the definition implies an élitist concept, for example, is not incompatible with social reaction. Nietzsche had a great concern for what he called the "most living".

Yeats made many assumptions about the past and critics who have not wanted to analyse his attitude to it have gone along with them. It is one thing to see and accept his prejudices for what they are, and another to try to conjure them away, or pretend that they were something entirely different. Yeats made practically no attempt to come to terms with twentieth-century society, and what attempt he did make failed. He is probably the last poet who could legitimately reject our modern civilisation without being guilty of intellectual and moral evasion. His poetic career, not merely his life, extended over a period of years in which great changes took place in the structure and nature of society. It would perhaps have taken a superhuman effort of adaptation to accept all the changes. His roots were sufficiently deep in the nineteenth century for him to be "the last romantic"; and, like Shelley, he was keenly aware of the shortcomings of the society in which he lived. But he could not see any constructive way out of the impasse. This quotation from a review by Raymond Williams of George Orwell's essays can equally well be applied to Yeats:

> "It is not the familiar historical case of the young radical becoming the mature conservative: that movement, in our time, has been no more than trivial. It is the more complicated case, very difficult to define, but quite central in our recent intellectual history, of the movement from anger to anger: from anger intersecting with a cause to an anger that is beyond causes and beyond attachments."[41]

In his last years it was this kind of anger which he sought, and which provided him with his greatest satisfaction:

> "Grant me an old man's frenzy,
> Myself I must remake
> Till I am Timon and Lear
> Or that William Blake
> Who beat upon the wall
> Till Truth obeyed his call."
> (*An Acre of Grass*)

Almost the last thing he wrote was a vindication of his own poetry: he urged Irish poets of the future to follow his example:

> "Irish poets, learn your trade,
> Sing whatever is well made,
> Scorn the sort now growing up
> All out of shape from toe to top,
> Their unremembering hearts and heads
> Base-born products of base beds.
> Sing the peasantry, and then
> Hard-riding country gentlemen,
> The holiness of monks, and after
> Porter-drinkers' randy laughter;
> Sing the lords and ladies gay
> That were beaten into the clay
> Through seven heroic centuries;
> Cast your mind on other days
> That we in coming days may be
> Still the indomitable Irishry."
> (*Under Ben Bulben*)

Yeats achieved what can best be described as a tragic stoicism, the belief that life is tragic but must be lived in a comic fashion, or, at least, joyfully. He believed, finally, that until the present era is reversed, the only thing a man of imagination can do is to dissociate himself from it:

> "Cast a cold eye
> On life, on death.
> Horseman, pass by!"

II

Wyndham Lewis

WYNDHAM LEWIS

I

LEWIS HAS BEEN the most prolific of all these writers on social and political topics. He has described himself as "a writer who is a novelist, a critic, a political pamphleteer ... who has been engaged in the analysis of what is obsessional in contemporary social life ... expressing abuses in art-politics; celebrating in fiction picturesque parasites; in weighing, to the best of his ability, contemporary theories of the State ... who has often found himself in conflict with the inveterate prepossessions of his age and country".[1] He has also been one of the most misinterpreted and misrepresented. *The Art of Being Ruled*, published in 1926, is mainly responsible for this, and yet the ideas contained in this book are fundamentally the same as those expressed in *Time and Western Man*, published in 1927, which was considered one of the best literary-sociological books of the time. In the former book, Lewis stated his principles more forcibly and applied them more directly to social and political questions. *Time and Western Man*, on the other hand, is an attack on Joyce, Gertrude Stein, Bergson, Spengler and Einstein. But the principles behind the two books are the same.

Lewis has been accused of writing *The Art of Being Ruled* as a justification of oppressive forms of government. What he did do in this book was to describe how, to his mind, the great mass of people had no interest in what form the government of their country took, and were incapable of deciding by whom, or how, they should be ruled. If forced to take an interest, as they are under a democratic system, they become miserable and neurotic. They wish to abrogate all responsibility for government, and so Lewis thinks it necessary and justifiable for the "intellectual" to assume that responsibility. In *The Art of Being Ruled*, he recognises himself as liable to make a mistake about democracy: "I feel that I slighted too much the notion of 'democracy' by using that term to mean too exclusively the present so-called democratic masses, hypnotised into a sort of hysterical imbecility by the mesmeric methods of Advertisement."[2] But, after correcting this, he is vigorously opposed to the democratic system itself, not merely to certain symptoms which may or may not be inherent in it: "At the root of the mechanical, subconscious obsession . . . is the reflection of political decay."[3] Lewis objected to the uniformity and standardisation that moulds separate individuals into indistinct masses. This hatred of the mass of people has often been stressed in Lewis's sociological writings, and has no doubt been compared with Nietzsche's concept of the botched masses. These two attitudes are very different, however. For Nietzsche, the mass of people did not deserve any consideration in themselves; he thought them intrinsically futile. Lewis, on the other hand, believed the mass had been degraded by the advance of technology and the growth of democracy. He probably had no great faith in their capabilities in any period of history, but thought they had been made worse by these agents. In *Monstre Gai*, the inhabitants of Third City are an irresponsible, imbecilic lot—what the inhabitants of a Welfare State made complete by technological advances might be like. Mannock is describing them to Pullman—"They are all nit-wits—their I.Q. level is so low that it might be said not to exist. But they get through life all right, which is mainly because they all, whether young or old . . . receive a pension, adequate to keep them at that café all day. Some of them may have been a little intelligent say 30 years ago—though I doubt it—but 30 years at that café . . ."[4] Lewis wrote this in 1954. Immediately after the war he had supported the Labour party, but now he despised it again and the passage echoes his feelings of thirty years earlier.

In *One Way Song*, published in 1933, a criticism in verse of the society between the wars, Lewis deplores the levelling-off of great and small in a democratic society, a process which sets standards of attainment and ability at a level which the majority can reach, a level which is despised by the more gifted minority, who, however, can do little to change things.

> "We are a little age, where the blind pygmy treads,
> In hypnotised crusades against all splendour,
> Perverts male prowess to the middle gender.
> We are a critic company what's more."[5]

In *Apes of God*, Lewis contrasts the truly "great" person with the imitators, the shams, the "Apes". This novel also reveals his contempt for the mass of the people, "who are characterised almost without exception by a pride in being not a *person*, but, as you have said, in being a *thing*".[6] He attacks democratic society in this way: "The 'great' is the incalculable, the 'small' is the calculable and safe. Such is 'Society'. It is an organised pettiness... or it is nothing. Society is a defensive organisation against the incalculable. It is so constituted so as to exclude and to banish anything, or any person, likely to disturb its repose, to rout its pretences, wound its vanity, or to demand energy or a new effort, which it is determined not to make. 'The small' is merely that constant and stable, almost dead thing, which can be measured and abstracted. 'The small' is the abstract. 'The great' is the concrete. What we call 'great'—that is the reality."[7] It is wrong to limit such criticism to democratic society. It is a charge which could be levelled at any society, even a revolutionary one, which tends to banish everything that is not revolutionary. In fact it is certainly more true of societies which are not democratic. Democracy at least attempts to treat each member of society as an individual with certain rights and responsibilities. Modern democracies have more consideration for the individuals which make up the mass than practically any other society in history. The aim of democracy is to end the state of affairs where the mass is a dead thing and not to be considered. To treat it so has been a principle of the ruling class in many past societies, and would become an important principle in the kind of society Lewis advocates.

II

One of his main criticisms of modern society is that it lacks stability. "The stable personality is indeed suspect... and stability of any sort at all is hated and is suspect... necessarily in a period of revolutionary change so absolute as the present."[8] He did not believe art can be produced in a society which lacks stability, and art was his first concern. His attempts to define a satisfactory society were chiefly carried on in the cause of art. The study of politics was a result of "a wish to find out under what kind of system learning and the arts was likely to fare best".[9]

Lewis was dissatisfied with the society which existed between the wars in England, first and foremost because art was neglected, and sometimes actively suppressed. He thought that modern industrial, democratic society had a disastrous effect on the arts, and that this in itself was enough reason for adopting some other form of society. "No artist can ever love democracy or its doctrinaire and more primitive relative, communism. The emotionally-excited, closely-packed, heavily-standardised, mass-units, acting in a blind, ecstatic union ... would be the last thing for the free democratic West to aim at, *if* it were free, and *if* its democracy were of an intelligent order."[10]

Lewis believed that the most important condition for intellectual success at any time is "solitariness of thought", and that today this is threatened by "mystical mass-doctrines". If the individual cannot separate his mind from the mass-mind, he cannot produce art.

The future of literature in particular is highly problematic in a democratic society: "Can language hold out in any degree against politics, when politics are so extremely fluid, and, inevitably, so indifferent to the arts engendered in words?"[11] What he is objecting to is the imprecise nature of democratic society and its doctrines, the "emotionally-excited mass-units", the "mystical mass-doctrines". Language is blurred because used for lying propaganda. This is the wrong atmosphere for the production of the kind of literature Lewis wants. The formation of art "institutes", Lewis thinks, shows how inadequate is democratic society as an environment for the artist. "An 'institute' ... is airy enough to satisfy the insubstantial conditions of the time. It is very accurately in conformity with the floaty character of the Zeitgeist."[12] Lewis associates this "floaty Zeitgeist" with democratic politics and romanticism in art.

In such an egalitarian society as Lewis describes, the artist is at the mercy of the "vast average"; at the worst, his books are seized and refused publication. In *One Way Song* Lewis deplores the fact that the truthful artist is suppressed; the sincere writer is dangerous to those in positions of authority, and, "in this political age", the young man who is suspected of being honest is held down. Lewis speaks in the guise of the "Enemy", the enemy of the Establishment, the enemy of those who

> "live by force—that imperfect force that is grounded
> On legal bluff, by wordslingers expounded—
> Extremely artificial."[13]

He thus assumes the "mask" of a hard ruthless attitude towards the society he dislikes and its leaders, who are materialists and businessmen and he frequently stresses that this tough attitude is necessary for solving modern social problems. The reason why the artist is suppressed is that he has vision and sympathy:

> "I am the man thus brought into contact with
> Misery, to see it, and make of it a myth."[14]

This is not the same "misery" which Spender and Auden, for instance, wrote about; it is not poverty or exploiting the poor that Lewis decried, but the change from a stable to an unstable society, the loss of contact with the tradition of the past, and especially the suppression of the "truthful artist".

> "And still and all, we know the invisible prison
> Where men are jailed off—men of *dangerous* vision—
> In impalpable dark cages of neglect,
> Invisible walls by self-protective sect
> Or cabal against the individual built,
> (At best with honorifics and lip-service killed.)"[15]

Lewis's colossal self-importance is hardly justified by this poem, which is very badly written, in spite of what Eliot says in the foreword.

Lewis believes that the mass-doctrines of democratic society inevitably result in a lowering of artistic standards. The democratic principle is to supply "what the public wants", and Lewis sees the contemporary public corrupted and degraded into semi-imbecility. Literature has suffered, he thinks, as a result of the mass-production of books, and the decay of values consequent on modern publicity techniques. The mass-public is the result of monopoly capital and mass-production, and provides a large market for the third-rate. Lewis firmly believed that people have deteriorated, that today a writer can be appreciated by a large public only by lowering his standards or by choosing inferior subject-matter, and he thought that Lawrence and Hemingway were two writers who had done this. This is certainly not true of Lawrence. He sometimes wrote badly because what he was trying to say can hardly be put into words, or because his "message" was more important to him than his technique. Also he often wrote rapidly, but he never, I think, lowered his standards to attract a wider audience. In *Lady Chatterley's Lover* he may have tried to gain a larger audience to do them good; but he would not think of this as lowering his standard. Lewis thought that Lawrence chose inferior subject-matter; naturally enough, as Lewis despised women (though he denied it), was disgusted by sex, and had no faith in the promptings of the solar plexus. But Lawrence's subject matter is often more fundamental and more interesting than Lewis's.

Lewis probably disliked Hemingway because he epitomised the love of action which Lewis associated with the modern age, and which Julien Benda had attacked in *La Trahison des Clercs*. Whether Hemingway deliberately lowered his standards, however, is difficult to say. His main interests in life were big-game hunting and bull-fighting, and he earnestly disapproved of "intellectuals" in Lewis's sense of the word. Lewis disliked this love of action, and probably also disliked Hemingway's prose style. I think Lewis is against Hemingway because he sees him as a renegade intellectual, and not because he writes badly. Hemingway's style is boringly narrow, and the final books are full of posturing and self-pity. But his was a fine style while it lasted.

Lewis contrasts the juvenile public taste, which he says affects all levels of modern society, with the eighteenth century and its aristocratic public. The idea that the writer needs to be appreciated by the whole of his society is one which he held only in the later part of his career. In *The Demon of Progress in the Arts*, published in 1954, he attacks Malraux as the champion of non-humanistic art, by which he means art which takes no account of the opinions of the public, writing or painting which is not done for any public *at all*. Before the Second World War, Lewis himself was not concerned with writing for a large public; but the war altered his social and political opinions a great deal. Immediately after it he supported the Labour government, and his attitude towards the general public softened and became more sympathetic. Apparently his artistic opinions were also somewhat changed. In 1950, he wrote that there should be "no breaking of the human bond at any time. Spiritually, as much as physically, there is no one who does not depend upon the average".[16] This is a complete reversal of his pre-1930 attitude to "the average"; probably the reason is that he went blind soon after the war.

During the inter-war years, at least, Lewis could see no hope for serious artistic production in a modern society: "So the fine arts, corresponding to no present need that a variety of industries cannot answer more effectively, the last survivals of the *hard* against the *machine* in every contest involving a practical issue, must, if they survive at all, survive as a sport, as a privilege of the wealthy, negligently indulged in—not any longer as an object of serious devotion."[17]

Here we have a specific contrast between Lewis's artistic principles and the society in which he lived. He makes a distinction between the "hard" (what exactly he means by this will be shown later) and the "mechanical". This can be roughly stated as a distinction between the working of the intellect and the functioning of a machine. The intellectual principle has been replaced in society by the mechanical, a change which, he thinks, makes "solitariness of thought", and therefore art, impossible.

III

It has been noted that Lewis stressed the importance of stability and the value of the intellectual approach to life and literature. He saw two conflicting principles in the arts, which can broadly be described as the "classical" and the "romantic". Moreover, he saw those two basic principles at war in politics and in society in general. In this context, they can be defined as authoritarianism and democracy. "The classical is the rational, aloof and aristocratical, the 'romantic' is the popular, sensational and 'cosmically' confused. That is the permanent political reference in these terms."[18]

Lewis's desire for an authoritarian government had the same basis as his desire for the "classical" in the fine arts. It is rather confusing though, because Byzantine mosaics are very unlike ancient Greek sculpture. Hulme's influence can be seen in this use of the word "classicism". He tended to lump together the diverse literary qualities of poets he liked as "classicism". He put Horace, Racine, the English Augustans and Shakespeare and the Elizabethans all together under this heading, and used Nietzsche's phrase "dynamic classicism" to hide the discrepancy. In the same way, Lewis described the literary qualities of writers he liked as "classical", and those of writers he did not like as "romantic". He attacked Joyce, for example, and said he was on the side of the "time-philosophers". Yet Joyce had great enthusiasm for the kind of forms Lewis wanted. It just seems hardly possible to write a novel which feels like a Byzantine mosaic.

Lewis says that by "classical" he means "something rigorous, hard and cold in the way of thinking; the rational rather than the emotional approach".[19] Yeats also often talks in this way about the kind of approach he wants to literature, but Lewis is more precise about it:

" 'The architectural simplicity'—whether of a platonic idea or a Greek temple—I far prefer to no *idea* at all or no *temple* at all. ... Nothing could ever convince my EYE—even if my intelligence were otherwise overcome—that anything that did not possess this simplicity, conceptual quality, hard exact outline, grand architectural proportion was the greatest art."[20]

In society what is needed "for the greatest achievements of the intellect, whether in art or science, is tranquillity and a stable order of things".[21] He contrasts this situation, which would be ideal for the artist, with the one existing in the twentieth century and the romantic ideal. He says Spengler is "for the 'Faustian Culture' (which resolves itself into modern Western Romanticism). That is 'far away' (or 'infinite', 'yearning', etc.), that hates the line, that loves the 'perspective', in which 'things' only exist in their relation to a misty, 'far-echoing whole', not for themselves".[22] Lewis dislikes imprecision in anything, particularly in the arts, as this leads ultimately to the destruction of the arts, to the destruction of "the line", that is, the properly defined. He associates imprecision with emotion, which will also destroy art if it is allowed to replace the intellect. He believes this is happening in modern literature. He deplores "the emotional—and hence decadent, imperfect, romantic—character of most art today".[23]

Before going on to discuss in detail what exactly Lewis means by this, we should note the political reference in the terms he uses. That is, we should be aware of the inter-relation between philosophic speculation and artistic philosophy on the one hand, and political philosophy on the other. Lewis himself was aware of this connection, and says that to have the "hidden cable connecting philosophic speculation with politics" exposed is a valuable and suggestive experience. He stresses the connection between art and literature and politics, and assumes that the arts today are politically useful. In other words, literature (he is probably thinking more of literature here than the other arts) can directly affect society and the forms of government : "But all art must be a political expression to some extent, and science exists owing to its usefulness. Politically it is extremely useful. And art today is more involved with science than at any former period."[24]

A little later in the same book he makes a closer connection between art and politics. "But all creative activity at the best of times must have been influenced, if not controlled, by political necessity." He does not think that this is necessarily a bad thing, but that in an age of continuous political revolution, the arts are bound to degenerate as the necessary stability and authority will be lacking. He believes that, before the end of the eighteenth century, politics were not so fluid and society was more stable than it is today; and he attributes to political causes the subsequent changes both in society and the arts. "In the eighteenth and seventeenth centuries there was the homogeneity of discipline, the like-thinking of a classical norm. The turning point was political; the age of political revolution was followed by the era of perpetual revolution in the arts."[25] He sees this discipline, this "classical-norm", as the antithesis of the intuitive mode of thinking and feeling. Revolutions, post-eighteenth-century movements both in art and politics, are contrasted with the classical principles of discipline and stability.

In 1954, apropos of the visual arts, where the effects of the revolutionary principle are most obvious, Lewis says that if this principle is carried any further the visual arts will disappear altogether. The point has been reached beyond which the visual arts cannot go technically without committing suicide. But Lewis disagrees with Malraux, who thinks that revolutions in the visual arts in the nineteenth century had a political implication; that is, painters rejected the values of a society they did not like, and this was reflected in their rejection of existing techniques in painting. Lewis thinks this merely showed they disliked the way in which earlier artists painted. But he has already said that revolutions in art have been the result of political revolutions. This statement has the same implication as Malraux's. If Lewis simply means that it is the *act* of challenging and rejecting certain accepted beliefs and principles that is the common factor in artistic and political revolutions, then it is difficult to see why he puts the turning point at the end of the eighteenth century. Surely artists before the French Revolution had rejected fashions and techniques which were current in their times. Jonson, Milton and Dryden did this. Chaucer's decision to write in English was politically significant, and he turned away from the allegorical technique.

If the turning point between an organised, disciplined ethos, and one in which revolutions are frequent, was a political revolution, then it seems probable that subsequent artistic revolutions did have political implications. This perhaps differentiates them to a certain extent from earlier changes in technique, and may account for their frequency. It becomes increasingly difficult to say how closely artistic and political beliefs were related the further we go back in time. But I think there was a great deal of buried politics in Dryden's taste. It is also likely that Milton's political and literary principles have a common basis. The austerity of his style, the linguistic discipline imposed by his "latinisms", the bareness and harshness of much of his poetry, are the literary counterparts of his Puritanism. Much of *Paradise Lost* evidently dramatises his Parliamentarian sympathies, even if in a puzzling way.

This would seem to contradict Lewis's thesis. When he says the turning point was political revolution, he means the French Revolution. But the Parliamentarian Revolution was a forerunner of the French Revolution in that it challenged an authority which had long been invested with Divine Sanction, and did so in the name of political democracy. Once such a supreme authority had been rejected, there was no longer anything sacrosanct. The difference in the effects of these two revolutions was that, although monarchy was eventually restored in both cases, the French Revolution had a much wider and deeper political influence, and was responsible, along with the industrial and technological revolutions, for an increased "politicalisation" of all aspects of human existence. All thought and action was increasingly interpreted in political terms. Today all thought tends to have a political implication, whether it is intended to or not : hence Malraux can say that the artistic changes in the nineteenth century were as much political as artistic. Lewis is in a dilemma here. He recognises the importance of political influence on the arts, but dislikes the idea that changes in artistic techniques have anything to do with politics. Since the beginning of the nineteenth century, all thought, including that embodied in literature, has had a greater political implication; this explains why Lewis, Eliot, Yeats and Lawrence are so concerned with social and political questions, while at the same time professing a dislike of political discussion.

There is a close connection, Lewis believes, between politics and the literature and philosophy of what he calls "modern Western Romanticism", exemplified, in particular, by the writtings of Bergson, Spengler, Gertrude Stein and Joyce. He says it "is almost impossible for any of the philosophers engaged in the task of putting the mind in its place, to express themselves without political analogy and phrasing".[26] Of the Impressionist painters he says, "there were politics implicit in these aesthetics it is true enough—the politics of the Plain Man".[27] This is equally true, he thinks, of the aesthetics of writers like Joyce and Stein. In *Time and Western Man*, Lewis is careful to dissociate himself from Joyce, and all that this writer stands for as exhibited in *Ulysses*. This book shows that Joyce's aesthetic principles are the antithesis of Lewis's. "It is a masterpiece of romantic art; and its romance is of the sort imposed by the 'time' philosophy."[28] That is, destructive of art in the long run. Lewis says the same thing of Stein's aesthetics as of those of the Impressionist painters. The following quotation also contains a direct statement by Lewis of the relation between "tendency" (in this case a democratic tendency), and literary style:

"In adopting the simplicity, and illiterateness, of the mass average of the Melancthas and Annas, Miss Stein gives proof of all the false 'revolutionary', propagandist plainmanism of her time. The monstrous, desperate, soggy *lengths* of primitive mass life, chopped off and presented to us as a never ending prose song, is undoubtedly intended as an epic contribution to the present mass-democracy. The texture of the language has to be jumbled, cheap, slangy and thick to suit. It must be written in a slovenly, straight-off fashion, so that it may appear to be more 'real'. Only the metre of an obsessing *time* has to be put into it. It has to be rhythmatised, and this proclivity both of Miss Stein, and of all those characteristic fashions of those for whom she writes, destroys the reality at best, giving to the life it patronises the mechanical bias of its creator."[28]

Here Lewis mentions, or implies, most of the literary and sociological phenomena he dislikes. Democratic politics, the "flow of consciousness" technique of writing, "time" philosophy, mass-movements, primitivism and the intuitive mode of being (champpioned by Bergson), and romanticism in literature (this is covered by "written in a slovenly, straight-off fashion") are all associated.

Although he is aware of the relation between democratic "tendency" and the literary technique of "romanticism", Lewis is apparently not aware of the relation between authoritarian "tendency" (fascism especially) and the technique of "neoclassicism". Or if he is, he never says so. Only once does he give any hint of such a relation, and this is in retrospect: "I had recognised that a great revolution was under way; that an entirely new epoch had begun, for England and for the world. It had its roots in those ferments of which Cubism, Futurism and Vorticism were intellectual expressions."[29] Here Lewis makes a definite connection between aesthetics and general social and political trends. He implies that the aesthetics of these movements, which are the counterparts in the visual arts of the writings of Lewis, Pound, Yeats and Eliot, had the same basis as the social ferment.

Lewis adopts an extreme intellectual approach to the arts. His novels are populated by ideas rather than by characters, and only rarely does he convincingly portray, or even attempt to portray, human emotions. Apart from ascetics, who are projections of his own character, there are practically no real people in his novels. The characters represent either intellectual concepts or social types. His most ambitious work, *The Human Age*, does not even take place on earth. The characters are all dead before the story begins. This frees him from the need to create convincing characters, and allows his mind to range freely over a variety of topics. His asceticism is also revealed in his prose style. He never chooses his words for their emotive power. He chooses them first for their intellectual content, their ability to convey abstract ideas; second, for their visual impact, their ability to provide a concrete, sharply defined image of what he wants to describe; third, for their ability to stand out by themselves, apart from the rhythm of either the sentence or the paragraph. His writing has little emotive power, and this is intentional. His prose style is an attempt to achieve precision and exactitude, even down to each individual word, and to exclude anything redolent of emotion, in an attempt to indoctrinate the reader with his own principles and beliefs. This is why he is better known for books like *Time and Western Man* and *The Art of Being Ruled* than for his novels. His style is eminently suitable for polemical writing; it is designed to be the artistic counterpart of his authoritarian political beliefs, as hard, austere, aloof and unbending as tempered steel.

In *The Art of Being Ruled*, Lewis adds a rider to the belief that the same principles hold good both in aesthetics and politics. This is that political problems had better be solved on aesthetic lines. In other words, art is the measure of all things, and political problems should be worked out by applying the same principles as one would in judging a work of art. He is discussing the problem of violence in society: "Where violence is concerned the aesthetic principle is evidently of more weight than the 'moral', the latter being only the machinery to regulate the former. One is an expedient, whose pretensions can easily be exploded : the other is the thing itself. As measure is the principle of all true art and as art is an enemy of all excess, so it is along aesthetic lines that the solution of this problem should be sought rather than along moral (or police) lines, or humanitarian ones. The soberness, measure, and order that reigns in all the greatest productions of art is the thing on which it is most useful to fix the mind in considering this problem . . . the exaggeration, emphasis, and unreality of all forms of common melodrama are all in the same class, and are vulgar first and evil because of that : the ethical canon must ultimately take its authority from taste. . . . Sadistic excess attempts to reach roughly and by harshness what art reaches by fineness."[30] This is a ridiculous attitude, but the passage serves to show the real weakness of Lewis's position. It is impossible to prove him wrong by logical argument; it is a question of sympathy. Before 1940, Lewis had very little human sympathy, either for individuals or for the mass of humanity. Like T. E. Hulme, he rejected humanitarian standards, but did not accept what Hulme called "absolute" ethical standards provided by religious dogma. He created his own "absolute" aesthetic standards, and said that any problem can be judged according to these standards. Problems concerning human behaviour, however, man's treatment of man, ought not to be solved according to aesthetic principles. The belief in absolute standards, whether aesthetic or religious, can cause and has caused the most atrocious human suffering. Lewis believed in the paramount importance of the arts; that artistic principles should govern one's attitude to moral and social problems. Such is the relation between his own artistic and political beliefs.

IV

The child-cult is another phenomenon which Lewis associates with modern democratic society; he relates it to the lowering of artistic standards and the decay of the "classical" principles, which reflect the decay of society. It follows the degeneration of the individual, as "a movement of retreat and discouragement— a part of the great strategy of defeat suggested to or evolved by our bankrupt society. Certainly there is a great deal of this discouragement and fear in it."[31] This ethos is expressed in Eliot's *Prufrock*. It is also reflected in the lives of the inhabitants of Third City in *Monstre Gai*. Pullman and Satters have managed to get into the city at the end of the Bailiff's retinue. They do not know whether or not this city is Heaven, but they soon discover it is not. This is obvious to Pullman from the look of the people there. "Something that struck one about all these people was that their faces were youthful. They were such as a young man would get if he had been young for a very long time, until the skin had come to look like parchment."[32] The citizens of Third City display the mental age they had reached in life on earth. Thus Satters, although he lived to be an old man on earth, appears as a fag, a great big baby who never did, and never will, pass the mental age of sixteen. The crowd in the city are similar specimens—"and always the black hole of the mouth". Vacuity is about their only characteristic. All this is the result of the child-cult. "If you banish altogether the mature, reduce everything to the childish, and keep it on ice for ... for a ... for a century, or even for two, three, or four decades ... it does produce something whose mindlessness verges on the mad."[33] Thirty years earlier, in *The Art of Being Ruled*, Lewis implied that it was the irresponsible, non-intellectual nature of the masses that made democracy inadequate, and which made a change to authoritarianism necessary. Here his opinion of the mass is much the same as it was earlier, but he now feels their hopelessness is the result of a bad system, one that deliberately fosters human futility for its own ends. The Bailiff is the arch-exponent of this technique. Mannock and Pullman are discussing the population of Third City. Pullman says:

"I find it uncomfortable to be in the company of this moronic majority. They are a very odd product indeed. How did they get like that?"

Mannock looked excited. He seemed very pleased at what his guest had said. "Well now," he continued, "what would you say was the philosophy of this place? And of course it is *contrived*, is it not—it is not natural for it to be like this. Is it an institution for the preservation and glorification of mediocrity? What he preaches, outside there, in the Camp, is that it is the *typical* that is valuable. The Bailiff has kept out of this place anyone of the slightest intelligence or character, anyone out of the ordinary. He has very thoroughly sifted the humanity presented to him at that Tribunal. Then there are these gangs of youths to which your fag has immediately joined himself. That is the Bailiff's doing. He is a great glorifier of 'Youth', of the immature, even of the childish. If you and Satterthwaite had gone up before him, our young hooligan lying on the bed in there would have been passed in, you would have been rejected. He does not, of course, say openly:

'I will pass in to the city the most perfect specimens of human nothingness I can find.' He has a lot of fancy talk about uniqueness. But what actually ensues from the deliveries of his magistracy may very well be examined in the Universal Café. And he deliberately wills it to be like that; that is what he aims at, and that is what he secures."

"The Bailiff, one would say—don't you think—was justifying the existence of this city. It is almost as if he had said 'there are very good men, and there are very bad men. Heaven is provided for the former, Hell for the latter; but is it a crime just to be the human average. . . ?' And it would seem that, through this insistence upon an ideal of averageness, he has produced a horrible nullity."

"That is wonderfully interesting. You really expressed that beautifully," exclaimed Mannock. "But, if you don't mind my saying so, that would be entirely to misread the motives of this man. He is not seeking after some perfection, and reaching nullity by mistake. Oh no, he has attained to nothingness on purpose." [34]

The tendency, as Lewis sees it, of modern democratic society to make imbeciles of the general public, is stated here in a celestial setting; and Satters is present throughout *The Human Age* to remind us of that "monstrous baby called 'the Public' ". But, after all, it is not true that democracy intentionally produces imbeciles. One might say that the predominantly commercial basis of modern society tends to do it; the trend is usually traced back to the success of Northcliffe, who created a taste rather than catered for one already existing. R. C. Churchill has shown that working class reading, though not widespread, was of a high standard in the nineteenth century. It is wrong to assume that Northcliffe's productions had widespread popularity because they were of a low standard; they were the first to be deliberately aimed at the new reading public.

Lewis wants some kind of separation between the creative man and the average man, but he insists that his motive is not personal. He believes the social structure should be "hierarchised" in the interest of everybody. "The ploughboy does not want to think but to plough." His viewpoint is cultural rather than social. He does not mean "the workers are happier in their muck", nor does he sentimentalise the worker's situation, as Eliot sentimentally idealises an industrial slum with its window boxes. He does not agree with Eliot's élite theories either. "All élite theories . . . suffer from a priggish taint, even a 'crème de la crèmishness'." In 1950 he denied any charge of despising the crowd, or of having an inhuman attitude to "the many"; he denied any similarity between his own attitude to the mass, and Nietzsche's attitude to the "canaille". For Lewis the difference between the creative man and the average man is that the intellectual way of life and work extend the horizons of the individual, whereas a butcher, for instance, is mechanical in his job; it needs no conscious intelligence, no imagination. Therefore, it is in the interests both of the ordinary man, and of art, that there be this separation. Lewis says that what he feels is a "bitter impatience with the philistine or the bourgeois which is very different in origin from a snobbish disdain".[35] This idea that, if a man's work is dull, he will be happier if he is given dull evenings as well, seems more like a long joke than a theory.

v

Lewis wrote *Time and Western Man* to try to counteract the influence of Bergson's philosophy of "Creative Evolution", and Einstein's Relativity Theory. He believed the whole movement to be democratic in essence, political in impulse and not genuinely speculative: "How far was Bosanquet right in identifying these attitudes in philosophy with specific political revolutionary idealism, and how far is the philosophic concept 'Time' in reality the old political 'Progress' transformed for the occasion?"[36] The quintessence of Bergson's philosophy can be stated as follows: (I have put this together from *The Philosophy of Change*, an essay on the philosophy of Bergson, by H. Wildon Carr.)

> "The impetus of life, the springing forward, pushing, insinuating, incessantly changing movement of life, has evolved the intellect to know the inert world of matter, and has given to matter the appearance of a solid, timeless existence spread out in space. Reality is not solid matter, nor thinking mind, but living, creative evolution. This reality is life. It is an unceasing becoming, which preserves the past and creates the future. Our ordinary idea that the reality of things consists in their being solid objects in space, the idea that underlies the whole of physical science, involves the conception of an unreal time. When we consider a living being, however, we find that time is the very essence of its life, the whole meaning of its reality."

Lewis was right in finding a close relation between the political concept of "Progress" and Bergson's "Creative Evolution". Bergson's version of evolution differs from Lamarck's in that he believed life has within it some driving force towards the highest forms, while Lamarck said it produces the forms which its environment makes it need. Indeed the political idea of progress was derived from this by analogy. But the whole of Bergson's philosophy is anathema to Lewis. His belief in the value of stability, which we have already noticed, is the antithesis of Bergson's "eternal flux". For Bergson, time is the essence of living things, and somehow part of the reality of all material things; Lewis rejects all this completely. With a touch of persecution mania, he describes an extremely widespread movement, including "time-philosophy", Einstein's theory of an expanding universe, and the idea of "Progress", which is fundamentally a political plot.

In *One Way Song* he complains that the accent in modern society is all on forward movement, progress, and he mentions the political implication of Einstein's theories:

> "An expanding universe, a bursting corn—
> An ever-budding, bigger and better system."

The consequence of all this is that we lose contact with the culture, values and experience of past ages. The "classical" principles which are not affected by time and which are applicable in any age are ignored: "six-foot of wall/twixt us and pastness". He says the "time-philosophers" have caused this break: "The 'time-philosophers' are still for me what they were then—men who presided at, and speeded the dissolution of an ancient culture."[37]

To explain his opposition to Bergson, Lewis says that time has no existence apart from things. It is not an absolute, and cannot be separated from change; indeed, the infinitesimal time-lag between a stationary object and a moving object will finally prove the downfall of the time-philosophers. In the meantime, however, the time doctrine is connected with action and violence; fascists have the word "action" always on their lips, and violence is their god. This is in *Time and Western Man*, written shortly after *The Art of Being Ruled*, and before *Hitler*, both of which are pro-fascist. Lewis, therefore, saw the dangers inherent in fascism right from the start, but this did not stop him from supporting it. In the late nineteen-thirties, Lewis said that he had not recognised the violent nature of German fascism in its early years. But these quotations show that he had. It was not until he saw the mass-hysteria which fascism aroused that he changed his mind about it. In fact, it was not the coercion or the atrocities of the Nazi regime that made Lewis withdraw his support. He did so when he saw that it had certain characteristics in common with what he called democracy.

What concerns Lewis even more than the effect of the "time-philosophers" on society, is their effect on the arts. They have not only destroyed an ancient, traditional culture, but have tried to undermine all those artistic ideals which Lewis upholds:

> "But no doubt what made me, to begin with, a painter, was some propensity for the exactly defined, and also, fanatically it may be, the physical or the concrete. And I do not think you have to be a painter to possess such inclinations. Many painters indeed, have no repugnance, it would appear, for the surging ecstatic, feature-less chaos which is being set up as an ideal, in place of the noble exactitude and harmonious proportion of the European, scien-tific, ideal—the specifically Western heaven."[38]

Lewis dislikes *Ulysses* because he believes it represents this "surging chaos"; and that it shows the same kind of "plain-manism" as Stein's novels, in that its hero, Bloom, is an ordinary, average, undistinguished human being. But he attacks it mainly because he associates it with Bergson's philosophy: "*Ulysses* is constructed on the most approved 'time' basis—that is, a basis of the fluid material gushing of undisciplined life."[38] He believes that the influence of Bergson's philosophy on literature is to make language imprecise. "Hostility to the word goes hand in hand with propaganda for the intuitional, mystical chaos."[39] By "hos-tility to the word", he means indifference to the precise use of language; having no interest in, or knowledge of, semantics and philology; using words for their evocative power rather than their intellectual power; and taking no account of their use and associations in literature and science. Lewis is fond of quoting Henry Ford's advice to young writers—get a dictionary and study the meaning of words. Joyce, especially in *Finnegan's Wake*, tries to do without traditional meanings of words, and tries to create his own language of sound and suggestion. This book, I think, can best be described as an experiment in the evocative power of language, but we are supposed to know the root mean-ings and pick out layers of puns; that is how the language is to evoke. Joyce was doing something similar in *Ulysses* only in not such an extreme way. Lewis's "classical" bias, his preference for the concrete, the clearly defined, the "hard", makes him reject writing of this kind, just as his asceticism makes him reject much of the subject matter of *Ulysses* as being unsuitable for literature.

In *Time and Western Man*, there is a lengthy criticism of Behaviourism, which Lewis sees as the counterpart in Psychology of the ideas of Bergson and the time-philosophers. The physiological explanation of psychological states, the idea that glandular action determines personality, is responsible for the destruction of the self, the ego, the personality, the mind, the psyche, or what Lewis calls "the thinking subject". He sees these psychological theories as pseudo-scientific evidence trumped up by the agents of this destructive force in art, politics and science. Consequently the brain emerges not as the "master tissue", but merely as the servant of the "vegetative apparatus", with the stress always placed on the primitive. He thinks that Bergson's philosophy has the same effect : "He has been the great organiser of disintegration in the modern world : it is he who has found all the 'reasons' . . . for the destruction of the things of the intellect, and the handing over to sensation of the privileges and heirlooms of the mind, and the enslaving of the intelligent—the affective nature."[40]

Lewis says that Nietzsche and Bergson share the responsibility for the poor state of the arts in twentieth-century society. They have caused a perversion of the artistic ideal, which has resulted in extreme and worthless movements. "The vulgar frenzy of Nietzsche, and Bergson's gospel of fluidity and illiquation form in about equal measure the philosophic basis of futurism and similar movements."[40] The social and political movements closely connected with these philosophers have exactly the same effect on the arts : "The fiery millenial zeal of the social revolutionary emotionally galvanising everything, and instilling the painter with a quite irrational belief in the rightness of his latest mannerism."[41] This belief in "Progress" is reflected in literature in writers like Shaw and Wells, and the communist poets of the nineteen-thirties.

In an attempt to uphold the principles by which he believes art flourishes, and to create conditions suitable for artistic production, Lewis sets up his "classical" ideal against Bergson's ideals. The contrast lets us see more clearly what he is aiming at. First, he is concerned with the concrete reality, and the "hard exact outline" of things. He calls the arts "the science of the *outside* of things". This is the exact opposite, he says, of Bergson's concern with "Life" which cannot be properly defined. " 'Life' (of the 'Up Life ! down art !' cry) means invariably the smoking hot *inside* of things, in contrast to the hard, cold, formal skull or carapace. The *emotional* of the Bergsonian dogma is the heat, moisture, shapelessness, and tremor of the vitals of life. The *intellectual* is the ectodermic case, the ideality of the animal machine with its skin on."[42] This is the view of the artist—the writer and painter—who is concerned with trying to communicate his observations of the external world as accurately as possible, as opposed to the view of the philosopher. But Lewis believes that the only hope for the arts and for society in general lies in a return to the ideals of the classical tradition. "All the health and sanity that we have left belongs to that world and its forms and impulses. . . . Today the issue is between that nature, or some development on it on the one side, and upon the other those forces represented by the philosophy of time."[43] The "neo-classic" movement in literature and the fine arts which included Lewis, Pound, Eliot and Yeats was the development he talks about. At one point he confidently asserts that it overcame Bergson's influence on the arts:

> "The influence of Bergson went down beneath the wave of formal enthusiasm that immediately preceded the War. In the arts that movement brought imagination back once more, banishing the naturalist dogmas that had obtained for fifty or sixty years. Impressionism was driven out, and the great ideals of structure and formal significance were restored."[44]

The fact that very few writers have been affected by this formal enthusiasm might be said to show how deep Bergson's influence had gone. I think, however, it is the result of political causes. The search for authority in the arts was conducted side by side with a search for authority in society. An extreme form of political authoritarianism, fascism, appeared at the right time to attract these writers. It had the added attractions of appearing to be a benevolent despotism, and to have an interest in the arts and the function of the artist in society. The political system as it developed in Germany and Italy under fascism, and in the Second World War, however, was sufficient to make most writers reject Lewis's ideas, even writers who might otherwise have agreed with him.

VI

In any discussion of democracy and authoritarianism, the question of the freedom of the individual inevitably arises. Supporters of democracy say that only under such a system are the rights of the individual preserved. Lewis does not deny that authoritarianism curtails the freedom of the individual, but he argues that democracy produces a wrong conception of freedom; that in a democracy, freedom and irresponsibility become synonymous. The child-cult, he says, is an attempt to achieve the complete freedom from responsibility which is the prerogative of the child. He makes a similar attack on the "artist-cult". Again and again between the wars Lewis attacked those people who had enough money to be able to play the part of an artist, without having artistic ability. His novel *Revenge for Love* satirises the pseudo-bohemian society of rich idlers who profess to be painters or writers, who rent studios, and make it impossible for real painters to find anywhere to live and work. These people undermine true artistic standards by producing third-rate work, and by providing a market for it as well. Lewis describes them as fellow-travellers who, with their upper middle-class backgrounds, profess allegiance to the working classes, but in reality have not the slightest connection with them, indeed despise them. The professional communist, Percy Hardcaster, is treated in the same way, and when he tells them a few home truths he is brutally attacked. This episode reveals a serious defect in Lewis's writing technique. He does not seem able to dissociate his personal animosities from his characterisation. He often creates characters who are representatives of some type which he dislikes, or of some philosophy or mode of thinking which he opposes, and then tries to win our support for his attitude by making them commit some thoroughly objectional action. One of the parlour communists kicks Hardcaster's stump where he has had his leg amputated; Kreizler, in *Tarr*, commits rape; and the Bailiff periodically allows his attendants to trample the petitioners to pulp. The last two books of *The Human Age* are full of such atrocities. A novelist ought not to assume that anyone who is temperamentally different from himself, or who holds different views, is also necessarily vicious in character.

Lewis, then, thinks that the issue of individual freedom is irrelevant, as most people do not want freedom anyway! "For in the mass people wish to be automatic: they wish to be conventional: they hate you teaching them or forcing them into 'freedom': they wish to be obedient, hard-working machines, as near dead as possible—as near dead (feelingless and thoughtless) as they can get without actually dying."[45] Freedom implies a choice between alternative courses of action, and responsibility for whichever course one chooses. Lewis says this is just what most people do not want; but that a disciplined, well-policed, herd-life is what they most desire. It is mistaken to think it inhuman to do away with individual freedom and responsibility for one's actions:

> "The ideal of obedience conceived by the Jesuits, so that, in their words, 'a member of their order should regard himself as a corpse, to be moved here or there' at the absolute discretion of the superior, has often been described as an 'inhuman' one. But is it 'inhuman'? For is it not what most people desire, to be dolls of a sort, to be looked after, disciplined into insensitiveness, spared from suffering by insensibility and blind dependence on a will superior to their own?"[46]

Hence Lewis thinks that autocratic rule is not inhuman. On the contrary, it is in the interest of the happiness of the people.

What form, then, is the supreme authority in society to take? The aristocracy can no longer assume this authority. They have lost all function in the modern world, Lewis believes. His satire *The Apes of God* depicts among other things the decline of the aristocracy. Lewis's attitude to this class is the complete opposite of Yeats's. He says that as a class they had outstayed their useful-ness and had grown to be preposterous parasites. Attempts have been made to identify particular individuals described in the novel, but this is of minor interest, because the work is political satire—"all social satire is political satire".[47] However, it is rele-vant that Lewis was thinking of Bertrand Russell. He sees Russell as a representative of the "humanitarianism of Liberal England", and he believes that the humanitarian ideal is no longer valid. It was the result of a spoilt and heedless prosperity which no longer exists, and was an effect of natural race egotism and aristocratism. Russell exhibits all the weaknesses of the society that he conventionally represents, and using Russell's own words to support his argument, Lewis describes him as "this 'tentative' and 'cautious' creature who is the kind of man of science who was so well described by Nietzsche, the man who was no longer able to will anything, even in his sleep; whose resolution had become entirely absorbed by his cautions and hesitations".[48] As a result, the aristocracy is politically dead. The *Apes of God* also satirises the numerous trivialities of Bloomsbury. The arty frauds are surveyed through the eyes of Daniel Boleyn, a gigantic young moron guided by Horace Zagreus who is supposed to unmask the frauds, but who is, himself, the arch-fraud. He is completely sterile, and when at his most brilliant, he is merely repeating the words of Pierpoint, a shadowy figure who dominates the novel but who never appears. What is most striking about this novel, of gigantic bulk and linguistic brilliance, is that Lewis/Pierpoint should expend so much energy on such trivialities.

The destruction of political authority is paralleled, Lewis thinks, by the destruction of the authority of the intellect, of "the like thinking of a classical norm". In his opinion, "the extinction of mind, the psyche, ran parallel to the libertarian process and the suppression of all visible authority".[49] He finds the same lack of authority in modern psychology, which, as we have seen, he associates with modern astronomy, democratic politics and "modern western romanticism" in literature. *Time and Western Man* contains a detailed attack on Behaviourism, which, he says, reduces a person to a set of predictable gestures; that is, it creates a mass of robots, or "things", The characters in *Childermass*, which could be described as *The Art of Being Ruled* dramatised, reflect this process. The Bailiff is the will behind the time-doctrines. He is the incarnate Zeitgeist, the representative of space-time. He embodies what Lewis saw as a definite, destructive intention behind these doctrines. The Bailiff denies any real personal existence to the people who come before him : "You persisted for a certain number of years like a stammer. You were a stammer, if you like, of Space-time. She...began saying 'Macrob' and she went on stammering 'Macrob' in a continuous present for the period of your natural life."[50] This also implies a connection between the "time doctrines" and the decay of language. He describes this decay—"Come now and I'll show you how it is that the words get melted, in gland-mud washing of de Swanee—bottom"—and follows this with a long parody of Joyce's style, which he mistakenly saw as evidence of the decay of language.

A more authoritarian form of society would, he thinks, have a salutary effect on psychological theories :

"The fashionable doctrines in psychology may be regarded as very much one with the social tendencies of the times. Is it too rash to assume that, with another kind of social structure, less deliberately fluid and destructive, more favourable to stability and to personal, secure and constructive achievements, we should have other psychological doctrines?"[51]

Such books as *The Art of Being Ruled, Time and Western Man* and *The Lion and the Fox*, record his desire for an authoritarian society. The last-named book is Shakespearean criticism, but the title itself hints at the different kinds of personal power which he believes to compete in modern society. One kind is typified by Iago—that of "the typical man of today"; that is, "pride in commonplace cunning". The other kind of power, the power that should be wielded by those at the head of an autocratic government, is the effect of the "natural law of what is due to character, creative genius, and personal power".[52] Lewis's Shakespearean criticism is similar to Bernard Shaw's, in that they both interpret Shakespeare in terms of their own philosophic concepts. Lewis sees Shakespeare's heroes (the opposites of the actual world) as "involved in a *real* action : whereas they come from, and naturally inhabit, an ideal world", and this is their tragedy. They are destroyed by a process stemming from human contact, but their real tragedy is that they are overcome by the small, the weak and the trivial : "in the pessimism of tragedy not only have the great always to be vanquished; but they have always to be overcome by trivial opponents who substitute a poor and vulgar thing for the great and whole thing that they have destroyed."[53] He implies that the hero is caught between two worlds—that of ideal austerity and asceticism, which is his natural environment, and the time-world. It is one of the inhabitants of this world who causes his downfall—Iago, representative of "the dark equivocal crowd saturated with falsity".

Lewis clearly tries to make Shakespeare himself into the ideal artist-hero type, contemptuous of society, even of life itself, his art the antithesis of life and action. Lewis describes Shakespeare as "a greater *hero* than any of the figures he depicted; in spectacular glory and renown no physical achievement could surpass his."[54] This hero figure is central to many of Lewis's books—*The Art of Being Ruled, Time and Western Man, The Diabolical Principle, The Apes of God, Childermass* and *One Way Song*. But Lewis's interpretation of Shakespeare's character and his artistic intentions is very one-sided and highly idiosyncratic.

VII

Lewis's ideas about power are clearly related to fascist ideology. His desire for the separation of the creative man and the average man, which we have noticed, is also close to certain fascist ideals, or at least, to ideals which the fascists adopted. Lewis says, "If the inflexible organisation (of society) severs it (the inertia of the masses) entirely from all free intelligences in the world, which it more and more isolates, then a new duality of human life (introducing perhaps a new species, and issuing in biological transformation), would result."[55] This idea is very much like Nietzsche's doctrine of the superman, and the Nazi doctrine of the master race. Lewis wants to breed a superior race which could organise society into a sensible pattern, while taking an interest in higher forms of life. This new breed would be the opposite of "that Abstract Man, that enlightened abstraction of a common humanity, which had its greatest advertisement in the eighteenth century. That No Man in a No Man's Land, that phantom of democratic 'enlightenment' is what has to be disposed of for good in order to make way for higher human classifications, which, owing to scientific method, men could not attempt."[56]

Lewis says that "classical" principles in the arts represent the "hard" as opposed to the "machine", and provide the unbending authority necessary for great art. In the same way he says that fascism provides the stern authority which is needed in society. The fascist "promises happiness to the masses as a result of his *iron* rule. But the iron is not hidden, or camouflaged as christian charity. He says that *one* politics in a country, *one* undisputed government will be for the good of the average man. And when these one-party states are centrally organised, as Italy is becoming, who can gainsay him?"[57] This kind of iron rule is not inhuman, he says, but is for the good of the people as a whole. "For the sake of the ruled—that is my argument—the ruler should be forced to rule by force, ostensibly, responsibly, as does the soviet or fascist government."[58] It is also for the sake of the cultivated interests, the arts. (It is likely, therefore, that it is the artist [Lewis] who is to force the ruler to rule by force, and tell him how to rule.) He believes that the leader who would emerge in a fascist regime would uphold the classical virtues of permanence and stability: "But the permanent state of mind of the revolutionary ruler will now be that of the philosopher; a more cultivated, in addition a more able, ruling class than Europe has ever possessed is promised."[59]

He should, apparently, be the antithesis of the democratic politician with his belief in progress, the opponent of the Bergsonian ideal.

I think, however, Lewis realised that the form which the fascist system took in its early days in Italy was only a façade:

"The political power that is taking command in the world today seems to have said to all those immature inoperative people, who were gradually forced away from the seats of authority, that they had for so long held in Europe, 'Run away and play!' Frightened and astonished, they ran away sure enough and are allowed to play also for a moment. But it will not be for long. That is why the fashions devised to fit this temporary situation should be disregarded when you are desirous of reaching some insight into the real tendencies of which they are only a caricatural, early phase." [60]

This was written in 1926. He did not, however, foresee the racial vendetta. He knew the evils which could result from racial antagonism; that race or nationality has, in the modern world, been recognised as a sanction for murder by every state. But he did not think these carried much force in modern society. "Race is the queen of the 'classes': but in Europe today its power is very slight." [61] Lewis was not guilty of the racial prejudice that is associated with fascism. He wrote *Paleface* in reply to Lawrence's books and essays about the Mexican Indian; it is a defence of the European intellectual tradition rather than an attack on the black man. Whether Lewis showed any anti-Jewish feeling is difficult to say. Bergson was Jewish it is true, and Lewis is certainly anti-Bergson. Julien Benda, from whom Lewis derived many of his ideas of the sociology of aesthetics, suggested in *Belphégor* that Jews were responsible for trying to force intellectual work into the realm of the emotions. He said there were two kinds of Jew; the severe, moralistic Jew—the Hebrew—on the one hand, and the Jew who is always greedy for sensation —the Carthaginian Jew—on the other. The second kind, he says, has a passion for "literature creative of emotion". Bergson would obviously fit into this category, and if Lewis had any anti-Jewish feeling, it was of the kind that Benda showed; that is, because of the supposedly bad effect that Jewish thought had had on the arts.

At times, however, Lewis describes the worst features of fascism with apparent relish, and some of the things he said about it can hardly be defended on the grounds of his concern for art and literature, or any other grounds. "In ten years, a state will have been built in which at last no trace of European 'liberalism' or its accompanying democratic 'liberty' exists. This will have been the creation of a tyrant or dictator, with virtual powers of life and death : for with his highly disciplined, implicitly obedient, fascist bands, no person anywhere will be able to escape assassination if he causes trouble to the central government, or holds, too loudly, opinions that displease it. As the press will be—is already—under the direct control of the central government, and its editors and responsible staffs appointed by it, death, imprisonment, or banishment can be inflicted on anybody, anywhere, without ruffling the surface of opinion—indeed, can occur, if required, without its being reported."[62] This is a deplorable attitude. Lewis foresaw exactly what the fascist state would become, and obviously was in sympathy with it in the 1920s. Lewis later attacked the Nazi regime in Germany, but not because of the cruelties it perpetrated, the complete domination of the individual by the state by means of secret police; he had foreseen these and did not consider them evil. He saw that fascism encouraged mass-movements more than democracy does. This is why he rejected it.

Lewis was apparently taken in by Mussolini's lip-service to creative writers. The Italian leader said that writers were important to the state and should have a say in how things ought to be run. In the passage quoted above Lewis obviously sees himself as one of the editors, or as a member of a responsible staff, if not the dictator himself. In such a society, if Lewis had not been a member of the ruling caste, he would have been the first to attack the government and also the first to be assassinated. He is stating, in an extreme form, the belief that a stable society is an absolute necessity for the production of great art. But if "death, imprisonment or banishment" is the price we have to pay to achieve stability, then this price is too high. The question of whether a stable society really is a necessity for artistic achievement will be discussed later.

Lewis goes so far as to insist that it is in the interests of the people to establish a fascist society. He says, "they would be thrown back on 'their own resources' and discover, it is to be hoped, their own reality," and adds, "even the fact that eventually the political order indicated above must lead to the establishment of a caste system does not seem a misfortune, once the caste system is there."[63] Lewis is in a hopeless muddle here. How can people be thrown back on their own resources if society is rigidly centralised, and all responsibility for government removed from the masses and put on to a ruling caste? Also, how can he say this is in the interests of the majority when on the previous page he says : "Can this poor man be the loser—has he anything to lose?—by his rulers shedding their pickwickian masks, the socialist noses, the kindly liberal twinkles of the European egalitarian masquerade, and appearing as men and women very like himself, only luckier; resolved, just as he would be in their shoes, to keep him finally in the gutter, and treat him, as he knows he would treat them, like a dog?" Lewis cannot believe in the democratic system because he cannot believe that anyone could have a disinterested concern for the well-being of the mass of the people. He assumes that anyone in a position of power would despise and maltreat the people over whom he had authority. Lewis himself is temperamentally devoid of broad human sympathy and assumes that everyone else is the same. His rejection of democracy and his support of fascism are based on a narrow conception of human nature.

He also believed that the fascist regime, resulting in a caste system, would produce a superior class of individuals by some means of biological selection. And of these he says : "Perhaps a really *perfect* group, or class, to prevent itself from dying of inanition, would favour war, as a stimulant."[64] The reflection, even at the time, cannot have enlisted support for his artistic ruling class. Lewis is again overstating his belief in the value of a stable society, or else his exasperation at the stupidity and philistinism of the average man. While such statements as these cannot be ignored, to place too much emphasis on them would not give a true picture of Lewis's attitude. For Lewis was usually against violence of any kind. In *Time and Western Man* he wrote, "all the doctrinaire barbarity of the sorelian and nietzschean spirit, leading to the 'blood-baths' of immense wars and revolutions, are like gigantic and ghastly prescriptions for the rejuvenation of some aged thing which had suddenly thrust itself among us".[65] A short time before, he had written this—"the senseless bellicosity of the reactionary groups of the 'Action Française' type may certainly result in far more violence, before long, than anyone is able to measure".[66]

He did recognise the fascist taste for violence—"Fascists have the word 'action' always on their lips. Violence is their god."[67] In *Childermass* the Bailiff is plagued by Hyperides and his band of followers. They form a political movement, the nearest counterpart of which in real life is fascism. One of the followers of Hyperides, called Alectryon, is of the 'steel helmet' type which

Lewis associates with the "Action Française". He also connects this type with the Germanic Gods, Odin and Thor. Lewis is sympathetic towards these people in so far as they are a corrective to the Bailiff's philosophy; here again, we see that the violent nature of fascism was clear to him from the beginning.

As a result of the spread of popular education, and improved communication techniques, says Lewis, "today there is no political, scientific or other charlatanry that cannot be put across them (the people). This power of imposition and suggestion put to good uses, and in the hands of people desiring the good of the mass, would be a marvellous instrument indeed."[68] This, I think, indicates the real weakness of Lewis's position regarding fascism. Most of his arguments in support of fascism presuppose that it is a benevolent system, that those in authority have the interests of society as a whole at heart. There is no reason to suppose that such an ideal position would be achieved under fascism, and the dangers of so much centralisation in the wrong hands are obvious. It is difficult to see how Lewis, of all people, with his view of human nature, could bring himself to believe in a benevolent despotism of this kind.

VIII

The answer is contained in Lewis's view of the artist or intellectual as leader of society. He believes that men as a whole will never be ready for a higher form of civilisation, and the organisation of society should, therefore, be left to those who have "a taste for other forms of life, or who were bred, by means of eugenics, to a different existence".[69] In *Monstre Gai*, Pullman states Lewis's position directly. "We—the human kind—here consist of a horde of idiots. In addition to this degraded caricature of man, there are perhaps a few dozen—perhaps a few hundred—men of intelligence. This more intelligent, this more sensitive handful, they are all we need to consider."[70] Lewis says creative men possess a personal power which makes them natural leaders. The qualities he stresses are "character, creative genius and personal power". "Had the best intelligences at any time in the world been able to combine, the result would have been a prodigy of power, and the result for men at large of the happiest."[71] This idea of the "hero" had attracted many intellectuals before Lewis subscribed to it; the novelty perhaps is in making him almost non-political: "This leader claims the authority of the function that he regards as superior to any mechanical dominion of physical force or wealth. . . . It is he and not the political ruler who supplies the contrast of this something remote and *different* that is the very stuff of which all living (not mechanical) power is composed."[72] But Lewis never says how this "living power" is to be recognised. Moreover, what is character, and who is to be the judge of creative genius? Lewis says "the prodigy of power" should consist of "free" or "best" intelligences. But who possess the best intelligences? Bergson, Einstein and Joyce could all reasonably be put forward as candidates. Lewis would instantly reject them, but that would be a purely arbitrary judgement. Even if an agreement could be reached on which individuals possessed personal power, a good intellect, creative genius and character, they would almost certainly represent such widely differing viewpoints as to make co-operation between themselves impossible. Even if we narrowed the field down to include writers only, it would be well-nigh impossible to decide which of them possessed these qualities. A "personal-power-and-creative-genius examination for writers intending to take up posts of political authority" hardly seems possible or desirable. To give artists greater control over specifically cultural matters seems to me a desirable and sensible thing to do. Poets, playwrights and novelists should be given greater opportunities to influence society as poets, playwrights and novelists—not as politicians. To become a member of a ruling political party, as Lewis suggests writers should, is to cease to be a creative artist; at least, if the work of administration is not to suffer. Neither of these tasks is a part-time occupation.

An imaginative writer can, of course, affect society by the influence which his books and ideas have on the minds of individuals. He can make them think as he does, and perhaps cause them to act in a way he would approve. Whatever one may think of politicians past and present, the mind of the creative artist is not often of the kind which could organise and regulate the workings of a real society. In *The Creative Element*, Spender says it was a fallacy of the pre-1930 writers to think that poetry can affect society. Certainly, Lewis thought that the imaginative writer can and does do this: "Now it is well enough to see in the man of words, words that possess so magical a power, the man ideally solitary, world-losing and world-forsaking, but possessed of a power to shake the earth from one pole to the other. Jean-Jacques Rousseau, with his books, certainly did that—tore up society by the roots."[73] I think that writers often have a political effect, and Lewis is very likely right in this quotation. Whether a creative artist is the right person to organise and run society, however, is another matter and more dubious.

Although Lewis thought it was democratic society and its allied artistic and philosophical trends which were destroying literature, he saw a paradox which he could not explain; neither could he see any way out of it, in 1926:

> "The destroyer cannot be at the same time the creator. The political impulses at work constantly distort the issue. The artist or thinker is apt to find himself making something, but ending it with dynamite, as it were. The political necessities underneath the surface are perpetually interfering ... with artistic creation or scientific research. The result is that all contemporary thought, science or art is spoilt, and its speculative integrity, its detachment, sacrificed. It also seems to acquire a mad, evil or hysterical twist. But also it frequently reaches a beauty that is new in Europe. That, I think, is our problem; and it is not easy to see an issue just yet."[74]

This would be Lewis's judgement on Yeats, Lawrence and Pound. While the poetry and novels of these writers contain great beauty, he would say that an evil or hysterical twist is shown in Yeats's aristocraticism and belief in historical cycles, in Lawrence's doctrine of sex and personal relationships, and in Pound's economics. This "mad twist", however, is not due to democracy but to the increasing complexity of civilisation; the fantastic progress of scientific research; the whole complex of industrial and scientific techniques; the vast areas of knowledge which are virtually unattainable to the creative artist, and yet upon which our society depends; and the mind's attempt to resolve the confusion of life in our society, and to come to terms with the baffling modern world. Van Gogh did not go mad because he lived in a democracy, but partly because he lived in a society which ignored the democratic principles in which he believed, and because he almost destroyed himself in trying to put his principles into practice.

After the Second World War, however, Lewis felt the situation had changed. It was no longer democratic society, or mass-advertising, or Bergson's philosophy that made conditions bad for art. It was the atom bomb, and the effect which the probability of universal disaster had on the human psyche. This is the position today. It is fundamentally different from that which existed before 1914, when politics, and war in particular, did not make as big an impression on the whole of a society, but only did so in those parts immediately concerned with the fighting. Lewis became aware of this difference. Of the Napoleonic wars he says, "The balls and festivities of the aristocratic life proceeded as usual in all parts of Russia outside of the reach of the French army."[75] This is not true today. The threat of annihilation is there to all society all the time. This has had a tremendous effect on the mind and temperament of the poet, or would-be poet, since 1945. The arts, indeed practically every feature of human life, appears trivial beside this overwhelming problem. Lewis says, "that is why talking about the alarming outlook for the fine arts appears so trivial a matter when one has finished writing about it. It is infected with the triviality of everything else."[76] This is the verdict of a writer and painter whose main concern throughout his life was with the arts, and the possibility of high art in twentieth-century society.

The poet cannot choose to ignore the problems facing society today, and concentrate solely on the inner life. The world is too much with us. Even if he managed for a while to put the H-bomb out of his mind, an evasion like this is not a good basis for literature. There is a strong possibility today that literature and the fine arts, all the great civilised forms of expression, will disappear altogether. Not only will the individual poet or painter cease to exist; the whole tradition of artistic expression will also cease to exist. The question is whether the poet can assimilate these possibilities and still write first-class poetry. It seems practically certain that those poets who reached maturity before 1945 cannot do this. Whether or not a new generation of poets, accustomed from childhood to the possibility of universal destruction, can succeed, time alone will tell.

III

Ezra Pound

III

EZRA POUND

I

After the end of the last war, Pound was taken back to the United States and tried for treason, but certified insane. Whatever his legal, medical and political position, his poetry has been unintelligible to most readers since he began the *Cantos*. There is a traditional notion that genius and insanity are akin; Pope probably meant by madness what we would today call eccentricity, the refusal to conform to accepted social, moral or intellectual standards; but then again, a modern doctor might call insane a variety of men of the past whose literary or philosophical stature is now undisputed. Rousseau, towards the end of his life, with his persecution mania, Blake, Nietzsche, Poe, the French Symbolists—all are fruitful soil for the modern psychoanalyst. Perhaps even Freud himself, for he too exhibits that characteristic of insanity which one suspects put Pound inside a mental institution—namely, being moved by certain compulsive obsessions.

A discussion of whether Pound was, or was not, insane may seem pointless now that he is free. But examination of the probable cause of, or merciful excuse for, his being certified—his obsessions—is relevant in that they affect his prose and poetry, and one might even say determine the nature and content of his work. Pound certainly knew what he was doing when he broadcast from Rome during the war. If he was mad at the time of his trial, that might be the effect of his post-war imprisonment. But in the *Pisan Cantos*, Pound appears more sane at that time, less driven by his obsessions, than at any other time since the First World War.

Pound was described as a "revolutionary simpleton" by Wyndham Lewis in *Time and Western Man*. It is easy to see what is meant. Once he has accepted some idea or principle, that principle becomes somehow part of his own vanity. Pound's weakness, however, is that he is easily taken in by the simplified idea, the specious method of reasoning, the easy remedy. This is especially true of his economic ideas. From the time that he "discovered" economics he thought that practically all the evils of modern society had an economic basis. This idea predominates in all his work except his translations. He frequently deplores the widespread ignorance of "economics", but the truth is that Pound himself had a very incomplete and distorted view of economics. One can place about as much faith in his economic ideas as in his translations of Confucius. Pound was unfortunate in approaching the study of economics through the writings of Major Douglas and Gesell. Their simplified, straightforward remedies for complex economic problems naturally attracted a mind like Pound's. Afterwards, when he came into contact with more academic economists, to whom the problems were more complex and the remedies not so simple, he could not understand what all the fuss was about, and came to the conclusion that they were in league with the bankers and financiers. For Pound, economic, and especially financial, evils cause the degeneration of society, allowing inept men to gain power, the defeat of the real capable leaders, such as Mussolini and Napoleon, the corruption of moral values, and, very important, the decay of the arts, which is most obvious in architecture and painting.

An examination of Pound's economic ideas is necessary as they form many of the themes in the *Cantos*, affect his conception of the relation between society and the arts, and are responsible in part for his fascist sympathies. Pound says the only economic problem which needs emergency solution in modern society is that of distribution: "We have got to clear up the economic mess . . . how much life can be cured by the very simple application of economic sense to reality (*abundance* of material wealth)."[1] The greatest evil, he thinks, is the stagnation of capital in banks, which results in a lack of purchasing power on the part of the consumer. "Counting money as a certificate of work done, the simplest means of keeping money distributed is to keep work distributed."[2] He believes the problem of labour and distribution can be solved together. He says Marxian economics were based on labour, and formulated at a time when a great deal of labour was needed. The new economics, however, are based on labour plus the complex of inventions. His first solution is to reduce the working day of paid labour so that everyone can work. He believes this would do a lot to keep credit distributed among the population. His second solution is the provision of honest certificates of work done. He says that no one should be able to sign cheques regardless of services rendered, and banks should not be able to charge interest on what they create out of nothing. If money is made the certificate of work done, it will do away with the greatest and most universal evil—usury. Pound adds a rider to all this, which is that the question of how measures are to be taken is a question of politics. Economics is merely concerned with *what* should be done. It is as well that he says this, because though his solutions have the advantage of simplicity, they are very impracticable. For instance, in this world of large-scale industry, expensive machinery, and techniques requiring capital investment, money clearly cannot be counted simply as a certificate of work done.

The Social Credit theory was propounded by Major C. H. Douglas, and in the 1930s the Social Credit Party was formed, its members wearing green shirts. Their plan was to distribute national dividends to all through central banks, and they attacked the existing financial system by trying to prove that it did not reflect the real credit of the community because some of the country's income was continuously being lost in the form of the interest charged by banks. By distributing dividends to everyone they thought that society's purchasing power would correspond to its productive power. Many people saw this theory as a solution to the problems of distribution, unemployment, inflation and devaluation, and Pound wrote Major Douglas's financial ideas into the *Cantos*:

> "I have of course never said that the cash is constant
> (Douglas) and in fact the population (Britain 1914)
> was left with 800 millions of 'deposits'
> after all the cash had been drawn, and
> these deposits were satisfied by the
> printing of treasury notes."
> *(Canto 38)*

This is bound to reduce the value of money:

> "Bank creates it ex nihil. Creates it to meet a need,
> Hic est hyper—usura."
> *(Canto 46)*

Banks not only create money out of nothing, they charge interest on it:

> "interest on all it creates out of nothing
> the b . . . bank has; pure iniquity

and to change the value of money, of the unit of
money.
METATHEMENON
we are not yet out of *that* chapter."
(*Canto* 77)

As the *Cantos* progress, these financial evils assume larger and
larger proportions in Pound's mind :

"and the two largest rackets are the alternation
of the value of money
(of the unit of money. . . .)
and usury   or lending
that which is made out of nothing."
(*Canto* 74)

He is not blaming individual money-lenders, Jews, financiers, but
is attacking the system of capitalism itself :

"and if theft be the main principle in government
(every bank of discount J. Adams remarked)
there will be larceny on a minor pattern."
(*Canto* 76)

This idea is repeated in almost the same words in *Canto* 78, and
follows a passage in which Pound repeats Mussolini's ideas on
money with approval and contrasts them with Churchill's and
the British government's :

"the root stench (is) usura and METATHEMENON
and Churchill's return to Midas broadcast by his liary.
'No longer necessary', taxes are no longer necessary
in the old way if it (money) be based on work done
inside a system and measured and gauged to human
requirements."
(*Canto* 78)

Pound thinks it unfortunate that Mussolini was

"hang'd dead by the heels before his thought in proposito
came into action efficiently."

The first step to be taken in remedying these evils is one which
we would expect a man of letters, or any other clear thinker, to
suggest, and one which recalls his association with Eliot. In a
letter written in 1937, Pound says he is concerned with defining
economic terms, this being necessary before any discussion can
follow. Pound sees a connection between the "obfuscators of language" and financial evils:

"And the betrayers of language. . . .
And those who had lied for hire;
the perverts, the perverters of language,
    the perverts, who have set money—lust
Before the pleasures of the senses."
                              (*Canto 14*)

The only solution is to examine the society in which these evils
occur, and discover their cause in the society itself, not in the
individuals who comprise that society:

"like an arrow
Missing the bull's eye seeks the cause in himself,
only the total sincerity, the precise definition,"
                              (*Canto 77*)

will solve these problems. The defining of economic terms is very
difficult and there is little indication that Pound ever got beyond
a superficial definition of the terms he uses. Not only is his
economic knowledge superficial, but the range of his interest is
narrow. Employment problems, he says, can be solved by limit-
ing the paid working day, so that no one person could do the
work of two or three, but anybody could earn enough to satisfy
his material needs. Although he sees distribution as the most
pressing problem, he is mainly concerned with the nature and
value of money, and the monopolistic money-lending activities
of financiers and bankers.

II

This concern with economics is not irrelevant to the study of
Pound's poetry or his theory of literature. In his later career, in
sharp contrast to the aestheticism of his early poems, he has
stressed the inter-relation between literature and economics. He
thought that unless writers studied modern economics, the theory
of Major Douglas, that is, and incorporated this study into their
imaginative writing, the literature being produced in the mid-
twentieth century would be worthless. In 1934 he wrote, "Capitalist psychology [is] a disease that has eaten thru every interstice
of the mind. . . . How much of capitalist literature can have a
meaning in 1950, I don't know. No one now writing can do anything of real interest unless they perform a few acts of mental
hygiene."[3] He also stressed the relation between literature and
economics as follows: "As a good reader you will refuse to be

bamboozled, and when a text has no meaning or when it is merely a mess or bluff you will drop it and occupy yourself with good literature (either belles lettres, economic or political)."[4] This principle as it applies to his own poetry is stated as follows: "I have all . . . to get economic good and evil into verbal manifestation, not abstract, but so that the monetary system is as concrete as fate and *not* an abstraction."[5] What he succeeds in doing in the *Cantos* is to create a succession of striking pictures of the misuse of wealth, to impress on the reader the flaws in modern Western European and American society. His diagnosis of causes and also his solutions, however, are disproportionate to the extent of the evil he describes. He is right as far as he goes, but one feels that there is much more to the problem than he sees.

It is economics, Pound thinks, that has altered the form of the novel. "Egoistic, psychological nuvveling has gone plop, because people who go on imitating Dostoievsky won't look at reality, i.e. what was economics, or inevitable 30 years ago is now plain god damn stupidity, and people not having the guts to think *what* the monetary system is."[6] This seems to be getting close to a Marxist conception of the relationship between society and literature. A novelist needs to understand why his story happened, but it is difficult to see why a writer should find out exactly what the monetary system is before he starts his novel.

Pound is overstressing one of his fundamental beliefs—that first and foremost the writer should concern himself with the state of society and ways of improving it: "what ultimately counts is the level of civilisation". He defines a good government as one that operates according to the best that is known and thought, and the best government as that which translates the best thought most speedily into action. It is the writer, and the poet in particular, who must provide such thought and knowledge. It is his duty to take an interest in social and political problems, and it is *artistically* necessary that he should incorporate these interests into his poetry: "I admit that economics are in *themselves* uninteresting, but heroism *is* poetic, I mean it is fit subject for poesy."[7] His heroes are economic heroes—John Adams, Thomas Jefferson, Malatesta, Mussolini (who attracted Pound partly because of his economic views). He sums up his belief that the study of society is one of the essential elements of poetry in the following words: "A lot of rot is talked and written on the assumption that political and economic laws exist in vacuo. I go on writing because it appears to me that no thoughtful man can in our time avoid trying to arrange those things in his own mind in an orderly fashion, or shirk coming to conclusions about them."[8]

Pound assumes that, if poetry contains this kind of interest, it can affect the world of affairs. Also he says that the arts are a nation's foreign office; only through the arts do nations gain any understanding and intimate respect for each other. (When it suited him, he chose to ignore Mussolini's extreme nationalistic doctrines.) This is doubtful, but he also says that literature may have good effects on international relations. Pound opposed nationalism in any form, and saw that it was becoming more prominent; he believed that a revival of cosmopolitanism in literature was necessary, to quiet the blood hatreds produced by racial theory.

If the poet is not also a social critic endeavouring to produce a better society, the arts will suffer; and degeneration of society brings a corresponding degeneration in the arts. This is a recurring theme in the *Cantos*, where a falling off in artistic standards is specifically associated with the incidence of usury in society: "An utterly stinking social order does its damndest to extirpate the arts, and then howls for pity when an artist gets wise."[9] Pound has described the effect of "an utterly stinking social order" in a really vitriolic attack on the society of post-war London in *Cantos 14* and *15*:

> "the invisible, many English,
>   The place lacking in interest,
>   last squalor, utter decrepitude."

The effect on the arts of this kind of society, with its profiteers and the "financiers/lashing them with steel wires", is disastrous:

> "The slough of unamiable liars,
>   bog of stupidities,
>   malevolent stupidities, and stupidities,
>   the soil living pus, full of vermin,
>   dead maggots begetting live maggots,
>   slum owners,
>   usurers squeezing crab-lice, pandars to authority,
>   pets-de-loup, sitting on piles of stone books,
>   obscuring the texts with philology."
>   (*Canto 14*)

This picture of London after the First World War is the equivalent of Odysseus's descent into Hell. Together with the *Usura*

Cantos, these form Pound's most violent attack on modern Western society. Apart from the bankers and financiers he is particularly hard on the publishers. Pound had found it almost impossible to get his work published in Britain. In *Patria Mia*, which, although not published until 1950, was written before 1913, Pound says that the problem of the social position of the arts is not one of popular ignorance or indifference, but of the harm done by pseudo-artists and the system of publishing. He believes the arts can thrive in the midst of a desert of popular ignorance. When he deplores the effect of modern mass-media, which in 1913 took the form of the popular magazine, it is not the effect on the general level of taste that concerns him, but the effect on writers who provide material for the magazine. He believes the increase in the machinery for the circulation of printed matter favours a sham, and false or careless expression. Pound is satisfied only by the highest art. He loathes people who do not care for the "master work", who set out as artists with no intention of producing it, who "make no effort towards the best", and who are content with publicity and the praise of reviewers.

The objection is that such a writer has destroyed his own values and standards. Pound sees no connection between the literary standards of the artist and those of society in general. The periodicals that he criticises are the high-standard ones, Harriet Monroe's *Poetry*, for example. The letters provide an interesting picture of an exasperated Pound trying to "educate" this woman in modern, "progressive" poetry. He is not concerned with trying to raise the level of taste of the public. He says that only "rubbing it in" has any effect on them. He corrects what he says are some misconceptions of the connection between art and the public in the past. The troubadours, for instance, did not introduce a popular art, but amused a highly cultivated audience. The Greeks were paid to go to the theatre or they would have stayed away, while Elizabethan drama was a Court affair. Pound thinks there is no authority higher than the writer's own artistic integrity, and his only duty is to his art:

> "Go, song, surely thou mayest
> Whither it please thee
> For so art thou ornate that thy reasons
> Shall be praised from thy understanders,
> With others hast thou no will to make company."
>
> (*Canto 36*)

He believes that the objection of the uneducated to foreign quotations in poetry is the same thing as class hatred working on the basis of money, by which he means that the objection is not based on principle; it is merely saying something is wrong because you have not got a share in it.

Basically, then, his doctrine is that of an artistic élite. In a letter dated December 19th, 1913, he says there are still half a dozen people in the United States (worth bothering about, presumably); shortly after he writes: "My problem is to keep alive a certain group of advancing poets, to set the arts in their rightful place as the acknowledged guide and lamp of civilisation."[10]

Pound is to be admired for his efforts to gain recognition for new poets; but what is one to make of an artistic élite writing for one another about economic problems, and trying, presumably, to influence votes by writing poetry that the ordinary reader cannot understand, without even caring whether he understands or not? Pound believed that the poet should be the acknowledged guide of civilisation, but did not think that his social obligation implied any artistic obligation. Yet if the poet is to be leader of society to the extent Pound envisages, there must be a more vital relation between the poet and the members of society than Pound's theory of poetry will allow. His theories of form and content in poetry appear to be incompatible. If poetry is to have a social function, then the form must be such as to allow that function to operate. Poetry cannot have a social function if it exists only in the rarefied atmosphere of an artistic élite. Of course, poetry need not be concerned with correcting social evils; but if this is what the poet is trying to do, and Pound is, then he needs to be intelligible to a majority of voters.

It is said that, in spite of greater opportunity, the reading public for poetry is no larger than in the nineteenth century. But this is doubtful; what is certain is that most modern poetry is difficult to understand. This may be because scientific and technical advances and the increasing complexity of society have affected all the arts, and the poets have reacted especially strongly. For whatever reason, the ideogrammatic method of Pound does away with narrative or any kind of connecting link, so that the reader is presented with a mass of images or statements which apparently have no connection. The separate ideograms often do not justify the effort needed to find out their significance. This is particularly true of those *Cantos* in which Pound deals with the political and economic history of the United

States. The content of the poetry does not seem to warrant this kind of presentation. After studying Pound's ideograms, it is annoying as well as unrewarding to discover that all he has been doing is breaking up the prose of John Adams or Thomas Jefferson into lines of verse. The poet should be able to assimilate his references into his imaginative conception of the poem as a whole. Here Pound is merely quoting, and at great length, economic and political views with which he sympathises. To know that Shelley, in writing about his "dome of many-coloured glass", has in mind the classical experiments of Newton with a prism, analysing sunlight into the colours of the rainbow, is to add another dimension to the image—the rise of science. To know that Pound is repeating the words of John Adams adds nothing to the significance of the poetry; it only shows that Pound is doing something in verse which has been done better in prose. Because of his concern with the social content of the poetry, his imaginative conception of the poem breaks down. He expects it to have a more direct effect on society than is possible.

Although Pound as an artist repudiates any obligation to individual members of society, he is very clear that society has obligations to the artist: "Five hundred people can get any kind of civilisation they want, up to the capacity of their best inventor and maker. But all they can do for him is feed, clothe and give him leisure and space to work in."[11] With a typical display of "ham", Pound says that society should chain an artist up, provide him with food, drink and women, and when he produces something, take it away from him. Another suggestion, less interesting but more worth discussing, is that artists should receive state subsidies. One thousand dollars per year should be settled on an artist of creative ability, and he should nominate his successor when he no longer has need of the money. This odd idea would make the award a vested interest. Not all writers are as altruistic as Pound is. He also maintained that schools of creation should be set up in universities. Many such schools have been set up in the United States, but they are unlikely to have satisfied Pound. Writers who have attended them tend to come out with a facile technique, a set of rules for "safe" writing. The plan is not likely to produce imaginative writers of what Pound considers the highest calibre. Henry Miller, for instance, was not considered to be in this class. Pound wrote of him in 1937: "I wish him luck. Certainly he comes after the real writers of whom there are . . . (numeral left blank)."[12]

Society has a duty to the artist, Pound thinks, not only because art is the finest flower of civilisation, but because it is a necessity. The individual members of society who are able to provide money for art have an obligation to do so and should be made to fulfil it. He says it is the duty of millionaires, just as it was with the aristocracy, to be patrons of art, irrespective of whether they have any appreciation of it. For Doctor Johnson, the main object of writing was to earn money; to Samuel Butler, money was important in that it provided leisure to do the things he wanted to do, particularly to write. For Pound, money is meaningless except in so far as it enables the artist to live and work in freedom. Furthermore, he thinks that the arts should be taught by practising artists and not by "sterile professors", and that literature is of paramount importance in the arts because painting and music schools need literature as a background.

Some artists have certainly had a rather literary conception of painting, and have struggled to express their artistic ideas in literary form, often taking literature to be the touchstone of the arts. Van Gogh, for instance, saw his pictures in relation to the naturalist trend in French literature. When one of his paintings was criticised because its subject matter was a dull grocer's shop and stark, stiff houses, he wrote to his brother, "I think to myself that Zola did a certain boulevard at the beginning of *L'Assommoir*, and Flaubert a corner of the Quai de la Villette in the midst of the dog-days at the beginning of *Bouvard et Pécuchet*, and that neither of them is trashy."[13] Thus Pound's idea is not impossible, though it is one which rather few painters have held.

III

Pound is especially concerned with the state of American society. Born into a nation fresh from a wide expansion of its frontiers, he saw unlimited possibilities for American civilisation; but also saw that it was at present severely limited. The values of big business were being applied to all spheres of life; Pound saw a sharp contrast between the material resources and progress of the American people and their parochialism in the arts. Nevertheless, he was convinced that a new spirit could reverse this position: "America has a chance of a Renaissance. Certain absurdities in American action are things of the surface and not necessarily symptoms of sterility or fatal disease."[14] He finds proof of this in the supremacy of American architecture, which will lead to fine works in the other arts, and stimulate an intellectual hunger for beauty. It seems paradoxical that a rotten society, which needs art to make it tolerable, is itself to be the cause of a new artistic upsurge. Pound says that commerce has produced this architecture, so that it seems that the basic evil in society is also going to cause the regeneration of society. All this was written before 1914. His view of American society was later to become more jaundiced, as the Babbitts became more numerous and powerful; but in *Patria Mia* there is a great deal of American braggadocio, itself largely a result of parochialism. He believed then that the Americans were the dominant people, and said that they would rebuild Venice on the Jersey mud flats and use it as a tea shop.

He is convinced of the future greatness of America, he says, because this sentence was used in an election: "The first duty of a nation is to conserve its human resources." Any nation which does this is bound to surpass one which tries chiefly to conserve its material resources. This is no doubt very true, but another credo of Pound is "deeds before words"; election slogans are not the best indication of what will get done. Later he thought the Constitution of the United States the greatest state document ever written, because it placed money in the hands of Congress. He still believed in the American system even after he associated himself with Italian fascism: "American government as intended and as a system is as good a form of government as any, save possibly that outlined in the new Spanish Constitution."[15] This was written in 1932, and it is clear that he was not opposed to democracy as a form of government, but rather to the abuses of wealth and power which are its hallmarks in the twentieth century: "Democracy run by clean men, decent men, honest men, could or should attain Kraft durch Freude quite as well as a dictatorship."[16] But in practice they have failed, because for the last century they have not made the people aware of the absolute rudimentary necessities of democracy, "the first being monetary literacy". However, in 1935, after ten years' experience of Mussolini's fascist regime, he questioned the validity of the democratic system in modern states: "The problem of democracy is whether its alleged system, its de jure system, can still be handled by men of good will ... and whether a sufficiently active segment of the public can still be persuaded to combine and compel its elected delegates to act decently in an even moderately intelligent manner"[17] Pound thought it irrele-

vant that elections are held in a democracy, while under Mussolini they were not, simply because, in the Western democracies,
the men who are elected are not the men who have the power:

> "Direct power prodigious ... boundless emissions.
> To whom is this power granted?
>   in a remote corner, a company.
> By whom directed?
>   By seven, by four, none by the people elected
> Nor responsible to them.
>   Encroaching on power of States,
>   monopoly absolute. ...
> Political as well as pecuniary. Such
>   a bank tends to subjugate government."
>   (*Canto 88*)

Pound is sceptical of the working possibility of democracy under
modern conditions, because he does not believe in the collective
sense of responsibility of elected delegates: "Man should have
some sense of responsibility to the human congerie. Very few
men have. No social order can exist unless at least a few men
have such a sense."[18] He saw the answer in fascism. The inability
of elected delegates to govern satisfactorily is set against the
"leadership" of one man who possesses this "sense of responsibility to the human congerie". Pound gives a specific reason for
preferring the Italian fascist system to the democratic system
as it has worked out: "Our democratic system is, for the first
time, on trial against systems professing greater care for national
welfare."[19]

This shows the extent to which Pound, along with many
others, was taken in by the socialistic façade of fascism, or to give
it its other name, National Socialism. Among the literary origins
of fascism, Carlyle contributed a socialist care for the proletariat,
mainly because he disliked industrialism and the nouveau riche.
One gets a better idea of how solicitous National Socialism was
towards the mass of people from Nietzsche's conception of the
bungled and botched masses. Many theorists around the turn
of the century offered an anti-democratic superman doctrine;
Pound felt that this ideal hero-leader had been realised in Mussolini, just as Lewis found him in Hitler. As Mussolini was the
embodiment of a theoretical idea, Pound felt it a duty to ignore
his obvious faults, and then his fascism appeared to be carrying
out Pound's recommendations in economics. Lewis realised his
mistake before 1939; Pound's illusions survived Italy's defeat

and Mussolini's death. The *Pisan Cantos* begin with a lament for Mussolini and his dead mistress. I am not saying that Pound ought to have changed sides because America won, but he expressed no regret till long after at the atrocities which took place under the fascists. He says of the allies:

> "Woe to them that conquer with armies
>   and whose only right is their power,"
>   (*Canto 76*)

—a criticism which seems most applicable to Italy and Germany.

In his book *Jefferson and/or Mussolini*, a justification of the Italian leader, Pound defends Mussolini against the charge of dictatorship. He writes, "Mussolini has steadily refused to be called anything save 'Leader' (Duce) or 'Head of Government'.... His authority comes, as Erugina proclaimed authority comes, 'from right reason' and from the general fascist conviction that he is more likely to be right than anyone else is."[20] This is not a satisfactory justification of authority. Yeats was nearer the truth when he wrote, "The best lack all conviction, while the worst/Are full of passionate intensity". This is what the Nazi leaders were full of, but it was not likely to make them the best leaders. Elsewhere, Pound says that "Mussolini's miracle" was the renewal of the sense of responsibility, and he insists that fascism is socialistic: "Given the possibility of intelligence against prejudice in the year XI of the fascist era, what other government has got any further, or shows any corresponding interest in, or care for, the workers?"[21] As Pound was the only one of the writers under discussion to work for a fascist country during the war, it may seem paradoxical to say that he was the most democratically-minded of them; but I believe this to be the case. He had a genuine concern for the underdog, whether individually or in the mass. He also had faith in the fascist leader as the champion of the ordinary man, a faith which was originally naïve and became downright stubborn. However, what was even more important to Pound than Mussolini's vaunted socialism was his idea that the mass of the people need poetry, an idea which he apparently shared with Confucius: "Great intelligence attains again and again to great verity. The Duce and Kung Fu Tseu equally perceive that their people need poetry."[22] Pound felt that Mussolini shared his own view of the importance of poetry; that it is not merely "culture" in the American sense (that is, has no obvious practical application), but a necessity: "Mussolini has told his people that poetry is a necessity *to the state* and Carlo Delacroix is convinced that poets ought to 'occupy themselves with these matters', namely credit, the nature of money, monetary issue etc. These two facts indicate a higher state of civilisation in Rome than in London or Washington."[23] Pound took this kind of statement at its face value, not realising that politicians of the type represented by Mussolini will always try to enlist the support of intellectuals, and if this fails, will suppress them. Mussolini was simply trying to get the support of the intellectuals when he insisted that they have a definite function in the state.

Pound was concerned with the condition of the mass of the people, and thus was more democratic than his fellow "neo-classicists"; but he did not believe that the good society can be achieved by any kind of socialistic activity within a democratic framework. He believed that "any scheme which demands the agreement of an infinite multitude of people is little likely to achieve itself"[24]; and had no faith in the ability of the mass to improve its own condition. Yet he had a naïve faith in the good-will of the hero-leader. He would not see that fascism was raw totalitarianism; that Hitler and Mussolini could retain power only by fostering a hero cult, with themselves as the objects of worship. One may blame him for this, but the motives behind his support of fascism were good ones. He thought a fascist system would benefit society as a whole and American society in particular. It is an indication of Pound's political unworldliness that he thought he could influence American society by making anti-American broadcasts from fascist Italy even after America was at war. It should perhaps be mentioned that he began these broadcasts before the United States entered the war. When she did, Pound tried to return to his native country but was refused permission. A few weeks later he resumed broadcasting. Still with America's interests at heart, he hoped she would lose the war because the resulting transformation of her society would be a great benefit for her. He continued to believe what he had said in 1937: "I am not writing Italian propaganda. I am writing for humanity in a world eaten by usury."[25] All this marks a kind of innocence in the artist, though it could not win him political immunity.

IV

Because of Pound's fascist sympathies, the *Cantos* raise Musso-

lini into a heroic figure alongside Confucius, Napoleon, Malatesta and John Adams. Mussolini's practical measures are
described in *Canto 41* :

> " 'Ma questo'
> said the Boss, 'è divertente.'
> catching the point before the aesthetes had got there;
> Having drained off the muck by Vada
> From the marshes, by Circeo, where no one else wd. have
> drained it."

Mussolini's money values were the same as Pound's :

> And the Boss said : 'but what will you do?
> Do with that money?'
> 'But! but! signore, you do not ask a man
> what he will *do* with his money.
> That is a personal matter.'
> And the Boss said : 'but what will you do?
> You won't really need all that money
> because you are all for the confino.' "

In the post-war *Cantos*, however, Pound says that this attitude
to money was the cause of Mussolini's downfall, and that the
same was true of Napoleon. After Waterloo, just as after the
First World War, no force could stand up to the money monopoly. He sees them as two great men, both with a large sense of
values, both crushed by the economic interests which are causing
the death of western civilisation :

> " 'and the economic war has begun'
> Napoleon wath a goodth man, it took uth
> 20 yearth to crwuth him
> it will not take uth 20 years to crwuth Mussolini."

This idea is repeated in practically the same words in *Canto 80*.
The *Pisan Cantos* open with an elegy on Mussolini, whose death
is reflected in the despair of the peasants :

> "The enormous tragedy of the dream in the peasant's bent
> shoulders.
> Manes! Manes was tanned and stuffed,
> Thus Ben and la Clara a Milano by the heels at Milano
> That maggots should eat the dead bullock . . .
> but the twice crucified
> where in history will you find it?
> Yet say this to the Possum : a bang, not a whimper,
> with a bang not with a whimper,
> To build the city of Dioce whose terraces are the colour of
> stars."

The great man's body has been defiled by the mob, as a bullock's that is eaten by maggots. Mussolini has certainly ended abruptly, but perhaps the reference to Eliot's *Hollow Men* indicates that his ideas on government and liberty have not been invalidated by his defeat and his death. Pound would still share his hatred of a government of anonymous men;

> "wherein is no responsible person
>   having a front name, a hind name and an address,"

and boasts of his calling liberty :

> " 'not a right but a duty'
>   whose words still stand uncancelled."
> *(Canto 78)*

More than once in the *Cantos* Pound attempts to justify his own broadcasts during the war by insisting that fascist Italy provided complete freedom of expression on radio and in the press, whereas the British radio ("Churchill's liary") and the British press were merely the organs of government propaganda :

> "Oh my England
>   that free speech without free radio speech is as zero
>   and but one point needed for Stalin."
> *(Canto 74)*

Pound simply refused to see the true situation. The British government was doing exactly what the Italian government was doing; that is, allowing freedom of radio speech to those whom it knew were in sympathy with its policies. The Italian government allowed Pound freedom of speech because it knew full well he was going to attack America and Britain.

He sympathised with fascism for the following reasons. First, his rejection of the liberal, democratic tradition; second, his diagnosis of the financial evils besetting that tradition, and his belief that National Socialism would correct them; third, his belief that poetry has an important role in society; fourth and last, his belief that an authoritarian, anti-humanist, anti-Romantic attitude is necessary both in literature and politics. Such an attitude, he says, is symbolised by the artistic ethos of medieval Constantinople :

> " 'Constaninople,' said Wyndham 'our star',
>   Mr. Yeats called it Byzantium."
> *(Canto 96)*

Pound was closely associated with T. E. Hulme, Gaudier-Brzeska
and Wyndham Lewis, and, to a large extent, shared their view
that the coming era would be "harsh, surgical, masculine,
authoritarian", bringing a reversal of the Humanist attitude in
politics and philosophy, and of the Romantic attitude in the arts.
This gives a real connection between fascism in politics and the
neo-classic movement in the arts, though it need not have worked
out as it did. In *Canto 78*, written while he was still in the concentration camp, Pound talks of,

> "keeping hand on the reins
>   Gaudier's word not blacked out
>   nor old Hulme's nor Wyndham's,
> Mana aboda,"

by which he must mean (unless he means that the war was fought
on aesthetic issues) that their intellectual, artistic and political
beliefs all form one "Weltanschauung" and are inseparable, being
based on the same principles. In *Thrones*, however, he regrets
that they were not firm enough in their support of fascism :

> "But the lot of 'em, Yeats, Possum, Old Wyndham
>   had no ground to stand on
> Black shawls still worn for Demeter in Venice."
>   (*Canto 102*)

(Demeter is here used as a symbol of the fascist ideal. She was
the Greek goddess of agriculture, and the National Socialists
placed great emphasis on the soil in their political tracts.)

Pound's poetic style also was clearly influenced by his association with Yeats, Hulme, Lewis and Gaudier-Brzeska. His ideogrammatic method is his attempt to achieve what Lewis called
a "conceptual quality", "hard, exact outline", while in the
Cantos as a whole he tries to achieve that "grand architectural
proportion" which Lewis said constituted the greatest art. There
is an immense range of material in the *Cantos*; and perhaps their
style is an attempt to reproduce the technique of Byzantine
mosaic art by means of language. Ideas, sentences, phrases, even
single words are juxtaposed without having any apparent connection. The connection can only be seen by viewing the finished
work as a whole; just as a mosaic looks jagged if viewed too
closely. As earlier chapters have shown, this poetic technique was
considered the artistic counterpart of a totalitarian political
philosophy. Also, what Hulme called "geometric art", thinking

especially of Byzantine mosaics, is an attempt to achieve permanence in fixity and rigidity, or even in abstraction. This is Hulme's own description, and it is what Lewis means by "classical art". Yeats, Lewis, Pound, and to a certain extent Eliot, tried to achieve a "geometric" literary form, an extremely difficult undertaking. It is the antithesis of what Lewis calls a "fluid, romantic" style, and what Hulme calls "vital art", which is produced when man is at one with nature, when there is a tendency towards humanism, romanticism and pantheism, and, as they were constantly at pains to point out, towards democracy.

V

The *Cantos* are Pound's epic : the poem begins with a deliberate imitation of the scheme of the *Odyssey*. But Pound's conception of an epic is different from Homer's, or anyone else's for that matter : "An epic is a poem including history. No one can understand history unless he understands economics."[26] Thus it follows that much of the poem is to be concerned with economics. Yet it is not a poem containing history for history's sake. Pound believes that the problems which need solving are fundamentally the same in any developed society. The same problems keep recurring, so the best way to solve them is to study other societies in other ages, to see exactly what the problems are, what attempts were made in the past to solve them, and how far these were successful. In *Cantos 1* to *52*, Pound examines the Italian Renaissance and the activities of governors of various cities, continually referring to modern Western society to compare the situation during the Renaissance, and its ultimate degeneration, with the situation in modern Europe and America. *Cantos 53* to *61* contain a potted history of Chinese civilisation and the careers and philosophies of a succession of emperors. *Cantos 62* to *71* describe the career, and report the political and economic ideas, of John Adams, second President of the United States. By the study of the economic history of different societies, Pound describes his ideal society, which has existed, in its essentials, at the time of Malatesta in the Italian Renaissance and in China in the eighteenth century, and can exist again with the intelligent application of the principles he advocates.

In the early part of the poem, Pound is concerned with the ultimate degeneration of the Italian Renaissance; he finds this in

twentieth-century England, America and France. He describes
the situation in Britain in Eliot-like fashion:

> "The old men's voices, beneath the columns of false marble,
> The modish and darkish walls,
> Discreeter gilding, and the panelled wood
> Suggested, for the leasehold is
> Touched with an imprecision . . . about three squares;
> The house too thick, the paintings
> a shade too oiled. . . .
>
> And the old voice lifts itself
>   weaving an endless sentence."
>   (*Canto 7*)

The verse suggests that ideals are dead, vitality gone, that any
values that exist are fossilised remnants of an earlier society. He
produces a similar effect with his description of decayed
twentieth-century Venice:

> "I sat on the Dogana's steps
> For the gondolas cost too much, that year,
> And there were not 'those girls', there was one face,
> And the Buccentoro twenty yards off. . . ."
>   (*Canto 3*)

But, soon after the First World War, both his attitude to London
and his poetic style show a marked change. He is now convinced
that financial evils are at the root of the trouble, and that London
in particular exhibits these evils:

> "Profiteers drinking blood sweetened with shit,
> And behind them . . . f and the financiers
>   lashing them with steel wires."
>   (*Canto 14*)

His style shows a rapid change to straightforward denunciation.
At the end of *Canto 14* he says who is to blame for economic
evils:

> "Monopolists, obstructors of knowledge,
>   obstructors of distribution."

As early as *Canto 12* he introduces the idea which recurs
throughout the poem, and which increasingly occupied his mind,
until it became an obsession which has affected his thinking on
practically every subject—the idea that usury is the root cause
of every social evil:

> "Directors, dealers through holding companies,
> Deacons in churches, owning slum properties,
> Alias usurers in excelsis,
>   the quintessential essence of usurers."

By usury, Pound means the charging of interest on loans by banks; the effect of this is that there is always a shortage of purchasing power—

> "And the power to purchase can never
> (under the present system) catch up with
> prices at large :"
>   (*Canto 38*)

the piling up of capital in banks which has the same effect,

> "And the general uncertainty of all investment
> Save investment in new bank buildings,
>   productive of bank buildings,
> And not likely to ease distribution :"
>   (*Canto 12*)

in fact the whole system of banking and international finance. The society is suffering from this misuse of wealth, and the condition of its arts shows how unhealthy it is. In any society in which usury is predominant, the arts suffer :

> "1694 anno domini, on through the ages of usury
> On, right on, into hair-cloth, right on into rotten building,
> Right on into London houses, ground rent, foetid brick work."

He sees the nineteenth century as "the age of usury", an age which culminated in the First World War, and produced this kind of society :

> "FIVE million youths without jobs
> FOUR million adult illiterates
> 15 million 'vocational misfits,' that is with small chance of jobs,
> NINE million persons annual, injured in preventable industrial
>   accidents
> One hundred thousand violent crimes. The Eunited States ov
>   America
> 3rd. year of the reign of F. Roosevelt."
>   (*Canto 46*)

Canto 45, the "Usura Canto", is the most complete expression of this idea :

"Stone cutter is kept from his stone
weaver is kept from his loom
WITH USURA
wool comes not to market
sheep bringeth no gain with usura...."

The great leaders of society had nothing to do with this kind of financial exploitation:

"Pietro Lombardo
came not by usura.
Duccio came not by usura."

The effect of usury on the arts is most obvious in painting:

"with usura the line grows thick".

In *Guide to Kulchur*, Pound writes, "a tolerance of gombeen men and stealers of harvest by money, by distortion and dirtiness, runs concurrent with a fattening in all art forms",[27] and says that future art critics will be able to tell from the quality of painting the degree of tolerance of usury in a society. He even names specific dates when the incidence of financial evils began to affect the arts:

"Wanting TAXES to build St. Peters, thought Luther beneath civil notice,
1527. Thereafter art thickened. Thereafter design went to hell,
Thereafter barocco, thereafter stone-cutting desisted."
(*Canto 46*)

Evidently, economic forces affect the arts, but sometimes they only decide which art form is to be most important in a particular society; in literature for example, whether the predominant form is to be poetry, drama, or the novel. But such economic causes are much more general and complicated than Pound assumes. What class of people constitute the audience, what are their interests and attitudes, has, before the twentieth century, to a large extent determined what form literature was to take. The reasons for the predominance of one particular group in society are often economic. The rise of the novel coincided with the increasing importance of the middle classes, and this had a variety of causes. The present-day financial system was developing at the same time, but this was only a part of the whole complex of economic developments and did not itself directly affect the arts. Moreover, when Pound writes, "with usura the line grows thick", he means that all the paintings became worse as the capitalist system developed; as he might say that Arnaut Daniel is better than all the nineteenth-century poets. It is a very sweeping value-judgement in the arts, and a dubious basis for an economic interpretation of society.

Cantos 8 to *11* describe the rule of Sigismundo Malatesta at Rimini in the fifteenth century, when Pound believes a cultural peak was reached. Malatesta had an enlightened economic policy, and was a patron of the arts, in a particularly generous manner:

> "I will arrange for him to paint something else
> So that both he and I shall
> Get as much enjoyment from it as possible. . . .
> You may say that I will deposit security
> For him wherever he likes. . . .
> So that he can work as he likes
> Or waste his time as he likes."
> *(Canto 8)*

This attitude is contrasted with the indifference to the arts in early twentieth-century London, described in *Canto 7*. *Canto 50* makes a specific reference to the effect of increasing industrialisation on the arts:

> "the first folly was planting factories for wool spinning
>   in England and Flanders
>   then England kept her raw wool, so that
>   damped down the exchanging
>   the arts gone to hell by 1750."

Now a poet can claim a certain amount of latitude in making his assumptions and proceeding to conclusions. But one cannot feel satisfied by this kind of statement either in prose or in poetry. For one thing, the arts had not "gone to hell" in Britain by 1750 —Blake and Turner are sufficient proof of this—and, moreover, textile factories could certainly not have exerted any great influence either on the arts or society in general as early as 1750. When he makes this kind of statement, Pound's rationality both as artistic and social critic is questionable. He is merely eking out his theory by making statements which are obviously false. His criticism of Western society after the Second World War—

> "the root stench being usura and METATHEMENON
> and Churchill's return to Midas broadcast by his liary,"
> *(Canto 88)*

implies that the problem is not peculiar to our society: those

> "who live by debt and war profiteering...
> in flat Ferrarese country seemed the same as here under
>   Taishan
> men move to scale."
>   *(Canto 77)*

The problem is a recurring one, but Pound wonders whether, after the second war, anything can be done to put matters right. He asks whether civilisation has ever reached such depths of iniquity:

> "is it blacker? was it blacker? ...
> is there a blacker or was it merely San Juan with a belly ache
>   writing   ad posteros
> in short shall we look for a deeper or is this the bottom?"
>   *(Canto 74)*

His own personal fortunes are correlated with the fortunes of Western society as a whole, and both are at a low ebb:

> "As a lone ant from a broken ant-hill
> from the wreckage of Europe, ego scriptor."
>   *(Canto 76)*

His solution is the spreading of Confucius's philosophy and its practical application to the problems of present-day society:

> "better gift can no man make to a nation
> than the sense of Kung fu Tseu."
>   *(Canto 76)*

Pound has tried to do this himself. In the "Chinese" *Cantos* he provides a panoramic view of Chinese history to show that the problems of civilisation recur, and that the most successful Chinese societies were those which upheld Confucius's ideas. In the *Cantos* dealing with John Adams (62–71), Pound gives a detailed account of the career and economic ideas of the President, treating his ideas as basic to any good society. Adams and Jefferson worked together to produce the American Constitution, which provides for government control of finance. Pound greatly admired the founders of the American Republic, who combined scholarship with action and provided a worthy illustration of the intellectual exercising political responsibility; both the Federalist and Republican parties had leaders who were as accomplished in scholarship as in politics, men like Adams, Jefferson, Albert Gallatin and Edward Livingston. The "Chinese" and "American" *Cantos* are an attempt to show universal evils working in society—greed, stupidity, selfishness, love of power—and the attempts of a few enlightened individuals to create a better society with constructive values. Pound attempts this by giving a generalised, but chronologically detailed, account of Chinese history, and a microscopic view of a short period of American economic history. Different situations are put side by side practically without comment.

A panoramic view, whether of history or anything else, is often the most impressive kind; but, if the subject is to be taken apart and examined piece by piece, the separate pieces must have significance and force in themselves. Pound is concerned with the complete effect of his poem. He sees it as one vast ideogram, which is made up of smaller ideograms, which are themselves composed of smaller ideograms put together without narrative. But the whole of the *Cantos* cannot be digested at once; therefore, the separate ideograms should provide some kind of satisfactory, complete experience within the experience of the poem as a whole. If this does not happen, the effort of reading the whole poem can hardly be made. It is not that the reader finds the text difficult to understand; this is not really an excuse for not making the effort; but that he finds any imaginative response impossible. This is where the *Cantos* fail. The smaller components of the poem are not always sufficiently interesting in themselves, either in content or expression. They do not provide a series of complete experiences which lead to the final complete experience of the poem as a whole. They only have any real significance when set against the whole poem, or by realising Pound's sociological ideas beforehand. We can understand that they are significant, but not feel that they are. One wonders whether the poem can be read straight through, for a first time, without skipping large expanses of semi-versified history.

In the *Cantos*, the narrative and descriptive passages of earlier long poems are largely replaced by passages dealing with sociological, economic, and political ideologies, and the theorising of different men of the past. These political parts are sometimes more readable than the "poetic" ones. But often the poetry gains nothing by merely reproducing passages of dry economic prose in free verse form :

> "that parliament
> hath no authority
>   to impose internal taxes upon us.
> Common Law. 1st Inst. 142
> Coke, to the 3rd Inst. Law is the subject's birthright
> Want of right and of remedy are all one,
> CONSTRUED that no innocent
>   may by literal construction be
> damaged actus
>   legis nulli facit injuriam."
>   (*Canto 64*)

A long poem must be sustained by intellectual content, by the imaginative use of words, by rhythmic pattern, and by passion, which may be of an intellectual kind. Pound certainly has this last quality, but has his poetry? He once envisages the doubt:

> "But it's a question of feeling,
>   Can't move 'em with a cold thing like economics."
>   (*Canto 19*)

As the *Cantos* progressed, up to the Second World War, they became increasingly doctrinaire and less interesting both as poetry and social criticism. Fortunately for the poetry, his experiences during and after the war had a profound effect upon Pound. The *Pisan Cantos* show a marked contrast with those immediately preceding them. We have thus to consider next Pound's alleged anti-semitism, his anti-liberal, anti-humanitarian attitude before the war, and his greater "humanitas" after the war.

VI

Anyone who has been associated with fascism runs the risk of being charged with anti-Jewish feeling. Moreover, Pound's ideas concerning finance would imply that he had little time for the Jews. The traditional occupation of exiled Jews is that of money-lender, and since the growth of international finance Pound sees them carrying on their tradition on a larger scale, under a respectable appearance. He says the power and importance of the Rothschilds shows how prevalent was the Jewish mode of thought, and Jewish financial interest, after the defeat of Napoleon. There is strong anti-Jewish bias in *Canto 52*:

> "Remarked Ben : better keep out the jews
>   or yr/grand children will curse you
>   jews, real jews, chazims, and neschek
>   also super-neschek or the international racket."

Then follow five lines which the publishers decided had better
be left out, but which Pound insisted should be indicated by
thick black lines. He probably went too far in attacking specific
persons. It has been said that Pound is not opposed to Jews but to
usury; that it is not the Jewish race as a whole that he opposes,
but some Jews because they misuse money. Even so, when he
says "it is nonsense for the anglo-saxon to revile the jew for
beating him at his own game",[28] this is not a vindication of the
Jews, but a further attack on British financiers.

  Canto 35 seems to indicate that it is not individual Jews that
Pound attacks, but the whole Jewish mode of thought and
feeling :

> "this is Mitteleuropa
>   and Tsievitz
>   has explained to me the warmth of affections,
>   the intramural, the almost intravaginal warmth of
>   hebrew affections, in the family, and nearly everything else. . . .
>   It must be rather like some internal organ,
>   some communal life of the pancreas . . . sensitivity
>   without direction."

This is nothing to do with finance, but is related to his rejection
of the humanist tradition, and the democratic system. Compare
it with these lines from *Canto 29* :

> "Languor has cried unto languor
>   about the marshmallow-roast
>   (Let us speak of the osmosis of persons)
>   The wail of the phonograph has penetrated their marrow."

"Osmosis" means the percolation of a fluid through a membrane,
causing intermixture. In applying the term to people, Pound is
referring to what he elsewhere calls "the general indefinite
wobble". (*Canto 35*.) The echoes of *The Waste Land* indicate
that Pound believes this general state of wishy-washiness is the
logical outcome of the liberal, democratic, humanistic attitude.
The operative phrase is "sensitivity without direction". Pound
believes what is needed both in art and politics is a greater sense
of direction; provided, in politics, by fascism, in the arts, by the

"neo-classic" attitude. He believes that the whole intellectual
tradition of Western society has been undermined and betrayed
since the rise of democracies, by what he believes is an associated
prevalence of Jewish thought:

> "Democracies electing their sewage
>   till there is no clear thought about holiness
>   a dung flow from 1913
>   and, in this, their kikery functioned, Marx, Freud,
>   and the american beaneries
> Filth under filth,
>   Maritain, Hutchins,
>   or as Benda remarked: 'La trahison'."
>   (*Canto 91*)

Here the poetry and the social criticism tend to deteriorate into
abuse of eminent Jews. There is no confusion, as there is elsewhere in the *Cantos*, as to whether these are Pound's own sentiments; obviously they are.

Whatever one feels about the connection which Eliot, Yeats
and Lawrence had with fascism, there is no denying that Pound
did lend himself to the purposes of a society which incorporated
the worst aspects of mass sadism. It is easy to condemn Pound
for this, just as it is easy to say that, had Yeats and Lawrence
lived, they would have dissociated themselves from the fascist
cause. Pound went furthest in support of fascism, and yet he was
the most democratically minded of these writers, in the sense that
he showed more genuine concern for the mass of the people than
any of the others.

Pound's rejection of Christianity is closely connected with his
anti-Jewish bias. Most of the tyrannies and stupidities of modern
life are, he says, based on Christian taboos, started by "that bitch
Moses". Christianity is a "Jew religion", and in 1940 he wrote,
"All the Jew part of the Bible is black evil. Question is mainly
how soon can one get rid of it without killing the patient." [29] He
does not describe what would be left of the religion after removing
all trace of the Jew. In a broadcast Pound made from Italy on
April 30th, 1942, he said, "Don't start a pogrom. That is, not
an old style killing of small Jews. That system is no good whatever. Of course, if some man had a stroke of genius, and could
start a pogrom up at the top . . . there might be something to
say for it. But on the whole, legal measures are preferable."
Emery, in his book *Ideas into Action*, says that, with these words,
Pound "dissociated himself from Dachau and Buchenwald, the

gas-chambers and cattle trains". He did nothing of the kind. His plan would make a difference to the number of Jews killed, but he did not dissociate himself from the principle behind the mass-murders; he merely said that killing big Jews is more important than killing small ones. It is difficult to deny anti-Jewish feeling to a person who can write, concerning the murder of millions of Jews, that "*on the whole*, legal measures are preferable". This throws some light on these lines:

> "From their seats the blond bastards, and cast 'em.
>   the yidd is a stimulant, and the goyim are cattle
> in gt/proportion and go to saleable slaughter
> with the maximum of docility."
>   (*Canto 74*)

There is no reason in the context of the poem to assume that this is Pound speaking, or that these are his sentiments. But then again, there is no reason to assume that they are not. The lines are in any case hard to stomach, and have to be interpreted in the light of Pound's earlier attitude. If this is Pound speaking, it is difficult to reconcile his sentiments with his greater "humanitas" in the *Pisan Cantos* as a whole.

Up to the time of his internment, Pound continued to reject the liberal-humanitarian attitude. "No one in society has any right to blame his troubles on anyone else. Liberal thought has been a mess of mush because of the tendency to produce this state of mind."[29] His was an extreme intellectual, authoritarian position. "The intelligence of the nation is more important than the comfort or life of any one individual, or the bodily life of a whole generation."[30] *Canto 30* opens with a lyrical attack on humanist ideals:

> "Compleynt, compleynt I hearde upon a day,
>   Artemis singing, Artemis, Artemis
> Agaynst Pity lifted her wail:
> Pity causeth the forests to fail,
> Pity slayeth my nymphs,
> Pity spareth so many an evil thing. . . .
> All things are made foul in this season,
> This is the reason, none may seek purity,
> Having for foulness pity
> And things growne awry."

He objects to the indecisiveness and the imprecision of humanist ideals. Values become blurred and tend to merge into a general tolerance of anything not obviously and directly harmful. The neo-classicist attack on the humanist tradition questioned certain accepted ideals: for instance, that man is the measure of all things, and that the right basis for all action is the greatest good of the greatest number. But Pound combined with the anti-humanist attitude a concern for the mass of the people: thus in *Canto 52* he writes of

> "The true base of credit, that is the abundance of nature
>   with the whole folk behind it."

His experiences in the Second World War fundamentally altered his ideas and his temperament. In one of his early letters he had said that he despised "patriarchal sentimentality". Like Eliot, he disliked this kind of affection, and wanted a harder, more intel-lectual approach to personal relations. In the first of the *Pisan Cantos*, however, he says,

> "is not that our delight
>   to have friends come from far countries
>   is not that pleasure
>   nor to care that we are untrumpeted?
>   filial fraternal affection is the root of humaneness
>   the root of the process
>   nor are elaborate speeches and slick alacrity."

"The process" is a movement towards the good life and the good society, and Pound evidently does not think here that they can be achieved merely by organised political schemes. While in the concentration camp he realised that direct propaganda was use-less, and he escaped, to a certain extent, from his nervous, highly intellectualised, social-reforming approach to contemporary problems:

> "Le Paradis n'est pas artificiel
>   but spezzato apparently
> it exists only in fragments unexpected excellent sausage
>   the smell of mint, for example
>   Ladro the night cat."
>   (*Canto 74*)

In contrast with Artemis's song in *Canto 30*, Pound mentions his own lack of pity in the past:

> "J'ai eu pitié des autres
> probablement pas assez, and at moments that suited my own
>   convenience."
>   (*Canto 76*)

His autocratic sentiments have been tempered by his own suffering, and, at times, he shows a sympathy for humanity which one would not have expected from his earlier writings. It improves his poetic technique:

> "Les larmes que j'ai créées m'inondent
> Tard, très tard je t'ai connue, la Tristesse,
> I have been hard as youth sixty years."
> (*Canto 80*)

While still to some extent clinging to his former ideals, with these echoes of the nineteenth-century French Symbolists, and of Yeats's later verse, Pound is beginning to realise that he has been wrong, that he had not known the nature of real suffering, and, therefore, could not appreciate or understand pity, tolerance and human sympathy. By the time he came to write *Canto 93*, published in 1957, he was even more aware of his earlier lack of human sympathy:

> "Ysolt, Ydone,
>   have compassion,
> Picarda,
>   compassion
> By the wing'd head,
>   by the caduceus,
>   compassion;
> By the horns of Isis-luna,
>   compassion.
> The black panther lies under his rose-tree.
> J'ai eu pitié des autres,
>   Pas assez! Pas assez!
> For me nothing. But that the child
>   walk in peace in her basilica,
> The light there almost solid."

It has been suggested that Pound has changed little as a person since his early twenties, that there is no central poem of spiritual crisis in his work comparable to Eliot's *Ash Wednesday*.[31] Perhaps not to the same extent, but the *Pisan Cantos* are Pound's spiritual crisis, where he turns away from the hardness of his youth and sees the importance of values which he had previously rejected, of pity and compassion for suffering or innocence—"the child in her basilica". He did not find a new set of values which were as effective intellectually and spiritually as were Eliot's. This makes it even more difficult and courageous to admit that the principles by which one has lived and thought for sixty years are perhaps mistaken principles, and to include this admission in a poem which has been largely concerned with expounding them. The fact that Pound does this goes a long way towards a final justification of the man and the poet. It does not make for a consistent poem; but a poem which is so long, and has taken forty years to write, had perhaps better not be perfectly consistent. Poetic development here is more important than poetic consistency.

IV

T. S. Eliot

IV

T. S. ELIOT

I

ELIOT HAS DENIED that he expressed the despair and the sense of futility of a generation in *The Waste Land*. But at least the poems, up to and including *The Waste Land*, describe certain psychological and spiritual attitudes, and show how these are revealed in the material forms of society. The obvious signs of the ugliness of twentieth-century industrial society—"a blackened wall", "empty cisterns", "trams and dusty trees", "the dull canal"—the continuous stress on its more unpleasant features— "the yellow fog", "the yellow smoke", that "lingered upon the pools that stand in drains", "soot" and "chimneys", "sawdust restaurants", "gutters"—all reflect the psychological states of the people who make up that society. The people in Eliot's poetry are representative of the different social levels, and their relationships reveal broken social bonds in a society which is rapidly being undermined.

Eliot's view of the disruption of society is stated in terms of failures between men and women, failures in love and marriage. In *A Game of Chess*, he describes two marriages at different ends of the social scale, but with a common theme, sterility. The causes are central to all Eliot's thinking about modern society. In the upper-class marriage we feel it is the absence of any kind of deeply felt faith, which would give meaning and direction to the couple's lives. In the lower-class marriage it is partly economic circumstance, but also, apparently, a failure to consider chastity a virtue and marriage a sacramental bond :

> "he wants a good time,
> And if you don't give it him, there's others will, I said."

The degradation of sexual passion is a common theme, and described most forcefully in *Sweeney Erect* :

> "This withered root of knots of hair
> Slitted below and gashed with eyes,
> This oval O cropped out with teeth :
> The sickle motion from the thighs

> Jacknifes upward at the knees
> Then straightens out from heel to hip
> Pushing the framework of the bed
> And clawing at the pillow slip."

Sweeney, "knowing the female temperament", goes on shaving. If reverence and respect are not present in some form, there is a tendency to become neurotic and hysterical, as in this woman's case, or completely indifferent. Eliot's poetry conveys that the monotonous, godless, soul-destroying atmosphere of modern civilisation takes not only reverence, but passion itself, from sexual relationships; perhaps he meant this by:

> "The goat coughs at night in the field overhead."
> (*Gerontion*)

In any case, *The Waste Land* gives the whole picture. The typist is "bored and tired"; the young man's vanity

> "requires no response,
> And makes a welcome of indifference."

The typist is

> "glad it's over.
> She smoothes her hair with automatic hand,
> And puts a record on the gramophone."

Nothing looks more monotonous than the label on a record going round and round, and this may provide an "image". The lives of these two have no vitality or meaning. Eliot believes that, with the break up of what is called the "organic society", "organic" relationships between people have disappeared. The difficulty of communication between individuals in modern society is treated at length in Eliot's later plays.

Another contrast between the old and the new, the vital and the non-vital, is contained in *Sweeney Among the Nightingales.* The characters have no identity. They are "the person in the Spanish cape", "the silent man in mocha brown". They have no vitality for passion of any sort, and even pleasure can hardly be provided by the antics of the drunken prostitute. She

> "Tries to sit on Sweeney's knees
> Slips and pulls the table cloth
> Overturns a coffee cup,
> Reorganised upon the floor
> She yawns and draws a stocking up."

These people are placed against the background of an earlier civilisation, or another kind of society, in which there was at least vitality:

> "The nightingales are singing near
> The convent of the Sacred Heart,
>
> And sang within the bloody wood
> When Agamemnon cried aloud,
> And let their liquid siftings fall
> To stain the stiff dishonoured shroud."

The "Convent of the Sacred Heart" is an example of an extremely orderly society, and carries the authority of the Christian faith, while Agamemnon exemplifies the vital world of heroic Greek tragedy. A similar contrast is implied in Part III of *East Coker*:

> "And we know that the hills and the trees, the distant panorama
> And the bold imposing façade are all being rolled away—
> Or as—when an underground train, in the tube, stops too long
>   between stations,
> And the conversation rises and slowly fades into silence
> And you see behind every face the mental emptiness deepen
> Leaving only the growing terror of nothing to think about."

In *The Waste Land* and the poems before it, therefore, Eliot depicts the decay of society, both in its outward and inward manifestations. He is clearly describing, like his friend Ezra Pound, important aspects of the society of post-war London. G. S. Fraser has said that *The Waste Land* is a poem about sexual failure, not about the state of general culture.[1] But it is nothing if not a symbolic poem and the sexual failure is the symbol of cultural decay and loss of faith. Eliot has this in common with Lawrence that they both use the degeneration of the sexual act as the symbol of the degeneration of a civilisation. Both believe that civilisation is determined by, and reveals itself in, mental and psychological states, and see sexual failure as the result and the most powerful symbol of psychological break-down —the result of the loss of "religious" faith, whether orthodox or unorthodox. *The Waste Land* gives Eliot's view of a broken world and his reaction, which was to look for a way of mending it.

The weakness of the symbolism in Eliot's case is that nowhere does he provide a picture of what he considers a satisfactory sexual relationship. Sex is always described in terms of a middle-aged degenerate and a drunken prostitute, or uninterested poseurs; in fact, in terms of failure. There is no reason, of course, why a poet should not do this, but such consistency tends not to make one accept the symbol but to suspect the attitude of the poet, to suspect that when he claims to describe a symptom of modern society, he is, in fact, describing his own personal reaction. There is little doubt that Eliot is disgusted by the mechanics of sex, which consist of ridiculous actions and postures. Yet these mechanics vary little from age to age, and even Greek heroes had to employ them. In fact, if one were to use Greek mythology in the way Eliot does, one might point out that Greek gods were reduced to the undignified practice of changing themselves into bulls and swans to satisfy their sexual appetites. Sweeney would be a more acceptable symbol of modern sexual degeneration if Eliot gave more convincing examples of sexual success than oblique references to Marvell's *Coy Mistress* and Day's *Parliament of Bees*!

II

Much of Eliot's theorising about society came long after the literary movement which caused it. He did, however, include political discussion in his editorial articles in the *Criterion* from 1924 to 1939. It was here that he began to popularise Hulme's ideas. In April 1924 he described Hulme as the forerunner of a new attitude of mind, which ought to be the twentieth-century mind—"the antipodes of the eclectic, tolerant, democratic mind of the nineteenth century". Although he was strongly anti-democratic and often expressed a preference for some kind of strict, authoritarian rule, Eliot did not openly sympathise with fascism to the extent that Lewis and Pound did. This was simply because he adhered to the principle of non-action, and refused to associate himself with political parties. In the *Criterion* for December, 1928, he wrote that the function of a political theory is to permeate society and all parties, not to form a working party. Russian communism and Italian fascism died, he said, "as political ideas in becoming political facts". This is an extreme intellectual approach to politics, and is simply a defence of the status quo. Eliot attributed the widespread enthusiasm for fascism to the "deterioration of democracy", which placed on men burdens they could not bear and took away those they could.

The general belief in the sameness of politicians, the remoteness of their work, the uselessness of the vote, brought a desire for a regime which would relieve people of the "burden of pretended democracy".

Eliot was not opposed to fascist ideas, but he preferred to approach them not through a political party, but through literature. Again in the *Criterion* for December, 1928, he wrote, "most of the concepts which might have attracted me in fascism I seem already to have found, in the work of Charles Maurras". He certainly seemed to derive many of his opinions from the Frenchman. Maurras thought that the principle of liberty results in chaos; religious liberty means that everything is challenged; political and social liberty leads to the enfeeblement of the individual and to anarchy, for it destroys the ties of family and tradition and upsets the state. True liberty needs authority, which is the product of fixed rules, habit and discipline. In society, a system with fixed rules of this kind entails hierarchy and stratification —a Platonic pattern, with each individual gaining happiness from the proper exercise of his own function. Organisation means differentiation, which involves useful inequalities. Maurras thought it necessary to relieve the mass of incompetent citizens from the responsibilities with which they had been overwhelmed in order to dupe them more easily. He regarded the electoral system as destroying authority, which should be the prerogative of the well-equipped, well-placed individual, who, if he had the ability, could dominate millions. For Maurras, this gifted minority was likely to be an hereditary élite.

Eliot did accept many of the ideas associated with fascism, but he preferred to derive them from a source more congenial to himself. This is also true of his anti-Jewish bias. Maurras and the Action Française movement were violently anti-semitic, and Barrès insisted that Jews should be deprived of political rights. The idea of metaphysical justice was abhorrent to Maurras because it was not only unnatural, but essentially Jewish. He said that Jews were responsible for the egalitarian principle because it came originally from Israel and had been introduced in the sixteenth century, when the Reformation had propagated the egalitarian mysticism of the prophets by making everyone read the Bible. Maurras insisted that plutocrats were the real rulers in a democracy, and that international finance, symbolised by the Rothschilds, was the basic evil in society. The jew (with a small "j"), figures prominently in Eliot's poetry up to and including

The Waste Land. He is the symbol of, and the reason for, the overriding insistence on money-making, and it is a recurring theme in the poetry that civilisation has rusted and decayed because of the effect of money power:

> "My house is a decayed house,
>   And the jew squats on the window-sill, the owner,
>   Spawned in some estaminet of Antwerp,
>   Blistered in Brussels, patched and peeled in London."

Again Eliot makes a person appear non-human. The Jew has not been born in a normal way, and his disgusting life does not deserve human terms. Eliot uses obvious puns to bring out the profit motive of Mr. Silvero, "with caressing hands" and the significant name, and of "the man with heavy eyes"—this probably means that he is a Jew—who

> "Leaves the room and reappears
>   Outside the window, leaning in,
>   Branches of wistaria
>   Circumscribe a golden grin."

The Jew, silver and gold are juxtaposed, and in this poem, *Sweeney Among the Nightingales,* there is a sharp comparison between the present civilisation, where such a juxtaposition is apt, and a nobler or fiercer previous one. There is a similar comparison in *Burbank with a Baedeker: Bleistein with a Cigar.* The sterility, ugliness and staleness of the modern world, with the Jew symbolising the materialist values, is contrasted with the order and strength which Eliot saw in antiquity, order being suggested by the "even feet":

> "The horses under the axletree
>   Beat up the dawn from Istria
>   With even feet. Her shuttered barge
>   Burned on the water all the day.
>   But this or such was Bleistein's way:
>   A saggy bending of the knees
>   And elbows, with the palms turned out,
>   Chicago Semite Viennese."

Such a person is a hybrid and therefore, Eliot thinks, cannot have any stability or sense of social cohesion and continuity. He believes this continuity to be essential for the survival of civilisation and culture (which has charge of values). If the continuity is destroyed, people become lonely, shiftless, frustrated and root-less. When Eliot writes, as part of a list, "Hakagawa bowing among the Titians", he presumably means that it is useless for a Japanese to study Titian; and, when he writes "Rachel née Rabinovitch", that a Jewess ought not to marry a Gentile. Certainly it is often hard to combine different cultures, but the idea that the Japanese ought not to see European paintings is silly. If the different levels and types of culture are to interact and foster one another, and Eliot says they should, then somebody has to become familiar with them.

The Jew and his commercialism, Eliot believes, have undermined the values of an earlier, more orderly society, symbolised by the Rialto:

> "The smoky candle end of time
> Declines. On the Rialto once.
>   The rats are underneath the piles.
> The jew is underneath the lot.
>   Money in furs."

Eliot seems particularly shocked because the Jew is rewarded and decorated for his activities. In the same poem, there is an ironic drop on to the first word of the last stanza:

> "Princess Volupine extends
> A meagre, blue-nailed, phthisic hand
> To climb the wasterstair. Lights, lights,
> She entertains Sir Ferdinand
> Klein."

This kind of anti-semitic feeling is traditional, even trite. The Jew has been the scapegoat for financial evils since medieval times. Pound is especially hard on him, and Eliot shares Pound's antagonism. The Jewish race has acquired a reputation for genius in matters of finance, and it cannot be denied that Jews often hold key financial positions in society. But to say that Jews are the cause of the importance of finance in the modern world is to misunderstand both the Jewish race and modern society. Europe, after establishing a capitalist society, which involved a great industrial revolution, had either to let finance be a major power or introduce widespread government controls. Jews are not only good at finance; probably no race is more widely gifted. It is the importance of finance in modern industrial society which has attracted exceptionally able Jews to make it their concern.

Also, dealing in money was made their tradition in medieval times, since they were forbidden to do almost anything else.

Eliot's anti-Jewish feeling, however, goes deeper than a dislike of economic adventurism. He looked to the Christian Church, rather than political movements, to impose order and authority in the years between the wars. Society appeared to be dissolving then; and he thought that tradition must be preserved or civilisation as we know it will disintegrate. Furthermore, unity of religious background is necessary for the preservation of tradition, and such unity is impossible, he says, if there are large numbers of Jews in society.[2] He is afraid the free-thinking of Jews strikes at the roots of Christian dogma, and destroys the premises on which religious orthodoxy is based. Therefore, he thinks it "undesirable" to have a large number of them. He does not say what we are to do with the large numbers that already exist. Eliot is not merely making a scapegoat of the Jew. He is saying that in a society such as he would like to see, the sense of tradition would be strong enough to make large-scale religious scepticism impossible. Thus, only the Jews with their instability and lack of tradition (as Eliot uses the word) will be likely to question religious orthodoxy.

If society existed in the form Eliot envisages, perhaps his fear of free-thinking Jews would be justified. But such a society can only be put forward as an alternative to the present one by ignoring realities such as the large number of free-thinking atheists or agnostics who are not Jews. If Eliot thinks that the problem they pose can be overcome by a continuity of tradition, why bother about the relatively small number of Jews? Surely they could also be absorbed into a tradition which was strong enough to eliminate the other social, economic and religious difficulties.

III

The idea of tradition is central to both Eliot's social and literary criticism. It is probable that he derived this concept from Maurras, for whom tradition was what had endured and must always be more important than the individual. There is a link here between politics and aesthetics; tradition did not include everything which had endured; it did not include humanitarian or Romantic ideas. Tradition was the transmission of the beautiful and true; order in the state was like beauty in the arts. Maurras found the model of a well-ordered system in classical

Greece, because beauty was identical with the idea of order—it
was composition, gradation, hierarchy. (Maurras' view of Greek
history was, in fact, limited to the Periclean century, a relatively
democratic period.) Eliot did the same and incorporated the idea
in his poetry. Many of Eliot's poems are imaginative restatements
of his views concerning society, and should be read in this light.
Yet the juxtaposition of Agamemnon and Sweeney and the
prostitute, although striking as an "image", has little of the
polemical force it is intended to carry, the examples are so obviously selective and weighted one way. The same is true of the
lines in *The Waste Land*:

> "But at my back from time to time I hear
>   The sound of horns and motors, which shall bring
>   Sweeney to Mrs. Porter in the spring."

where there is an implied comparison between Sweeney's attitude to seduction and Marvell's. An allusion of this kind must
be able to sustain the intellectual, as well as the imaginative,
conception of the poem. One is justified in making this kind of
criticism if the poet has a social concern as well as an artistic
purpose, and if the bias which results from the use of selected
examples is typical of the poet's thinking as a whole.

Eliot is keenly aware of the "contemporaneity of the past",
both past literature and past societies. Society should be so organised as to preserve the national culture in its traditional form.
But the continuity of tradition has been broken, he says, and the
immediate necessity is its re-establishment. This will provide the
necessary "order and authority" for a new framework within
which democracy can function again. Thus his political views
are derived from his theory of history and tradition. The past
exerts a living influence on the present, and the present alters
the whole picture of history. The interaction of past and present is
implied in the opening section of *East Coker*. The scene is a present-day country lane, down which a van passes in the daytime,
but from which ancient rites can be seen at midnight, "if you
do not come too close". Such ancient, pagan rites are part of
lower cultural levels,

> "Lifting heavy feet in clumsy shoes,
>   Earth feet, loam feet, lifted in country mirth,"

and so a certain detachment from them (the repeated "do not
come too close"), is necessary. The long tradition is reflected in

the archaic spelling—no doubt this marks a quotation, but tracing it does not seem likely to be much help :

> "The association of man and woman
> In daunsinge, signifying matrimonie—...
> Two and two, necessarye coniunction,
> Holding eche other by the hand or the arm
> Whiche betokeneth concorde."

The common idea of time is inextricably involved with material objects, in contrast with the "timelessness" of the human soul. "In my beginning is my end." But

> "In succession
> Houses rise and fall, crumble, are extended,
> Are removed, destroyed, restored, or in their place
> Is an open field or a factory, or a by-pass."

These different forms of society succeed one another, and Eliot may be presumed to think that the present one is not all that it should be, because the traditional wisdom and experience of the past are ignored. It is a false conception of "Progress", Eliot says, which society in general, and social reformers in particular, hold. It has come to mean increased material benefits, industrial expansion, equality of possessions, rights and privileges. The social reformers of the twentieth century in the main derive their faiths from Marx and Darwin. The past, for them, is not important in itself, but only in so far as it has produced the present state of affairs, and may give some indication of what might be ahead in the future.

Eliot rejects this idea of "Progress", which he associates with the ideas of liberalism, democracy and, in particular, socialism. In part two of *The Dry Salvages* he writes,

> "It seems, as one becomes older,
> That the past has another pattern, and ceases to be a mere
> sequence—
> Or even development : the latter a partial fallacy
> Encouraged by superficial notions of evolution,
> Which becomes, in the popular mind, a means of
> disowning the past."

Eliot thinks the collective experience of past generations cannot be ignored, and has a significance for us which is more than mere academic exploration. He believes

> "That the past experience revived in the meaning
> Is not the experience of one life only
> But of many generations—not forgetting
> Something that is probably quite ineffable :
> The backward look behind the assurance
> Of recorded history."

The past should be a living reality; but he adds a warning :

> "There is, it seems to us,
> At best, only a limited value
> In the knowledge derived from experience.
> The knowledge imposes a pattern, and falsifies,
> For the pattern is new in every moment.
> (Part II of *East Coker*)

This was perhaps meant to belittle the experience of the individual, compared to the tradition; but it must also imply that any return to an earlier form of civilisation is not likely to succeed; at least, any deliberate attempt, based on the ignorant decisions of men about what is best to do, is bound to fail. A return to an earlier form must, apparently, be the result of natural causes.

Precisely because the value of "the knowledge derived from experience" is limited (such is the answer to Eliot), we must try to go forward by means of practical social reform. It is not enough to say, as Eliot does, that practical social reform is useless because we cannot tell what the new society will be like to live in, and because new evils are bound to be created. In his introduction to *Notes towards the Definition of Culture*, Eliot has this to say about Harold Laski :

> "[He] was convinced that the particular practical and social changes which he desires to bring about, and which he believes to be advantageous for society, will, because they are so radical, result in a new civilisation. That is quite conceivable : what we are not justified in concluding, with regard to his or any other changes in the new social framework which anybody advocates, is what the new civilisation will be like : so many other causes operate than those we may have in mind, and the results of these and the others, operating together, are so incalculable, that we cannot imagine what it would *feel* like to live in that civilisation.[3]

What we can say is that certain evils which exist in our society ought to be destroyed. Society would then be better, inasmuch as those evils would no longer exist. A succession of such changes will probably cause new evils to appear, but this ought not to deter us from doing the best we can. Eliot prefers to go back to something which has worked (however inefficiently) in the past; or, at least, to leave things more or less as they are rather than risk radical changes, even though they would be improvements so far as we can see.

The real weakness of Eliot's position is that he takes the tradition of the English people to be something it is not. He evidently admires the achievements in literature, and in colonial expansion, since the mid-sixteenth century. But he does not see that economic expansion, together with the rise of democracy and individualism, were what made these achievements possible. He denounces individualism, laissez-faire economics and financial adventurism, and yet cannot understand why the English in general do not like Kipling. He cannot see that Kipling's work is the meeting-point for all the worst aspects of the principles which Eliot says he despises. The truth is that the English people understand their tradition better than Eliot does, and this understanding makes them dislike jingoism and aggressive national patriotism.

IV

"The image of a society organised in terms of value is recurring and inevitable."[4] In every society, of course there must be values of one kind or another. Raymond Williams here was referring to values other than materialistic, not merely the idea of "getting on". In trying to create such an image, Eliot is following a tradition at least as old as Burke, which continues through Cobbett, Mill, Ruskin, Arnold and Morris to the present day. The tone of his writing shows that he is aware of this tradition. *The Idea of a Christian Society* and *Notes Towards the Definition of Culture* seem to be an attempt to recapture the spirit of the nineteenth-century writers. Both essays recall Arnold's method of writing, in contrast to the more specialised criticism of the twentieth century. This more specialised interest is the result partly of an increasing concern with practical politics, partly of the recognition that the writer is not a special "kind" of person who has little to do with the practical side of life; that is, a reaction against aestheticism.

Partly because he generalises so freely, Eliot's writing, like Arnold's, has an appeal to the layman which is lacking in more

detailed political writers. He speaks of social reform with contempt, and tries to define a society which will dispense with
social reform, one that will be adequate, without any change,
for all time. Such writing is bound to lack the appeal of immediate applicability. Mr. Williams, discussing Ruskin, writes: "the
failure was one of realisation. His society was an image without
energy, because the necessary social commitment could not or
would not be made."[4] This means that it was a practical im-
possibility to realise the kind of society that Ruskin wanted. Industrial development had progressed too far. This quotation
could be applied equally well to Eliot. He does not seem fully to
understand the complex structure of modern society, or to recognise that there can be no going back. Social change can now
come about slowly and gradually through the efforts of men
who are concerned with particular social evils. Either this or
Marxist revolution, which, in this country, seems as unlikely
as a return to feudalism. Eliot half realises that industrial society
has developed to an extent which makes a return to an agrarian
society impossible; the decisive factor is the population. Yet he
cannot give up this ideal altogether. He thinks that the majority
of people should be settled in the country, and a balance kept
between industrial and agricultural development. Modern society
"shows a marked contrast with the past, when the happiest lands
were those where conflict between men and environment brought
out the best in both". But this balance between industrial and
agricultural development, with the majority of the population
settled in the country, is just as impossible today as a return to a
medieval form of society was in Ruskin's time. With the immense
increase in population, England has to rely more and more on
industrial techniques, because its first need is still food. Eliot's
seems to be a case where conscious imitation of a literary technique has led to adoption of the ideas which were expressed in
that technique, though they evidently no longer apply.

Eliot sets himself the task of finding what values ought to
apply in every society:

"The most important question that we can ask, is whether there
is any permanent standard by which we can compare one civilisation with another, and by which we can make some guess at the
improvement or decline of our own. We have to admit, in comparing one civilisation with another, and in comparing the different stages of our own, that no one society and no one age of it
realises all the values of civilisation."[5]

This shows an advance on the attitude of the nineteenth-century medievalists. They offered a different way of life, while Eliot is chiefly offering a new set of values. They tended to idealise all the features of an earlier way of life, ignoring the less admirable ones—the lack of sanitation and medical facilities, the harsh legal penalties and the abuse of judicial procedure. The recognition that "no one age . . . realises all the values of civilisation" should prevent us from over-idealising more primitive kinds of society.

Writers like Cobbett, Carlyle and Ruskin were genuinely trying to provide a way of life which would be satisfying and rewarding to the people themselves. But Eliot approaches society with a preconceived idea—that of "culture". The difference is this. Carlyle and Ruskin, for example, said that society was not what it should be. It should be organised so that everyone could live a fuller, more vital existence. One of the results would be the creation of great works of art and literature. Eliot, on the other hand, says that great literature is not evident in modern society because it is dull, ugly, mechanical and "worm-eaten" with the idea of equality. If society is organised so that each person has a definite function according to his abilities and background, great works of literature will result from the healthy state of the different levels of culture.

In using "culture" to mean a whole way of life, Eliot is following a nineteenth-century tradition. But, as Raymond Williams says, he replaces what was formerly vague by a definite and deliberate intellectual method. His meaning of culture is practically synonymous with civilisation. Work, methods of relaxation, religion, social and political customs are all as much a part of culture as books, paintings and music:

> "If we look at the several activities of culture listed in the preceding paragraph [refinement of manners, learning, philosophy, the arts], we must conclude that no perfection in any one of them, to the exclusion of the others, can confer culture on anybody. We know that good manners, without education, intellect or sensibility to the arts tends towards mere automatism; that learning without good manners or sensibility is pedantry; that intellectual ability without the more human attributes is admirable only in the same way as the brilliance of a child chess prodigy; and that the arts without intellectual context are vanity. And if we do not find culture in any one of these perfections alone, so we must not expect any one person to be accomplished in all of them; we shall come to infer that the wholly cultured

individual is a phantasm; and we shall look for culture, not in any individual or in any one group of individuals, but more and more widely; and we are driven in the end to find it in the pattern of society as a whole."[6]

He says the mistaken view that culture is the prerogative of the higher classes is no longer tenable. No one class or group of people can be regarded as the guardian of culture. It can only be possessed by society as a whole. The different social, political, religious, artistic or scientific groups are only concerned with that specific element of the whole culture which it is their function to uphold.

This is a sound idea, and one that is eminently tenable today. It is an improvement on the idea that culture is, or has been, or should be, the prerogative of one or more élites. R. C. Churchill, in *Disagreements*, has pointed out that members of the labouring classes shared in what might be called "intellectual culture" in the nineteenth century. The cultural tradition of the lower classes is something that the Marxist poets of the 1930s overlooked. They assumed that the lower classes would, as a result of a Marxist revolution, begin to share in the cultural traditions of society, from which they had previously been barred. They either forgot, or chose to ignore, that some of the very greatest writers were born into this section of society—Langland, Bunyan, Cobbett, Blake, Turner, Burns, and Lawrence, for example. All these occupy important places in a specifically literary tradition, the last place one would expect to find men who had been barred from the cultural traditions of society.

Eliot emphasises that different levels of culture must exist, but his unwillingness to exemplify leaves the reader in the dark as to what these different levels are:

"What is important is a structure of society in which there will be, from 'top' to 'bottom', a continuous gradation of cultural levels: it is important to remember that we should not consider the upper levels as possessing *more* culture than the lower, but as representing a more conscious culture and a greater specialisation of culture."[7] He also points out the value of interaction. The higher level of culture must be thought of as valuable in itself, and as an enriching of the lower levels; thus the movement of culture would proceed in a kind of cycle, "each class nourishing the others". But what Eliot is really doing is pleading the cause of minority culture. In effect, he says exactly the same as those people who, in the past, believed culture to be the prerogative of a select few. Their idea of culture is the same as what Eliot calls the "more conscious part of culture", and he makes clear this is not for the masses: "to aim to make everyone share in the appreciation of the more conscious part of culture is to adulterate and cheapen what you give".[8] In theory he believes contact between the cultures to be necessary. In practice he finds it disastrous, and he is only concerned with the higher levels of culture. He is profoundly disturbed by the lack of good poetry in modern society, and by the reduction of Christian dogma to the principle of "love thy neighbour". The responsibility for these things rests in the hands of a select few, and the higher level of culture must not be diffused—"for it is an essential condition of the preservation of the quality of the culture of the minority, that it should continue to be a minority culture".[9] A good interpretation might perhaps be found for this sentence, but bad ones are evidently possible; and, indeed, the text seems to assume them.

Eliot associates the diffusion of the higher levels of culture, which causes their decline, with the democratic ideal; and he says that those social reformers who disagree with him should stop paying lip-service to culture:

"If they [the essential conditions for the growth and survival of culture] conflict with any passionate faith of the reader—if, for instance, he finds it shocking that culture and equalitarianism should conflict, if it seems monstrous to him that anyone should have 'advantages of birth'—I do not ask him to change his faith, I merely ask him to stop paying lip-service to culture."[10]

But if Eliot wishes to preserve the high level of minority culture by keeping it that of a minority, he must stop paying lip-service to the members of lower levels, their culture and their happiness. His position with regard to good literature is fundamentally the same as that of the writers with whom Eliot was associated before the Second World War, and they certainly never considered it necessary to justify themselves to the masses. Eliot's is a legitimate view, and can only be attacked, as it was formed, from preconceived notions of the relationship between literature and society. His position, with society in the state it is in today, is not untenable; if a man believes that great literature must continue to be written, whatever the cost to society, he will not feel that the position needs any other defence.

V

D. H. Lawrence

D. H. LAWRENCE

I

THERE IS A tendency among literary critics to call it a waste of time to concern oneself with what a writer is saying, rather than the way in which he says it. But if he is trying to define specific social evils, and provide remedies for them, then it is what the writer is saying that is important. D. H. Lawrence went so far as to say: "It seems to me that even art is utterly dependent on philosophy: or if you prefer it, on a metaphysic. The metaphysic or philosophy may not be anywhere very accurately stated and may be quite unconscious, in the artist, yet it is a metaphysic that governs men at the time, and is by all men more or less comprehended and lived."[1] It is important, therefore, to find out what this "metaphysic" is. Critics often sympathise with a writer's diagnosis of human or social evils, but merely tolerate his recommendations as the whims of a mind struggling out of its depth. This is perhaps inevitable; it is easier to agree on what is wrong than on ways to put it right. Critics, again, often agree that the "spirit" of such writers as Carlyle, Ruskin, Arnold, and in this century Yeats and Lawrence, is the right one. They mean, perhaps, that the writers make a full imaginative response, and recognise that fundamental evils can only be cured by a change in values, not by political legislation or social organisation.

This attitude is to some extent shared by the writers themselves. Yeats was content to leave specific remedies to practising politicians, although he had little faith in them, and Eliot leaves much of the organisation to his drab society to those who, he says, know best about such things. But this leads to an impasse. The politicians whose job it is to find remedies are often blatantly ignorant of what is really wrong. Neither would it help much to tell a Member of Parliament to go and read Yeats, and then work out a scheme of moral and political reform. If diagnosis and remedy are to correspond in any way, imaginative writers who are concerned with the problem of the individual in society must state their case with more practicality.

Lawrence is the most doctrinaire of novelists and cannot be

criticised solely as an artist. His novels exist as records of his
own psychological problems, and as he was pre-eminently the
product of the society into which he was born, they are the
problems of man in present-day society. His novels present his
beliefs concerning social and personal relationships in our modern
industrial society, and the difficulties which confronted him are
to a large extent those which still confront us today. If we ignore
all this, or make no attempt to realise the basis in experience of
Lawrence's opinions, then the novels are both meaningless and
distasteful. Passages of rare beauty become irrelevant, or somewhat noxious, if we ignore or completely reject his "message".
His books are a mixture of pure fiction, autobiography, the imaginative presentation of his own psychological conflicts, and
straightforward discussion of his ideas about social and personal
relations. They are first and foremost expressions of his beliefs
and attitudes, whether or not he was aware of this at the time
of writing. He thought of himself as a prophet rather than as an
artist, and did not even make the occasional violent rejection of
the lot of the artist which is common among great imaginative
writers. This is probably because writing was comparatively easy
to him. Only in the matter of the banning of his books did he
feel any resentment about his occupation. Murry thought that
Lawrence preferred the role of prophet to that of artist for
sociological reasons:

"He really did tower by a head and shoulders above his con-
temporaries by this very recognition that the necessary conditions
of great 'art' are lacking in our age."[2] This is only partly true.
Lawrence thought of himself as a leader, rather than an observer,
of mankind. He wanted to create not works of art but a great
humanity, where "to live one's animal would be to create oneself, in fact, be the artist creating a man in living fact". Art
would then be the final expression of man, not the be-all of man
but the climax. Some men would end in artistic utterance, and
some would not; but each one would "achieve that piece of
supreme art, a man's life".[3] To bring this about, a change is
needed in the human psyche, but Lawrence continually stressed
that psychological and social changes are intimately connected.
In his books he tried to define the process by which such a "great
humanity" could be created. He did not believe in evolution but
in what he called the "rainbow-change of ever-renewed creative
civilisation". Lawrence himself realised what a hard task he had
set himself, and knew that he would be only partly successful

because of the nature of his "message" and the difficulty of
communicating it. "I believe I am only trying to stammer out
the first terms of a forgotten knowledge."[4]

II

As early as 1915 he conceived the idea of trying to change the
face of English society, and this ambition remained with him
for the rest of his life. The only friends he wanted were those
who were willing to put everything into an effort to bring about
a "a new unanimity ... a new movement for the pure truth, an
immediate destruction—and reconstructive revolution in actual
life"[5] in England at that particular time. He also hoped to
bring about a change in European civilisation in general, because
he believed England was the determining factor for Europe,
"the vital core of the whole organism". People might have been
more sympathetic towards his ideas on the regeneration of European society, if his globe-trotting had not led him to believe that
the initial impulse must come from unexpected places. "Though
England may lead the world again ... she's got to find a way
first. She's got to pick up a lost trail. And the end of the lost
trail is here in Mexico."[6] Several writers in this century have
tried to find a social climate satisfactory to their needs, with odd
and sometimes disastrous effects. Eliot came to England and tried
to organise society on traditional lines that he did not understand; Auden went to the United States imagining it to be free
from imperialism. Pound went to fascist Italy imagining it to
have a just money system; but Lawrence just kept on going.
For one whose "Englishness is his very vision" to pick Mexico,
of all places, as the end of the trail leading to the regeneration
of European society, is almost beyond serious consideration.

Lawrence never did find a social climate in which he could
live satisfactorily. This is simply because it did not exist. Society
is made up of individuals, and the material forms of society are
outward manifestations of human attitudes and relationships.
Lawrence's misfortune was not that he could not find a satisfactory society, but that he could not form satisfactory personal
relationships with other individuals. Either, then, Lawrence was
acutely maladjusted, or such vital and creative relationships as
he desired between individuals are impossible in our modern
world. Lawrence realised his predicament, and concluded that
there was something radically wrong with modern civilisation.

His love ethic is his attempt to solve the problem, an attempt to create new personal relationships between man and woman, and man and man, which would change the nature of society.

More than once Lawrence made plans to set up a small colony of a few personal friends, situated in some remote spot, having little connection with the outside world. Florida and the slopes of the Andes were two suggested sites, but none of his plans came to anything; although he did live quietly for a while in Mexico. It is hard to see what Lawrence hoped to achieve by hiding himself away. One who takes upon himself the role of saviour of society ought to accept that his place is in that society, however much pain and disappointment his undertaking may cause him. Lawrence's experiences during the First World War intensified his hatred of modern society. Later he tried to excuse his deficiencies in the crisis by denouncing the society which imposed such experiences. Lawrence was obviously right; there is something radically wrong with a civilisation in which wars are fought on such a scale, and so frequently. But to rage and stamp one's foot at being medically examined does not do much good. Lawrence did not oppose the war on strict pacifist principles; he could hardly be said to have opposed the use of physical violence. He simply did not like being prodded with a stethoscope and being told to put his lights out. His letters during the First World War amount to a bad-tempered rejection of humanity in general. Everyone seems to be out of step except Lawrence himself: "It is a damned life. I curse my age, and all the people in it. I hate my fellow men most thoroughly. I wish there could be an earthquake that would swallow up everybody except some two dozen people."[7] His self-pity and his efforts at self-justification are made more difficult to accept by this attitude towards the fellow men who were at least trying to make the best of a very bad job. His attacks are aimed as much at people as at society, and are often vicious and trivial at the same time: "I wish one could be a pirate or a highwayman in these days. But my way of shooting them with noiseless bullets that explode in their souls, these social people of today, perhaps it is more satisfying. . . . Let them cease to be. Let them make way for another, fewer, stronger, less cowardly people."[8] Lawrence had cause for grievance at the way he was treated during the war, but his letters reveal a viciousness of temperament; one often senses it in the novels too.

This period of his life is imaginatively re-created in the "Night-

Mare" chapter in *Kangaroo*, where he describes his emotional reactions to the crisis even more forcefully, and tries to justify himself on grounds of principle. But he is so bitter that the principles put forward as the basis of action, or non-action, are unconvincing. Somers sees himself as a strong man of principle, refusing to be carried away by what he calls "mob-spirit" : "Somers tiresomely belonged to no group. He would not enter the army, because his profoundest instinct was against it. Yet he had no conscientious objection to war. It was the whole spirit of the war, the vast mob-spirit, which he could never acquiesce in. The terrible, terrible war made so fearful because in every country practically every man lost his head, and lost his own centrality, his own manly isolation in his own integrity, which alone keeps life real. . . . Practically every man being caught away from himself, as in some horrible flood, and swept away with the ghastly masses of other men, utterly unable to speak, or feel for himself, or to stand on his own feet, delivered over and swirling in the current, suffocated for the time being. Some of them to die for ever. Most to come back home victorious in circumstance, but with their inner pride gone; inwardly lost."[9] War is the greatest destroyer of illusions; the men who take part in a war are not likely to have any illusions as to its causes, or the methods used in fighting it. But it is ludicrous for the man who stays at home, wanting to play pirates instead of fighting, to twist the situation in this way, and to claim for himself "manly isolation in his own integrity." His claim of moral superiority has no foundation at all.

III

Lawrence's criticism of contemporary society usually has a sounder basis. He is concerned at the superficiality of modern life amid all its mechanical attainments. He says that civilisation is revealed in sensitive life rather than in inventions, and that "culture and civilisation are tested by vital consciousness. Our conscious range is wide, but shallow as a sheet of paper. We have no depth to our consciousness."[10] He believes that in this respect we are far inferior to the Ancient Egyptians, the Etruscans, the Hindus of the Indus. The price men pay for stripping themselves of their emotional and imaginative reactions is boredom and deadness. "Our bald processes of thought no longer are life to us." He calls this process "idealism". "By idealism we understand the motivising of the great affective sources by means of ideas mentally derived. As for example the incest motive, which is first and foremost a logical deduction made by the human reason, even if unconsciously made, and secondly is introduced into the affective, passional sphere, where it now proceeds to serve as a principle for action. This motivising of the passional sphere from the ideal is the final peril of human consciousness. It is the death of all spontaneous, creative life, and the substituting of the mechanical principle."[11] He thinks that mentally derived ideas penetrate the unconscious, and that psycho-analysis reveals them and misinterprets them as integral parts of the unconscious, therefore as affective motivising forces. For instance, he rejects the idea that the incest-motive is inherent in the human psyche, saying that it has been implanted by men who have found the relation between themselves and their wives less satisfying than that between themselves and their mothers.

To counteract Freud's ideas he tried to re-define the "unconscious". He called Freud's conception of it "the inverted reflection of our ideal consciousness". He tried to discover "the true unconscious where our life bubbles up in us, prior to any mentality. . . . It is pristine, not in any way ideal. It is the spontaneous origin from which it behoves us to live". Lawrence saw a connection between what he called "idealism" and the advance of science and technology, which had made any kind of deep emotional response impossible; the trouble with modern man is that the "great divine dragon is inert. We cannot wake him to life in modern days." His "dragon" is another word for the "Libido" or "élan vital". By using this ancient symbol for human consciousness, he implies that we must get back to the consciousness that existed before modern scientific discovery, which has given us a wrong conception of the universe.

Whatever feeling exists in our age, Lawrence sees as "sentimentality and false feeling". The radio, the film, the press and current literature all produce counterfeit emotion; true personal relations cannot exist; there has never been an age of greater mistrust between persons, under a superficial social trust. This is quite genuine, but it exists only between individuals. As far as social groups are concerned, there is no trust, only conflict. In *The Plumed Serpent*, Ramon says, "Victims and victimisers. The upper classes craving to be victims to the lower classes; or else craving to make victims of the lower classes. The politicians, craving to make one people victims to another. The Church, with its evil will for turning people into humble, writhing things that shall crave to be victimised."[12] This is an exaggerated picture, but one that Lawrence often presents. Conflict between social groups, he seems to have thought, is not due to a clash of interests but a positive desire for oppression, or perhaps a nervous exasperation with the conditions of life. George Orwell had a similar idea—that the great phenomenon of this century is the rise of the power-mode as an end in itself. It has nothing to do with another belief of Lawrence, to be discussed later, that men must now submit to the power of superior individuals. Orwell recognised that the will-to-power, in this century, operates through mass organisations, for example a state-controlled press and radio, and a political police. For Lawrence, power is invested in the individual by reason of his superior qualities, not his control of mechanical agencies.

Whether or not Lawrence is right in the above quotation, and he may well be up to a point, he does not realise that the enmity has developed from a clash of economic interest, for example between different social classes. If there is a "desire for victimisation", it is the product of centuries of economic and political struggle. He comes near to recognising this in *A Propos of "Lady Chatterley's Lover"*, where he says that blood connection used to hold the classes together, and is still apparent in Defoe and Fielding, but absent from the works of Jane Austen and the novelists after her. It was not "blood connection" which held the classes together. What blood connection was there between the nobility and the peasantry? Before the time of Defoe and Fielding, it was common interest which held the squire and the peasant together, as far as they were held together. After the Industrial Revolution, their interests were opposed and their connections severed. Lawrence's timing is right, but his diagnosis is wrong.

Lawrence believed that the nineteenth century and the middle classes are responsible for society being what it is today. He hated the nineteenth century, "the century of the mealy-mouthed lie", for its materialism, its faith in scientific discovery and in the externals of life, and its hypocrisy. "The bourgeoisie, with their greedy dead materialism, have made morality and family and affection and trust all suspicious and repulsive."[13] This kind of attitude produces what Lawrence called "the fixed thing"— fixed society, fixed homes, fixed money, even fixed love. These he could not stand. He was sensitive to what is unsatisfactory and tedious in life and society, especially in so far as it was particularly unsatisfactory for his own needs and temperament. Here, as often, Lawrence is only half right. When society itself, and the attitudes of individuals within that society, become fixed, then there can be no development of either, no change in values. But the violence of Lawrence's attack is itself enough to show that some kind of stability is necessary. The most obvious objection to the kind of society that Lawrence would like to establish is that anarchy is always just round the corner. A whole society cannot always be on the move, and the individual needs of a man like Lawrence can only be fulfilled because society is to a large extent fixed and stable.

He is more convincing when he discusses the attitudes of mind in a society which is too rigid. Writing about Dostoievsky he suggests that the men who represent the will, the "pure mental, social, rational, absolved will", Ivan Karamazof, Pyotr Stepano-vitch and Gavril, for example, represent the last stages of our social development, the human being become mechanical, and having no personal relationships: "When Stepan talks with the devil, the devil is a decayed social gentleman—only that. The mechanical social forms and aspirations and ideals, I suppose, are the devil."[14] Whether or not such men represent "the last stages of our social development" is debatable. Pyotr Stepano-vitch seems to me a sneaking, secretive schemer, and likely to be found in any kind of society, plotting his petty revolutions. Law-rence thought that the prevalence of such attitudes is the main problem facing society. However, he did not underestimate man's social instinct; in fact, though his sexual creed has won most attention, he said that sex fulfilment is not as important as the fulfilment of man's social function, and that a man's ultimate desire is for great purposive activity. A man feels lost without this sense that he is creative—"When he makes the sexual con-summation the supreme consummation, even in his *secret* soul, he falls into the beginnings of despair."[15] On the other hand, if you make purposiveness the one supreme activity in life, you drift into emotional sterility. Instead, "you have got to base your great purposive activity upon the intense sexual fulfilment of all your individuals. That was how Egypt endured. But you have got to keep your sexual fulfilment even then subordinate, just subordinate to the great passsion of purpose."[16] This purpose is to create a better society. The great purpose of manhood is to achieve "a passionate unison in actively making a world". This is difficult in the modern world because each man is isolated in his

own ego. The individual cannot link up with the "social unconscious". In *Apocalypse* Lawrence describes the dual nature of
man; "Man is individual only in part of his nature. In another
great part of him he is collective."[17] But, in present-day society
the collective self is not allowed to function, because every man
regards every other as a menace, a threat to his being.

Individualism, the sense of isolation, class-consciousness, result
from a lack of feeling of community with one's fellow men. The
intellect plays no part in the kind of relationship Lawrence wants.
For Lawrence the main source of consciousness lies in the solar
plexus, and it is from there that personal relationships must grow.
The intellect only impedes this growth : "No human being can
develop save through the polarised connection with other beings.
This circuit of polarised unison precedes all mind and all knowing. It is anterior to and ascendant over the human will. And
yet the mind and the will can both interfere with the dynamic
circuit, an idea, like a stone wedged in a delicate machine, can
arrest one's whole process of psychic interaction and spontaneous growth."[18] He says that we suffer agony from the failure
to establish and maintain "vital circuits between ourselves and
the effectual correspondent, the other human being, other human
beings, and all the extraneous universe". This is the cause of
most modern psychiatric disorders.

Sir Clifford in *Lady Chatterley's Lover* is meant to be a pure
product of our civilisation. He has lost all sense of human contact except that of usage; he is a symbol of the "death of the
great humanity of the world". The same is true of Gerald Crich
in *Women in Love*. There is a sharp contrast between Gerald's
attitude to the miners and his father's. Real sympathy and understanding existed between the old man and his employees; but
they are of no more significance to Gerald than the pieces of new
machinery which he installs to increase production. He is concerned only with the job of reconstruction; given any kind of
mechanical or administrative challenge, he will succeed. But in
his personal life, one tragedy follows another. The will to destruction rules all his personal relationships, from the killing of
his brother in childhood to his own death in a cold, snow-filled
world.

The problem of Gerald's personal relationships implies special
reference to the civilisation in which they are worked out. The
same is true of Skrebensky in *The Rainbow*. He is an example
of the kind of social man that Lawrence saw in Dostoievsky's

novels. Skrebensky believes in the greatest good of the greatest
number: "One had to fill one's place in the whole, the great
scheme of man's elaborate civilisation, that was all. The whole
mattered—but the unit, the person, had no importance, except
as he represented the whole." But the "whole", the community,
is "an abstraction from the many, and is not the many themselves". The futility of Skrebensky's attitude is shown in this
conversation between him and Ursula.

> "What do you fight for, really?"
> "I would fight for the nation."
> "For all that, you aren't the nation. What would you do for
> yourself?"
> "I belong to the nation and must do my duty by the nation."
> "But when it didn't need your services in particular—when
> there *is* no fighting? What would you do then?"
> He was irritated.
> "I would do what everybody else does."
> "What?"
> "Nothing. I would be in readiness for when I was needed."
> "It seems to me," she answered, "as if you weren't anybody—
> as if there weren't anybody there, where you are.... You seem
> like nothing to me."

Skrebensky is a failure as a lover, and the author insists that this
is because he accepts the social function as the ultimate meaning of life. There are many examples of such failures in Lawrence's novels, often portrayed convincingly. But there are few,
if any, convincing portraits of people who are successful in their
personal relationships. Lawrence asserts that Birkin's marriage
to Ursula Brangwen is the kind of ideal relationship he wants.
But why it is any more successful than Gerald Crich's and
Gudrun's is not clear. Lawrence cannot convincingly describe an
ideal relationship. Tom Brangwen is another failure who has
surrendered his life to the social and industrial function. His
marriage to Winifred Inger, who represents modern woman,
lacks any kind of vital relationship and this is shown through
their industrial environment. "He wanted children. Neither marriage nor the domestic establishment meant anything to him. ...
He would let the machinery carry him; husband, father, pit
manager, warm clay lifted through the recurrent action of day
after day by the great machine from which it derived its motion.
As for Winifred, she was an educated woman, and of the same

sort as himself."[19] In *The Rainbow* and *Women in Love*, Lawrence is particularly concerned with "the machine" and its effect on men's lives. "The machine" is represented by the pit, but we must take it to mean, in its wider sense, the whole of industrialised civilisation, with its accompanying organisation and regimentation of life. The men resent the machine, but in spite of this, they grow to feel secure under its shadow, to rely on it. "But she knew moreover that in spite of his criticism and condemnation, he still wanted the great machine. His only happy moments, his only moments of pure freedom, were when he was serving the machine." This is also the attitude of the miners who work for Crich. As contact between individuals becomes more difficult, man turns to the impersonality of the machine and its uncomplicated existence. The effect on the human psyche is exactly the same as what he calls "idealism". "An ideal established in control of the passional soul is no more and no less than a supreme machine—principle. The ideal is but the god in the machine—the little fixed machine principle which works the human psyche automatically."[20] Lawrence was acutely aware of the contrast between the old, organic agricultural society and modern mechanical and industrial society. The contrast was thrust upon him as a child, and he has vividly described the differences of the two societies. But he was chiefly concerned with the different psychological attitudes which they caused; he kept asserting that the old organic relationships between men had been destroyed by industrial society. He also said that personal relationships had become more complex; it is more likely that they had become much cruder and flatter. Lawrence's idea that something dramatic has just happened to consciousness seems rather journalistic; what he describes, if he is right about the cause, must be as old as towns.

In many of Lawrence's novels we find a contrast between "dark-consciousness", or "sense-awareness", and the intellectual consciousness of modern civilisation. It is found in the conflict between Mellors and Sir Clifford in *Lady Chatterley's Lover*. To make the contrast more obvious, Sir Clifford is paralysed from the waist down and is sexually dead, a disembodied intellect. *The Rainbow* describes a development, from the elemental life and relationships of the earlier Brangwens to the increased consciousness of the younger Brangwens. The relationship between Ursula and Skrebensky is self-conscious, and merely destructive. It is sometimes said that Lawrence failed in his attempt to portray upper-class life and people. In fact he often failed in his attempts to portray any kind of person, except projections of his own personality. Skrebensky is a type rather than an individual—a European aristocrat who should possess a natural leadership, but who has lost all sense of function; like Sir Clifford, he represents social man at his worst. After Ursula has rejected him, she is nearly trampled to death by a herd of horses, but she gets a satisfaction from this experience which was lacking in her affair with Skrebensky. As the end of a novel this is rather unsatisfactory, but it illustrates the desire of Ursula, and of Lawrence, for greater "sense-awareness" but for less conscious sex-relations. In *Fantasia of the Unconscious,* he says that a dream about horses surging round a person indicates that "the spontaneous self is secretly yearning for the liberation and fulfilment of the deepest and most powerful sensuous nature".[21]

In *Women in Love* the spiritual roots present in *The Rainbow* have disappeared; indeed, Brangwens in the later novel have no real connection with the farming Brangwens. The development from the old, physical, to the new, mental consciousness has been completed in three generations, replacing the old organic relationships either by highly conscious personal relationships or by lifeless social ones. Even that between Ursula and Birkin only becomes satisfactory through an effort of the will. " 'There's somewhere where we can be free. . . . It isn't really a locality, though,' he said, 'it's a perfected relation between you and me and others' " (p. 308).

The relationship between Gudrun and Gerald Crich is destructive, because Gerald represents a deadly social system and a life-destroying energy. His attitude and relation to the miners is purely negative:

> "He saw the stream of miners flowing along the causeways from the mines at the end of the afternoon, thousands of blackened, slightly distorted human beings with red mouths, all moving subjugate to his will. . . . They were all subordinate to him. They were ugly and uncouth, but they were his instruments. He was the God of the machine" (pp. 214–215).

The pits, the ugly houses, the machinery are outward expressions of the modern personality, of which Gerald Crich is the fullest expression, destroying the countryside, the individuality of the human being (for which Lawrence had a religious veneration), even the wonder of life itself. Lawrence describes how the men changed as they came into contact with "the machine" and its ego-bound master:

"The joy went out of their lives, the hope seemed to perish as they became more and more mechanised. And yet they accepted the new conditions .... They were exalted by belonging to this great and superhuman system which was beyond feeling or reason. ... Their hearts died within them but their souls were satisfied. ... It was the first great step in undoing, the first great place of chaos, the substituting of the mechanical principle for the organic, the destruction of the organic purpose, the organic unity, and the subordination of every organic unit to the great mechanical purpose. It was pure organic disintegration and pure mechanical organisation. This is the first and finest state of chaos" (p. 223).

This is a powerful diagnosis of the modern industrial and social machine, and the attitudes it produces. But we must remember that men invented the machines, and men feel this curious attraction for them; there must be a change in the attitudes of the men, if the machines are to be destroyed.

IV

While it is true that Lawrence wanted a return to an earlier form of human consciousness, especially in sexual relations—what he called "phallic-consciousness", which would allow two people to meet on some level other than that of their mental consciousness or ego, and yet allow them to remain intrinsically individual— he did not as yet advocate a return to a form of pre-mental consciousness. He thought that some of the coloured races, he specifically mentioned South Sea Islanders, are inferior to the white races in that they have never developed this mental consciousness: "We know we cannot live purely by impulse. Neither can we live solely by tradition. We must live by all three, ideal, impulse and tradition each in its hour. ... Man always falls into one of three mistakes. In China, it is tradition. And in the South Seas it seems to have been impulse. Ours is idealism."[22] This corrects impressions gained from elsewhere in Lawrence where impulse seems all. Indeed, a high degree of intelligence and personal integrity seems to be necessary before this new form of consciousness can be achieved. He indicates that Birkin and Ursula achieve the kind of thing he wants, although the reader does not learn what it is. It is achieved by a conscious effort of the will.

Lawrence believed that they had only to will this change for it
to happen, though it is either above or below the level of mental
consciousness. This is a very improbable picture, and he ought
to have known better, recognising as he did the strength of
the unconscious and the lasting effects on the personality of
a social and intellectual environment. We are given the same
message in *The Rainbow, Women in Love* and *Lady Chatterley's
Lover*; there must be a new spirit in society, totally negating the
spirit of industrial society, and religious but not Christian. But in
none of these novels does he indicate how his message could be
applied to existing society; he seems to presume that it can be
willed into existence. We need not doubt that new attitudes
would destroy the present external forms of society, but may
naturally ask how the attitudes can be changed while the forms
persist.

The main point of Lawrence's diagnosis is this: we are increasingly dependent on the machine, and it imposes social
arrangements which make impossible the vital, creative, personal relationships in which life reveals itself most fully. His beliefs about sex are a result of this profound concern at the state
of English society. He believed that sexuality was the purifying
force which could regenerate such a society because it was an
essential part of his belief that the social pattern reflects the
sexual pattern: "No great motive or ideal or social principle can
endure for any length of time unless based upon the sexual fulfilment of the vast majority of individuals concerned."[23]

Thus, he thought that the most catastrophic thing about modern
civilisation is that the sexual act has become ugly and degrading.
Unless a new spirit exerts itself, the sexual act can never be the
creative and regenerative force that it should be. The present-day
attitude to sex is a legacy of the nineteenth century: "In public, in
the social world, the young are still entirely under the shadow of
the grey elderly ones. The grey elderly ones belong to the last
century that has tried to destroy humanity. . . . They dominate
in society, in the press, in literature, everywhere. And, naturally,
they have the vast mob of the general public along with them."[24]
The century that had created the conditions of industrial society
had also created the attitudes which were prevalent in it; and the
sexual taboos of the nineteenth century were still dominating the
young. When such taboos were removed, however, or when some
people managed to emancipate themselves from them, the effects
were equally distasteful; a superficiality about sex, or even in-

difference to it—a rejection of its "mystery" : "Then keep the
girls apart from any familiarity or being 'pals' with the boys. The
nice clean intimacy which we now so admire between the sexes
is sterilising. It makes neuters. Later on, no deep, magical sex life
is possible."[25] Lawrence thought sex important because, in the
modern world, the sexual act was the sole remaining source of
wonder. In every other sphere of life, he said, the sense of wonder
had been destroyed, and human consciousness become composed
entirely of social images. The sexual attitudes of present-day
society, even if there is more flouting of the taboos, are no
healthier than in Lawrence's time; if his remedies were needed
by early twentieth-century society, they are needed still.

There is much to be said for Lawrence's criticism of the sexual
relationships between individuals. If his account makes them
more important than they seem in most people's lives, that is
simply because they are usually not of the vital, creative kind
which Lawrence wanted. He also wanted to recapture a sense
of wonder of the universe, to regain that sense of association
with the cosmos which was felt by pagans before Christianity :

> "It is a question, practically, of relationship. We *must* get back
> into relation, vivid and nourishing relation to the cosmos and
> the universe. The way is through daily ritual, and the re-awaken-
> ing. We *must* once more practise the ritual of dawn and noon
> and sunset.... This is an affair of the individual and the house-
> hold. Then the ritual of the seasons with the Drama and Passion
> of the soul embodied in procession and dance, this is for the ...
> whole community. And the ritual of the great events in the year
> of stars is for nations and whole peoples."[26]

He felt nostalgia for the pagan world and its living cosmos—
before science "explained" it all. He was more concerned with
man's idea of the cosmos than the scientific truth. If ignorance
and superstition have a salutary effect on man's life and consciousness, then he preferred ignorance to knowledge. "False,
inorganic connections" must be destroyed, especially those related to money, and "living organic connections", with "the
cosmos, the sun, the earth, mankind, the nation and the family",
must be renewed. When Lawrence said that science had removed
the sense of wonder from the universe, he did not mean that
science had made it easy to understand how the universe works
and how it is constituted. After all, our present picture of the
universe is more baffling than any previous one. What he prob-

ably meant was that science has destroyed a sense of inter-relation between the individual and the universe.

V

Lawrence differs from the other writers under discussion in that he is not concerned to the extent that they are with the role of the artist in society. He is not first and foremost the artist, trying to create a society in which great works of art would be produced and appreciated as the supreme manifestation of life. Like the others, his literary style derives from the same principles as his sociological beliefs; yet his conclusions are different. His literary style is founded on a belief in freedom, that spontaneity is needed in literature as in life:

> "There is poetry of this immediate present, instant poetry, as well as poetry of the infinite past and the infinite future. The seething poetry of the incarnate Now is supreme, beyond even the everlasting gems of the before and after. In its quivering momentaneity it surpasses the crystalline, pearl-hard jewels, the poems of the eternities. Do not ask for the qualities of the unfading timeless gems. Ask for the whiteness which is the seethe of mud, ask for that incipient putrescence which is the skies falling, ask for the never-pausing, never-ceasing life itself. There must be mutation, swifter than iridescence, haste, not rest, come-and-go, not fixity, inconclusiveness, immediacy, the quality of life itself, without denouement or close. There must be the rapid momentaneous association of things which meet and pass on the forever incalculable journey of creation: everything left in its own rapid, fluid relationship with the rest of things."[27]

It is not only his free verse which reflects his metaphysic, but his prose style also. Most of his novels were improvised in the sense that he did little planning before starting to write. He preferred to let his words and rhythms keep the effect of immediate composition, and when he did re-write his novels, he re-wrote whole passages or chapters, declining to make minute corrections of style.

In common with the other writers discussed, he thought that the conditions necessary for great art are lacking in the modern world. He saw no hope, he once wrote in a letter, "that people will want sincere work from any artist".[28] He blamed industrial society, with its mechanical attitudes and counterfeit emotions, and scientific discovery, because he thought they removed the sense of wonder from life. Without this, there can be no imaginative reactions. He also blamed democracy because it contains a wrong conception of human nature; for although people are better off materially in our modern democracies, he said, they are nowhere so "absolutely impoverished in life" as in the most absolute democracy. Elsewhere, he wrote: "It seems a strange thing that men, the mass of men, cannot understand that *life* is the great reality, that true living fills with vivid life. . . . They think that property and money are the same thing as vivid life. Only the few, the potential heroes or the 'elect', can see the simple distinction."[29] What "vivid life" meant to Lawrence was the reason why he believed himself to be one of the "elect"; it was the strength of his imaginative reactions and his ability to communicate them. Elemental feeling does not seem to have been particularly strong in him. Thus he has much in common with the authors who wanted an artistic élite, though for different reasons.

Lawrence violently rejected the democratic politics of modern industrial society. He mistrusted "the mob" who, he said, were individually weak but would rule if they were not ruled by the strong; and then their motto would be—Down with the strong! He had no faith in the democratic electorate or the working man, thinking him unfit to elect the ultimate government of the country. The miners (representatives of the working man in general, chosen because he knew them personally) understood mentally only industrialism, wages and machinery. All their collective thinking was in these terms only, which in the long run was bound to produce something like Guild socialism. They were unable to appreciate any "pure, ulterior truth". The only way out was to conquer these people, to think beyond them, act beyond them and know beyond them: "It is the business of very few to understand and for the mass, it is their business to believe and not to bother, but to be honourable and humanly to fulfil their human responsibilities. To give active obedience to their leaders, and to possess their own souls in natural pride."[30] He thought that twentieth-century society was gauged to the level of the lowest individual, "full of contrivances to prevent us being let down by the meanness in ourselves". Basically, Lawrence was pleading the cause of a minority; perhaps this was the only thing a man in his position could do, but it need not have carried him to such large political claims.

Modern democracy, Lawrence believed, is the result of the

Christian doctrine of "love thy neighbour", and pure Christianity cannot fit society at large. The collective whole must have some other inspiration. He said that the will of the community of Christians was anti-social, almost anti-human, revealing from the start a frenzied desire for the end of the world, the destruction of humanity altogether, and then when this did not come, a grim determination to destroy "all mastery, all lordship and all human splendour". The religions of renunciation satisfy only the individual side of man's nature. To satisfy his other side, the collective side, there must be a recognition of the power-spirit. "Accept it, recognise the natural power in the man, as men did in the past, and give it homage, then there is a great joy, an uplifting, and a potency passes from the powerful to the less powerful. . . . Give homage and allegiance to a hero, and you become yourself heroic, it is the law of man."[31] Lawrence believed, like Yeats, that the end of the Christian era was approaching, that some great revolution was imminent. He repeatedly stated that a great destructive revolution was necessary, saying, in 1915, that it would happen in the next ten years. This Nietzschean belief in the power-mode is incompatible with democracy, which is the result, he said, of the Christian elevation of the poor, the meek, the humble. They have risen up and exerted their will against the few who are strong. Democracy is merely a system which allows the majority, who are weak, to elect rulers and invest *authority* in these, instead of recognising natural *power* in the individual. We are bound to ask why this recognition is expected to work better than democracy, and Lawrence was so vague as to what natural power may be, and how we are to recognise it, that we are left expecting it to be worse. At least, in a democracy, we do know more or less why we prefer such and such an individual. Lawrence himself seems to doubt how we are to recognise the superior individual and in what lies his superiority. In a criticism of Fenimore Cooper's *White Novels*, for instance, he wrote: "I feel I'm the superior of most men I meet. Not in birth, because I never had a great-grandfather. Not in money, because I've got none. Not in education, because I'm merely scrappy. And certainly not in beauty or manly strength. Well, what then? Just in myself. When I'm challenged, I do feel myself superior to most of the men I meet. Just natural superiority."[32] He found this feeling hard to explain, and the reader may doubt whether he succeeded. In most men a feeling of superiority which has no intelligible foundation is called vulgar conceit. I do not think this is true of Lawrence. Though he avoided claiming superiority as an artist, he believed that life reveals itself most fully in imaginative reactions. He felt superior because of the vitality and strength of his imaginative reactions, and his ability to communicate them : "But let a question arise, let there be a challenge, and then I feel he should do reverence to the gods in me, because they are more than the gods in him. And he should give reverence to the very me, because it is more at one with the gods than is his very self."[33]

It is implied that the artist, by the force of his natural superiority, is a leader of men, the supreme manifestation of human existence, and in his essay *Why the Novel Matters*, he stressed the superiority, not only of the artist in general, but of the novelist in particular : "Being a novelist, I consider myself superior to the saint, the scientist, the philosopher, and the poet, who are all great masters of different bits of man alive, but never get the whole hog."[34]

In *Apocalypse*, he says that when men come together to do something, power comes into being; it is inevitable that one man should be the master, the leader. Great joy is derived from recognising this principle, and in paying homage to the leader, the lesser man is made heroic also. This is the highest form of collective being. At the end of *Aaron's Rod* this question suddenly comes to the surface, but is left unresolved. It is taken up and discussed in *The Plumed Serpent* in the relationship between Ramon and Cipriano. The latter is more of a success in the social world; he is a general in the army, although in Mexico this is not saying much. But he is clearly a good general, a first-rate organiser, a brilliant horseman and has complete authority in his own sphere of activity. But he defers completely to the power of the other man, because, as Lawrence would say, the gods in Ramon are more than the gods in Cipriano. Ramon is the antithesis of the social man. He lives in an isolated hacienda, is completely out of sympathy with his wife and two sons, and shows a certain childish naïvety which contrasts sharply with Cipriano's social cynicism. But Ramon is the vital force behind their religious revolution, and no one knows this better than Cipriano.

Lawrence had introduced this subject in *Kangaroo* in the relationship between Somers and Kangaroo himself. F. R. Leavis finds it difficult to see why Somers was so attracted to Kangaroo, and Lawrence does not provide reasons. It is because Kangaroo represents the "idea of love, self-sacrifice, humanity united in love, brotherhood and peace", the Christian-democratic attitude which is Somers's religious, social and cultural heritage, but which he insists is dead and from which he is trying to escape. He is still drawn towards Europe and its great tradition, but he finally rejects it in rejecting Kangaroo. Somers cannot pay homage to Kangaroo in the way Cipriano pays homage to Ramon, because the power invested in the Australian is that of a dying civilisation and its outworn attitudes, not the power of natural superiority: "One must have aristocrats, that we know, but natural ones, not artificial."[35] For Lawrence, power is invested in the individual in varying degrees, and the problem is to discover where the power is incarnated. In *Kangaroo* he is rather vague about this because he obviously does not know himself just what he does want. Nevertheless, the book contains a consistent and powerful attack on democracy:

> "The real sense of liberty only goes with white blood. And the ideal of democratic liberty is an exploded ideal. You've got to have wisdom and authority somewhere, and you can't get it out of any further democracy." (Chapter 5.)

> "Freedom! Not for this sub-normal, slavish humanity of democratic antics. But for the world itself, and the Mutigen." (Chapter 8.)

He uses "democratic" as an adjective almost devoid of any precise meaning but simply as a term of abuse, and he has, he says, "a dread, almost a horror of democratic society, the mob". This horror has been aroused by the First World War—"no man who has lived through this can believe again absolutely in democracy". (Chapter 12.) Lawrence's fine invective about "mob-spirit", "democratic mongrelism", "manly isolation", cannot disguise the fact that his hatred of democracy was largely the effect of highly personal and emotional, not intellectual, causes: because he was married to a German woman; because they were treated badly during the war; and because he felt himself humiliated by being medically examined and declared unfit for service. He was not able to blame the war as war; he had to produce some abstraction which was responsible for making this war a special kind of war, aimed specifically at the destruction of the superior individual. (If he was treated badly, he did not help matters by his own antics in Cornwall, singing German songs, for instance, when the authorities were anywhere about. This is a harmless enough practice in itself, but one which inevitably assumes other proportions when one's country is at war with Germany, especially if one is already under suspicion.)

There was, in fact, a latent pro-Germanism in Lawrence : "If a man is to be brought to any heel, better a spurred heel than the heel of a Jewish financier. So Richard decided later, when the years let him think things over, and see where he was. Therefore when the war came, his instinct was against it." (Chapter 12.) His political attitude was not as original or unorthodox as he would have us believe. He equated democracy with the rule of Jewish financiers, and he even "gradually came to believe that all Jews, and all Celts [typified by Lloyd George] even whilst they espoused the cause of England, subtly lived to bring about the last humiliation of the great old England". (Chapter 12.) It needed a Jew, he said, to produce the "last step in liberty", the Theory of Relativity, and like Lewis, Pound and Eliot, he believed the whole liberal-democratic tradition to be essentially Jewish in nature. Kangaroo, the representative of this tradition, is himself a Jew. He did not mention men like Einstein and Marx by name alone; they were "the Jew, Einstein", or "Marx, the Jew". This is simply a device to imply that whatever is thought wrong with the individual is symptomatic of the group, class or race to which he belongs. It can also be a process which leads one to believe that what is implied is true. A dislike of Jewish financiers, or Einstein's mathematics, or Jewish free-thinkers can result in anti-semitism.

What Lawrence became increasingly certain about in writing *Kangaroo* was the need for aristocracy, authority, rule, based on the natural superiority of certain individuals. He insisted that Europe was really established on the aristocratic principle. Remove the sense of class distinction, of higher and lower, and you have anarchy. The control of all supplies should be put into the hands of sincere, sensible men who were still man enough to know that manhood isn't the same thing as goods. "Somebody must have power, so those should have it who don't want it selfishly, and who have some natural gift for it, and some reverence for the sacredness of it." (Chapter 5.) He thought that the white man with his democracy, his equality, his Christianity had lost all understanding of real power, the natural power of the superior individual, the hero. He himself was groping towards "some other living relationship. But what? He did not know.

Perhaps the thing that the dark races know : that one can still feel in India : the mystery of lordship. That which white men have struggled so long against, and which is the clue to the life of the Hindu. The mystery of lordship. The mystery of innate, natural, sacred priority. The other mystic relationship between men, which democracy and equality try to deny and obliterate. Not any arbitrary caste or birth aristocracy. But the mystic recognition of difference and innate priority, the joy of obedience and the sacred responsibility of authority." (Chapter 6.) It was inevitable in the development of his "metaphysic" that his next journey should take him to a place like Mexico.

In *Kangaroo* Lawrence gets little further than distinguishing between the kind of power he does want, and the kind he does not want; that is, the "mass-bullying" of both Christianity and democracy. He claims that the "dark god" which invests power in the individual is not a tyrannical god, but it is difficult to justify this claim from the novels. In *The Plumed Serpent* the execution of Ramon's attackers is made into a ritual to satisfy the gods of which these two men are supposed to be the living incarnations. It could be argued that such a ritual murder, in Mexico, would be a return to an older civilisation in which blood-sacrifice has been a fairly recent reality. There is no doubt, however, that Lawrence was fascinated by the idea of blood-sacrifice, even human sacrifice; he felt its "attraction" not only in Mexico, but in Cornwall :

> "The Cornish night would gradually come down upon the dark, shaggy moors, that were like the fur of some beast, and upon the pale-grey granite masses, so ancient and Druidical, suggesting blood-sacrifice. . . . The spirit of the ancient, pre-Christian world, which lingers still in the truly Celtic places, he could feel it invade him in the savage dusk, making him savage too, and at the same time, strangely sensitive and subtle, understanding the mystery of blood-sacrifice : to sacrifice one's victim, and let the blood run to the fire. . . . He no longer wanted to struggle consciously along, a thought adventurer. He preferred to drift into a sort of blood-darkness, to take up in his veins again the savage vibrations that still lingered round the secret rocks, the place of the pre-Christian human sacrifice. Human sacrifice ! He could feel his dark, blood-consciousness tingle to it again, the desire of it, the mystery of it." (*Kangaroo*, Chapter 12.)

Lawrence quite deliberately associated blood-sacrifice with the worshipping of the "hero", in whom the dark god is manifest :

"There's got to be meeting: even communion. Well, then, let us have the other communion. 'This is thy body which I take from thee and eat,' as the priest, also the God, says in the ritual of blood-sacrifice. The ritual of supreme responsibility, and offering. Sacrifice to the dark God, and to the men in whom the dark God is manifest. Sacrifice to the strong, not to the weak. In awe, not in dribbling love. The communion in power, the assumption into glory. La gloire." (Chapter 14.)

All this cannot be ignored, nor is it merely symbolism. *The Woman Who Rode Away*, written at the same time as *The Plumed Serpent*, is specifically concerned with human sacrifice, the voluntary sacrifice of a white woman to the ancient Indian gods. This may well symbolise that "the power of the world, which she had known until now only in the eyes of blue-eyed men . . . was now fading in the blue eyes, and dawning in the black". Yet Lawrence himself stated in a letter to Martin Secker in 1925, that *The Plumed Serpent* was not a symbolic book, but that he meant literally what he said about a return to the old gods and primitive life forms. Nor did he advocate this return for the Indians only, but insisted that it applied also to European civilisation. He fully realised the implications of what he was advocating. Cipriano says to Kate, "Get used to it that there must be a bit of fear, and a bit of horror in your life, and marry me, and you will find many things that are not horror. The bit of horror is like the sesame seed in the nougat, it gives the sharp wild flavour. It is good to have it there." (Chapter 16.) She manages to do this with a vengeance:

"When she thought of him and his soldiers, tales of swift cruelty she had heard of him : when she remembered his stabbing the three helpless peons, she thought : Why should I judge him? He is of the gods. And when he comes to me he lays his pure, quick flame to mine, and every time I am a young girl again, and every time he takes the flower of my virginity, and I his. It leaves me insouciant like a young girl. What do I care if he kills people? His flame is young and clean." (Chapter 24.)

She eventually comes to understand the new relationship between men which is going to cause the regeneration of civilisation:

"She understood why Ramon and Cipriano wore the white clothes and the sandals, and were naked, or half-naked, as living gods. It was the acquiescence in the primitive assertion. It was the renewal of the old, terrible bond of the blood-unison of man, which made blood-sacrifice so potent a factor of life. The blood of the individual is given back to the great blood-being, the god, the nation, the tribe."

One cannot dismiss this aspect of Lawrence's writing; it is the extreme to which his emotionalism can quite logically be carried. The fact that he himself went to that extreme does much to destroy sympathy for his ideas. This whole concern with blood, blood-sacrifice, human sacrifice is near-lunatic. If Lawrence had not caught malaria and been forced to leave New Mexico, he might well have lived longer; he might also have lost his sanity.

What is peculiar is that, for Lawrence, if the individual believes completely in his actions, and acts with sincerity and according to his conscience, then what he does must be right, even if violence, suffering and death are the result: "The way to immortality is the fulfilment of desire. . . . If you want to go to war, go, it is your righteousness. Because what intimation of immortality have we, save our spontaneous wishes?"[36] Or, as Lawrence puts it in *The Plumed Serpent*, "The executions shocked and depressed her. She knew that Ramon and Cipriano did deliberately what they did: they believed in their deed, they acted with all their conscience. And as men, probably they were right." (Chapter 24.)

It is easy to see how close this is to the rule of violence. Society becomes impossible if the moral code of each individual is to fulfil his spontaneous desires, and Lawrence should have realised it. However one may try to "explain away" the passages of crude violence in Lawrence's novels, there is no ambiguity about this passage: "Don't tell me there is no Devil; there is a Prince of Darkness. Sometimes I wish I could let go and be really wicked —kill and murder—but kill chiefly. I do want to kill. But I want to select whom I shall kill. Then I shall enjoy it."[37] This kind of thing is hard to stomach, and naturally affects one's attitude to the rest of his ideas. It is clear that the satisfying of a spontaneous desire such as this cannot be tolerated in any organised society. Once you admit that the individual is capable of real evil, which Lawrence does, then complete freedom to fulfil one's desires is an impossible principle.

Lawrence's dilemma is that of every highly conscious and intelligent person who wants to recapture something of the elemental, spontaneous life which is below the level of mental consciousness, and yet who mistrusts the mass of humanity. To whom do his principles apply? Are they to apply to a select few who will appreciate the new conditions, or are they to apply to everybody? There is a lot of double-talk about psychology in Lawrence. The claim that the consciousness situated in the solar plexus is superior to mental consciousness inherently cannot be justified to the mind. Apart from these paradoxes, the style of Lawrence is vague. While a man is "a true human individual, there is at the core of him a certain innocence or naïveté which defies all analysis, and which you cannot bargain with, you can only deal with it in good faith from your own corresponding innocence or naïveté".[38] This kind of relationship is what Lawrence wanted, and he believed that it would come if his ideas were accepted. But in the absence of this "innocence or naïveté", the plan will produce chaos and violence. The difficulty of interpreting Lawrence's work is that he was trying to communicate something to the intellect which, he was always stressing, was beyond the intellect. This gives scope for widely differing interpretations of what he actually meant, and the conclusions will depend as much on the reader's temperament as on what Lawrence wrote.

VI

Lawrence's views on social leadership are inherently close to the fascist conception of society: "For the mass of people knowledge *must* be symbolical, mystical, dynamic. This means you must have a higher, responsible, conscious class: and then in varying degrees the lower classes, varying in their degree of consciousness."[39] Like Lewis, Lawrence thought that the lower classes should be relieved of all responsibility. They should not even learn how to read or write. "The secret is to commit into the hands of the sacred few the responsibility which now lies like torture on the mass—let the few, the leaders, be increasingly responsible for the whole. And then let the mass be free: free, save for the choice of leaders. Leaders—this is what mankind is craving for."[40] This is not the strict, authoritarian society that Lewis, for instance, advocated. Lawrence said he wanted the individual to be as free as possible, free, certainly, from the restrictions and the coercion that Lewis seemed to think would be good for him. But their ideal of a ruling class is fundamentally the same, although they differed greatly as to how it would rule. Lewis concentrates his discussion on one side of the situation, the act of depriving people of their say in government, while Lawrence concentrates his attention on the effects which he sees, namely a freer, fuller life, unburdened by cares and tensions which he says are too much for the average person. What he failed to appreciate was that, in the modern world at least, most other freedoms stem from the freedom to choose one's leaders.

Lewis and Lawrence did, of course, differ completely in their attitudes to the intellect. Lewis could never have agreed with the second half of the following quotation: "Symbols must be true from top to bottom. But the interpretation of symbols must rest, degree after degree, in the higher, responsible, conscious classes. To those who cannot divest themselves again of mental consciousness and definite ideas, mentality and ideas are death—nails through their hands and feet."[41] Lawrence anticipated the fascist emphasis on ritual and symbols. In *The Plumed Serpent* the semi-religious, semi-political movement seems to consist of ritual and symbols, and very little else. In politics, the casting off of mental consciousness leads straight to the mass hysteria of the regimes of Hitler and Mussolini. Belief in the power of a natural leader, in "dark gods", in irrationalism and racialism, had disastrous results in the 1930s, when Nazism gave them perverted political forms.

Lawrence wanted society to be organised in a rigid hierarchy —in the shape of a cone or a pyramid—the fascist conception of society:

"The next relation has got to be relationship of men towards men in a spirit of unfathomable trust and responsibility, service and leadership, obedience and pure authority. Men have got to choose their leaders and obey them to the death. And it must be a system of culminating aristocracy, society tapering like a pyramid to the supreme leader."[42]

Ramon in *The Plumed Serpent* receives uncritical obedience and has this kind of pure authority. It is a view commonly held that in democratic society some individual must have responsibilities forced on him which would prove too much for the vast majority. Lawrence went further than this and asked that these responsibilities should be taken off the shoulders of ordinary men and put on his own. He wanted to take over the "responsibility for general affairs", which he said saps the life of most men, the responsibility for the future, for "thought and direction". He saw himself as some kind of messianic saviour of society.

In his last book, *Apocalypse*, a vigorous attack on democracy, he says, "Deny power and power wanes. Deny power in a greater

man and you have no power yourself. But society, now and for-
ever, must be ruled and governed."[43] A few pages later he writes,

> "Every peasant was consummated in the old dash and gorgeous-
> ness of the nobles and in the supreme splendour of the Tsar.
> The supreme master, and lord and splendid one; they might see
> him with their own eyes, the Tsar. And this fulfilled one of the
> deepest, greatest and most powerful needs of the human heart.
> The human heart needs, needs, needs, splendour, gorgeousness,
> pride, assumption, glory and lordship".[44]

This is an echo of a passage in *Kangaroo* in which Lawrence
describes the balance which is necessary between the "flow of
love" and the "flow of power". The world, he says, has gone too
far in the first direction, where the weak, the woman, the masses
are dominant. The balance can only be kept by stern authority,
the unflinching obstinacy of the return-force, power:

> "When the flow is power, might, majesty, glory, then it is a cul-
> minating flow towards one individual, through circles of aristo-
> cracy towards one grand centre. Emperor, Pope, Tyrant, King:
> whatever may be. It is the grand obeisance before a master."
> (Chapter 16.)

Lawrence's views about personal power and innate priority were
largely his attempt to rationalise and justify the sense of his own
superiority. Bertrand Russell, who knew him well, said that Lawrence imagined that he would be the supreme leader when a
dictatorship had been established. Russell also said that Lawrence had developed the whole philosophy of fascism before
the politicians had thought of it,[45] that Lawrence was "an ex-
ponent of the cult of insanity" of the between-wars period, of
which nazism was the most emphatic expression. There is no
doubt that Lawrence's homicidal tendencies and his belief in
"blood" are reminiscent of the worst features of German fascism.
He deserves sympathy when he struggles to describe entirely new
and much better personal and social relationships, but a certain
viciousness of temperament, together with the evasiveness of his
style, do much to counteract the sympathy.

Summing Up

SUMMING UP

I

IT HAS BEEN said that totalitarianism has had an innate attraction for an able minority of literary intellectuals as far back as Plato.[1] In the 1920s and thirties, however, it was not only a minority of literary intellectuals who were attracted by fascism. The extensive support for fascism had two main aspects: the pragmatic support of a large number of people, including politicians, with widely varying ideas and backgrounds, and the ideological support of mainly intellectuals and writers, who were responsible for providing fascism with all kinds of ideologies, most of which were rationalisations of their own prejudices.*

The pragmatic support for fascism had the following causes. First, there was an increasing dislike of the negative aspects of democracy. One of the dilemmas of a constitutional government is that the law makes clear what one cannot do, but not what one ought to do. The democratic process is a tentative, conditional process, and avoids direct commitment beyond the preservation of freedom. Between the wars this seemed to many people to be evidence of mere aimlessness, indecision and confusion. They felt that they were living in a sluggish society, and admired the apparent dynamism of fascist states; they wanted to put an end to the welter of confusion by some kind of decisive action. The Weimar Republic, culminating in mass unemployment and soaring inflation, was taken by many people to be the epitome of democratic society. "What an intellectual Babylon of voices, that Weimar Republic! Talking of decline, of crisis, of doom—but joyful talking. Philosophers demonstrating that there was no longer time for any philosophy, sociologists unmasking all creeds, values, moral standards as 'ideological', economists calmly proving that five or six million unemployed had come to stay... legists affirming that the very notion of

---

* It would seem to be desirable to summarise the arguments put forward in previous chapters, and this will inevitably involve a certain amount of repetition.

natural justice was a hoax, and that any positive law, duly codi-
fied, was as good as any other—far too many people assiduously
sawing off the branch on which other people or they themselves
were sitting."[2] Men like Rauschning, Strasser and Thyssen described nazism as a national awakening, a surface discipline and
order, a vast display of energy and achievement which lifted
men out of the humdrum atmosphere of daily life. Intellectuals
in Germany welcomed the substitution of real authority and
German Volkstum for "weak" and "cosmopolitan" parliamentary democracy.[3] The widespread feeling of contrast between
fascism and democracy is summed up in these words: "Why did
reaction succeed in gaining control of Prussia? On the one side
there was weariness, on the other vigour; on the one side democrats, on the other soldiers; one side went riding every morning,
the other sat wearily among its papers."[4] Hoesch said that many
of the English admired the autocratic nature of nazism, and
were impressed by German discipline and efficiency, as opposed
to the indolence of the British, while Arnold Wilson thought that
the English would do well to study and adopt aspects of nazism
—the energy and the burning flame of patriotism of the young
Germans, for example.[5]

Second, the fear of Communist Russia and of a socialist revolution in Britain was an important element in pro-fascist sympathy. Many people in the 1920s and thirties saw Communist
Russia as the greatest danger and welcomed Hitler as the pro-
tector of European civilisation against the Reds.[6] They believed
that only a united Britain and Germany could resist the threat,
and Anglo-Saxondom was revived as a concept of racial and
ethical solidarity, Teuton versus Slav. People thought communism, not nazism, the great threat to the British Empire, and
wanted an economically strong Germany to avoid economic
collapse and to uphold the value of exports. The affair of the
Zinoviev letter indicates the strength of anti-Soviet feeling in
Britain. Some people thought French weakness worse than Nazi
excesses because this could be exploited in Moscow. There was
a revival of Francophobia—"Rather Hitler than Blum"—which
was strengthened by the idea that the Franco-Russian alliance
had been an important cause of the First World War. Lord
Lothian, for instance, thought Anglo-German friendship necessary to resist Franco-Russian dominance in Europe. Conservatives who supported Franco feared that a Republican victory in
the Spanish Civil War would mean that Spain would go Com-

munist and thus trade would be harmed. But the most surprising aspect of pro-fascist feeling was the support given to Hitler's Germany by British Communists, who saw it as a means of avoiding a capitalist attack on the Soviet Union by the Western Powers.[7] It has also been suggested that pacifists in the 1930s were pro-fascist. As it worked out in practice this is probably true; if you hinder one side, you help the other. George Orwell, however, said that pacifists were consciously pro-fascist, that their attitude was not as innocent as it was supposed to be, pointing out that many French pacifists went over to Hitler after the fall of France, and claiming that there was an overlap of membership between the Peace Pledge Union and the Blackshirts.

Third, Germany lay on many consciences after the First World War and the Treaty of Versailles. A sense of guilt drove men into a one-sided relationship with Germany, in which she was always given the benefit of the doubt. In the early years of nazism it was a common opinion among intellectuals in Britain that, since the victors had imposed harsh terms on Germany, the victor nations had no right to oppose Hitler, who was only expressing the German people's rejection of those terms.[8] It was even said that the Treaty of Versailles was responsible for internal persecutions in Germany, because it had driven the country into anarchy. There was a real desire in Britain for peace at almost any price, but although appeasement was a strong emotion, not something taught, it was, nevertheless, an attitude of mind rooted in pro-Germanism.[9]

Fourth, Mussolini and Hitler seemed to provide the decisive, dynamic leadership which many people wanted. Support for the relatively mild Italian form of fascism provided the basis of the support for nazism, the widespread sympathy and admiration for Mussolini and his system being extended to Hitler when he came to power. Lloyd George thought Hitler a born leader, a magnetic, dynamic personality with a single-minded purpose, and wished that Britain had such a man at the head of its affairs.

Fifth, the anti-semitism of the Nazi regime obviously appealed to those people in all countries who harboured that particular prejudice. "Anti-semitism as an old, deeply-rooted and ubiquitous phenomenon in the Western world could serve better than anything else to galvanise and diffuse pro-Nazi sentiment throughout the world."[10]

Finally, there were those people, particularly the literary intelligentsia, who saw the problem as essentially a cultural one. Confronted with cheap national newspapers, radio, films, they thought they saw a massive decline in cultural standards and attributed this to the spread of democracy. Fascism, violently anti-democratic, also seemed to them to be a modern counterpart of earlier hierarchic societies in which authority, stability and inequality had provided the soil of flourishing artistic cultures. Many of the intelligentsia were as much concerned with the cultural history of the German people as with the contemporary political situation, and political sympathy was very much a part of cultural sympathy.[11]

II

Modern literature often reveals a consciousness of the destructive principle in modern society, and this is especially true of the five writers discussed here. Theirs was a moral or aesthetic concern which sometimes involved them in politics. When a writer becomes immersed in political ideology or a specific social programme, it sometimes has a bad effect on his work. The magnificent language and vivid visual effects of *Apes of God* might be said to be wasted on subjects which the author considers trivial and insignificant. In *Childermass*, on the other hand, Lewis includes the social, political and intellectual phenomena which he dislikes, and yet does not make the novel merely a statement of his preferences. Pound's dislike of bankers and Jewish financiers becomes too obtrusive in the *Cantos*, while those describing parts of American history, though sometimes more readable than the "poetic" parts, are too long and too detailed. In the 1930s, Auden adopted a political position and wrote from it, but his poetry was not affected to the extent that Pound's was by political dogma.

In *The Twentieth Century*, June 1951, Stephen Spender wrote that Orwell had thought it impossible to see any coherent attitude that Lawrence could have taken up after 1939. He might even have found himself having to support the Nazis. But he differs from Lewis, Pound and Eliot in that he was offering his experience of living as a formula for saving society. He belonged more to the epoch of individualist literary prophets while the other three belonged to the 1930s, when it was thought that individual sensibility, however important, was not a force which could itself alter society. Co-ordinated social and political measures were thought necessary, even though opinions differed as to what form the measures should take—varying from Eliot's Christian, platonic concept of society to the Marxist ideology of Auden and Spender. The difference between Yeats and the Communist poets of the 1930s is not that they were interested in society while he was not; he was. The difference is that they had committed themselves to a political party and were interested mainly in social conditions, while Yeats, Lewis, Pound and Eliot were really interested in society only in so far as it would allow the arts to flourish. Their interest in social problems stemmed, as we have said, from their interest in the arts, and their plans were worked out on the basis of providing good literature, and not necessarily a "good" society; that is, one in which the majority of its members live full, free and satisfying lives. The desire to influence society in order to create a suitable background for his own writing is characteristic of each of these writers. Moreover, they based their political and social criticism on the same principles as their imaginative writing and literary criticism. They transferred their value-judgements from aesthetics to politics. It worked out differently in Lawrence's case, as his literary principles were very different from those of the other four. But he, like them, advocated a rigidly hierarchised, anti-democratic society, and the transfer of value-judgements from literature to society is the same. David Daiches, in *Critical Approaches to Literature*, says that it is wrong to transfer value-judgements of society to literature. He means that it is wrong to say that in a good society the literature will be good, or if society is bad, the literature must be bad. It is often thought a Marxist position to hold that nothing good can come out of a corrupt society. But it is also wrong, and more dangerous, to transfer value-judgements the other way, from literature to society. The desire for "classical" order, discipline, strict rules and hardness in literature led Yeats, Pound, Lewis and Eliot to demand the same in society. They were within their rights, and it need not have worked out badly; but the process was not likely to produce good political judgement.

There was the same connection between the political and literary principles of the Augustan poets of the eighteenth century, but they supported the social system under which they lived. In seventeenth-century France and eighteenth-century Britain there was no question as to what form the political or literary authority should take; but by the end of the nineteenth century the established, dominant aristocracies no longer existed, and the romantic and aesthetic movements in literature had made the individual artist's sensibility the sole arbiter in matters of form, style and content. The neo-classicists stressed the importance of order and authority but could not satisfactorily explain what it was or how it was to be achieved, either in society or literature. They were attracted to fascism because it promised to provide a clearly defined ruling élite, whereas in a democracy the responsibility lies with no one or with everyone. "Intellectuals have not in front of them any organised group or class or caste bearing the final responsibility for society. . . . [They] have been accustomed since immemorial times to work in the interest and through the medium of a king or a dynasty, or an oligarchical class. . . . It seems cruelty to have responsibility without power, precisely when the intellectual is most fettered by his need of adjustment to democratic society."[12] Like many others they were impressed not only by Hitler and Mussolini as hero-types, but by the promise of a more active, decisive role which fascist leaders said writers and artists should play in political affairs. One of the main causes of frustration of men like Lewis and Pound was that while the improvement in the artist's social status, and more important, the sense of his moral superiority which culminated in the aesthetic movement, made them see themselves as leaders of society, the increasingly esoteric nature of the arts tended to alienate society as a whole. Their own attitude to the public could only mean that the public in a democratic society could not seriously consider them as political leaders, while fascism, which at first seemed to be the antithesis of a mass movement, appeared to promise political responsibility for creative artists who supported the regime.

The desire for authority, together with the belief in the superiority of the creative man, led them to advocate the rule of the artist-hero in politics. They wanted responsibility for affairs; they wanted political power for themselves because they genuinely thought that they were the men most suited to wield it. Like Ruskin, they believed that the arts should be an active guide to society, and therefore to political action. Political economy, Ruskin said, is "a system of conduct and legislature, founded on the sciences, directed by the arts, and impossible, except under certain conditions of moral culture".[13] The idea that the writer should be the leader of society was stated most directly by Lawrence. He thought that it was not only the "artist" or the writer who should be the leader of society, but Lawrence himself. To quote again from *Fantasia of the Unconscious*, "I would like him to give me back the responsibility for general affairs, a responsibility which he can't acquit, and which saps his life. I would like him to give me back the responsibility for thought, for direction. I wish we could take hope and belief together. . . . I would like him to give me back books and newspapers and theories. And I would like to give him back in return his old insouciance, and rich, original spontaneity and fullness of life."[14] Lawrence here at least professed to want power himself for the benefit of the majority. The others did so for the benefit of the arts. The danger is to become preoccupied with power itself, rather than the ends to which it can be put, and they all, to a certain extent, were imaginatively guilty of this.

Because these five writers thought they saw a society developing in which there could be no good art, they attacked the democratic, humanitarian ideal. They criticised the humanist principles of their time, the belief, for example, that man is the measure of all things, or that one should act for the greatest good of the greatest number. The main effect was something that none of them wanted except Eliot; that is, a Christian revival, if not among society in general, at least among many intellectuals. Joyce, although he was associated with the "neo-classicists", supported the ideals of humanistic liberalism while he attacked its vulgarities. He had experienced a "paternal" society in his childhood in Ireland, with the authority provided by the Catholic Church, and he had no enthusiasm for a fascist one. Orwell thought that people like Yeats who hated democracy, science, machinery, the ideas of human equality and progress, in fact the modern world in general, were necessarily gathered under the wing of fascism because this was the one movement that consciously attempted to formalise these phobias.

Writers like Lewis and Pound, however, were completely mistaken in equating fascism in politics with "classicism" in literature. They failed to realise early enough the irrational stress of fascist ideology, which was the antithesis of the intellectualism and rationalism of the art and literature they called "classical". It is possible that these writers did not realise that a totalitarian regime will repress writers and artists who do not uphold the government in power. It is more probable that they did see this, but were so intent on propagating the literary and political beliefs they themselves held, that they were quite willing to see different opinions suppressed. Pound and Lewis, in particular, were totalitarians in that they would have suppressed anything to which they were opposed, not only in the practical sphere—Pound suppressing Jewish financiers—but in the intellectual sphere—Lewis suppressing behaviourism and Bergson's philosophy. They developed and refined their prejudices into a political philosophy.

Lewis, Pound and Eliot were looking for that absolute certainty, what William James called emotional "sumptuosity of security", which is most easily reached through revealed religion. Hulme tried to postulate the same *a priori* absolutes in politics as in his religion. He regarded original sin as the central insight of Christianity, and saw literary classicism as the creative recognition, and authoritarianism as the political recognition, of the fact of original sin. This connection between religious and political authoritarianism is also evident in nineteenth-century German thought where the state becomes the concrete reality of the religious abstraction, God. Totalitarian ideology becomes a substitute for religion, not merely in providing form and authority for a set of beliefs and prejudices, but because it was invested with God's authority by seminal minds like Hegel. Men like Lewis and Pound, whose pessimism was based on a sense of man's feebleness rather than a belief in original sin, were forced to look to a political system for that absolute certainty that politics can never provide. The result was their addiction to authority, organisation, hierarchies, which alone, outside the arts, could give meaning and significance to man's life. In Germany it has been thought that man exists for the state, not the state for man, and social and political ideals have been regarded as ends in themselves. The separation of ideal from individual has been accompanied by a confusion of means with ends.[15] The same is true of writers like Yeats, Lewis, Pound and Eliot, who in spite of their concern with social and political problems adopted an essentially aesthetic position. Oscar Wilde in gaol can be compared with Pound in the prison camp—"I have been hard as youth sixty years." Neither of them had seen any need for human sympathy or understood the nature of human suffering. Literature becomes an end in itself; man creates something more important than man, that is great "art". The individual is insignificant in the face of the magnificence of the impersonal ideal. Art does not exist for man, man exists for art, therefore society must be organised so that the arts will flourish. The individual is sacrificed to the cultural ideal.

III

Each of these writers attacked the democratic system because it lacked the kind of stability he wanted. With the possible exception of Lawrence, they believed that great art is impossible without social stability. For Lewis, social stability depends on minority rule. For Yeats, the stable society is synonymous with aristocratic rule; and this would help great art because patronage would free the artist to work and let him meet people with good manners. The image of the stable society is constantly recurring in the *Cantos*, as Pound describes what he considers to be good forms of society in the past. It was largely an economic stability that Pound wanted, but he believed that other kinds of stability depend on that. Eliot thought that small, closely knit, mainly agricultural units would provide the necessary stability. Lawrence also regretted the destruction of the agricultural basis of society, and the increasing industrialisation and mechanisation, not only of society but of individual human life. Occasionally they idealised the Middle Ages as a time when a static society produced great works of art, culminating in the poetry of Chaucer. Nothing, however, could be further from the truth. The Middle Ages as a whole were not stable, and the late Middle Ages were a time of bewildering change : "It [the thirteenth century] was followed by a period of exhausting wars, economic difficulties, and the gradual, bewildering break-up of its code of values. Late medieval England experienced disillusionment, and a desire for new aims and new verities. There were radicals convinced of the need to abolish what they considered the corruptions of the existing order, bitterly opposed by alarmed conservatives who felt that if concessions were made the whole structure of faith and society would collapse. There were complaints that the lower classes were becoming outrageous in their demands, and that unscrupulous capitalists were squeezing out the craftsmen and causing unemployment. Preachers vigorously denounced the selfishness and ambition of their own time, and what seemed to them its exclusive love of pleasure and display. There was a widespread feeling among thinkers and writers that the time was out of joint; and in late medieval literature and art there runs a strain of melancholy, a preoccupation with death, a sense of coming disaster."[16] The Black Death came to England in the fourteenth century, and the Peasants' Revolt took place in 1381 owing to a complex combination of political, social and religious factors. "It affected

areas as far apart as Hampshire and the Scottish borders, Wirral
and Norfolk."[17] In the midst of all this Chaucer was writing, and
there was a great deal of building in the splendid new perpendi-
cular style. Had Yeats and Eliot lived in the late Middle Ages,
they would probably have attacked their society as fiercely as
they did twentieth-century society, since "the rise of the yeomen
and gentry broke up the old village community and made the
hierarchical conception of society more and more unreal".[18]

Lewis placed great emphasis on some kind of stability in philosophy, which he called the "like-thinking of a classical norm",
but just what he meant by that is likely to remain for ever a
mystery. He seems to have placed the destruction of this "classical
norm" somewhere in the nineteenth century, and equated it with
the rise of democracy and political revolutions. Again the Middle
Ages are often taken to be an era when philosophy was static,
Aquinas remaining the undisputed authority. A. R. Myers, however, writes: "Scarcely was his *Summa Theologica* finished, than
two Oxford Franciscan friars initiated the process of destruction
which eventually led to Descartes and the downfall of medieval
philosophy."[19] The rival philosophies of these two friars, Duns
and Ockham, "dominated the universities of Western Europe
until the Renaissance". It is impossible to think of any time
since the Renaissance when there have been the kind of static
and universally held beliefs which Lewis assumes. Even if we
interpret "classical" literally it is hard to find a "norm", certainly before Aristotle. Thales, who was alive in 585 B.C., believed that everything is made of water. After Thales, Heraclitus
believed in the concept of eternal flux, universal change. He was
shortly followed by Parmenides who said that nothing ever
changes. Empedocles, who was living in 440 B.C., first stated the
theory of the four elements, earth, air, fire and water, while at
the same time Leucippus and Democritus first put forward the
atomic theory. Aristotle's ideas did acquire an authority which
lasted for centuries, but very few great works of art have been
inspired by them.

The greatest period of Greek culture is the age of Pericles, a
hundred years before Aristotle flourished. This was preceded by
a period of strict aristocratic rule. Pericles, however, was a
moderate democrat, and under him Athens prospered. Bertrand
Russell writes: "The city increased very rapidly in wealth and
also in culture, and, as invariably happens at such times, particularly when wealth is due to foreign commerce, traditional

morality and traditional beliefs decayed."[20] This was the great age of Greek drama, and the time when the great Athenian temples were built, a comparatively democratic, fluid, free-thinking era. Stability was not necessary then for the production of great art.

1793 in England saw the beginning of twenty years of war with Revolutionary and Napoleonic France. There followed a period of violent social change : "With its violent disturbances of economic life, and its mood of 'anti-Jacobin' reaction against all proposals for reform and all sympathy with the claims and sufferings of the poor—the war formed the worst possible environment for the industrial and social changes then in rapid progress. . . . Man had acquired formidable tools for refashioning his life before he had given the least thought to the question of what sort of life it would be well for him to fashion."[21] During this period of social upheaval, English poetry revived; it had become practically moribund by the end of a period of relative social stability. The romantic movement was a revolt against received and standardised ethical and aesthetic principles. The poetry of Wordsworth, Byron, Keats and Shelley, and the paintings of Turner, were not freak occurrences produced in spite of great social, political and ethical changes, but were largely the result of such changes, or at least an integral part of them.

In this respect the Elizabethan era is the counterpart of those years at the turn of the eighteenth century. Myers writes of "the fascination of watching new life, new techniques, new forms of society, new modes of thought and expression unfolding in the old order, until in the sixteenth century the new culture became self-assertive and mature—destroying much that was of value in the old order, but also fashioning an England which was to advance to fresh triumphs of hand and mind".[22] Elizabethan and Jacobean England was particularly plagued by the problem of inflation. Economic stability, therefore, however desirable it may be, is not, as Pound said it is, necessary for artistic creation.

The Italian Renaissance shows most clearly that social stability is not a prerequisite of great art. Bertrand Russell has said that "the moral and political anarchy of fifteenth century Italy was appalling, and gave rise to the doctrines of Machiavelli. At the same time, the freedom from mental shackles led to an astonishing display of genius in art and literature. But such a society is unstable."[23] It is difficult to see why so many writers have thought that stability, whether social, political, moral or philosophical, is a prerequisite of artistic creation. It is probably that the bewildering changes which have occurred during the last 150 years have made many writers long for an undisturbed pattern of thought and existence. Some of them assumed that the slower pace at which life was lived before 1800 indicated the kind of stability they idealised. Arnold thought that the breaking down of park railings by a London crowd was a symptom of the degeneration of civilisation. What would he have said about the Peasants' Revolt?

Twentieth-century writers such as Lewis, Pound and Yeats realised that there was no hope of a return to an earlier form of civilisation, so they hoped for a stability provided by totalitarian regimes. Totalitarianism, however, depends on mental shackles which make continuous artistic excellence impossible. It produces the rigid attitude to the arts illustrated by recent controversies in Russia; and this is what will destroy the arts, if anything will.

IV

Many twentieth-century writers have decided that culture has been sacrificed to democracy; the spread of culture has meant that the level of the masses is raised, but that the level of the élite is lowered. Eliot and Pound, in particular, sometimes claim to write only for a small group, mainly consisting of other poets, because they despair of finding any public of sufficient intelligence to understand them, or with enough discrimination to appreciate their poetry. This, they think, is because democratic sentiment, an enemy of literary standards, has triumphed; and it did so because of the levelling-off processes of mass-production and standardisation. F. R. Leavis is very much in agreement with them. He says that the best writers are now appreciated only by a very small group, most probably other artists, this being the result of levelling agencies—radio, films and the national press. Previously the best writers—Shakespeare, Milton, Fielding, Byron, Hardy—provided art which was of high standard and yet widely popular. It "appealed at a number of levels of response, from the highest downwards". He says that modern literary experts such as J. B. Priestley are "anti-highbrow", "highbrow" being a word which did not exist before this century. The fact that the levels of response to Shakespeare's plays reached from the highest to the lowest, however, proves nothing in itself.

The important point is not how low you can go in the social scale while still getting a response to Shakespeare, but how low you can go while still getting a sensible response which shows some discrimination in the playgoer. I think one would find this response to be more widely present in different levels of society today than it was before this century. Thus not all levelling is to the lower level.

Many writers also believe that a democratic system must inevitably result in a lowering of artistic standards. Lewis, however, although he once firmly held this opinion, later realised that he was wrong: "I feel that I slighted too much the notion of 'democracy' by using that term to mean too exclusively the present so-called democratic masses, hypnotised into a sort of hysterical imbecility by the mesmeric methods of Advertisement."[24] The fundamental principle of democracy is that everyone should have the chance to achieve standards which are higher than under a feudal or aristocratic system, for example. The idea that democracy as a system deliberately fosters mediocrity is wrong. T. B. Bottomore has pointed out that we have, as yet, no direct experience of the way of life of an egalitarian society, and can do no more than estimate the probability of its being able to create and preserve a high level of culture. We may reasonably expect, however, that such a society in which leisure is widespread and individuals are encouraged to develop their talents would at least be as creative as those of earlier periods.[25] The levelling ought to be upwards not downwards, and the spread of education, in particular higher education, is surely achieving this. If, during the last twenty years in particular, we have seen a decline in the very highest level of artistic production, one cannot accept that it has been brought about by the tastes of a mass audience, which are after all extremely varied and difficult to assess.

"Machine culture," typified by the popular press or television, is, moreover, not a democratic process, as R. C. Churchill has shown in his book *Disagreements*. There is no reason at all to equate machine culture with democracy as a political system; in fact, if it tends to destroy standards of literacy, then it is an anti-democratic phenomenon. The Yellow Press is often said to have suited exactly the taste of the new reading public, just as the worst specimens of the popular press of today are said to suit the taste of the mass public. But how does anyone know this? Mr. Churchill has also convincingly shown that the history of English culture is predominantly democratic, and that newspapers produced and read by the lower classes before North-cliffe were reliable and well-informed. "How did the Conservative Party and Northcliffe know what the public's taste was? The new journalism was supposed to fit exactly the new reading public (so far as it was new). The new journalism was deliberately vulgar and sensational: are, then, the Bible and the *Pilgrim's Progress*—the staple reading of many of the previous 'lower orders'—also vulgar and sensational? Is Dickens vulgar and sensational? The new journalism was deliberately unreliable and sketchy on political affairs: were, then, Cobbett's *Register* and Hetherington's *Poor Man's Guardian* also unreliable and sketchy on political affairs? O'Connor's *Northern Star* may have been, but that was a paper written by the upper classes for the working man. The actual newspapers written and read by the lower classes—Cobbett's, Hetherington's and others—were most reliable on political matters, serious and well-informed, like the best of the upper-class newspapers. The truth is that neither the Tory chiefs nor the future Lord Northcliffe knew anything or cared anything about the literary tradition of the English people. They based their policy on other lines."[26] To say that the Yellow Press was the inevitable result of the spread of education and the rise of a mass reading public is completely false. Some of the lower classes had been illiterate, so nobody could have known their tastes. Many of the others had been fond of the Bible, Bunyan and Dickens, and had read newspapers written by Cobbett, Place, Hetherington and Lovett. Northcliffe regarded a newspaper as an article of commerce, caring nothing for literary tradition or standards, and success for his venture was ensured by revolutionary methods of distribution and by pressure of advertisement.

Alongside the growth of democracy has gone the growth of empiricism and the development of logical analysis, which is concerned with tightening up philosophical thinking, with destroying imprecision and vagueness. Lewis, among others, however, associates democracy with imprecise thinking and anti-rationalism, epitomised by Bergson's philosophy. Lewis was right to object to emotionalism and the destruction of the intellect; but he was wrong to equate these with democracy. Russell, equally unfairly, stressed that Bergson had the opposite effect: "The main effect of Bergson's philosophy was conservative and it harmonised easily with the movement that culminated in

Vichy."[27] Democracy more than other political systems discourages anti-rationalism. It encourages the populace to choose its leaders on grounds of individual merit and the policy they put forward; the choice is based on explanation, discussion and reflection (there will also be irrelevant grounds for choice, but so there would in any society). One could not say so much for a choice based on a belief in personal power, or inherited ability, or inherited wealth and position, or the superiority of a certain type of person, the "artist-hero", for example. Lewis did not recognise this. Lawrence did, but, of course, he accepted and even encouraged irrationalism. Eliot is confused by seeing the reality of the situation but by being unable to accept it. His is a modern version of Plato's commonwealth, where the rulers have authority chiefly by reason of birth, background and training, with a vague provision for the promotion of the more able, but lower-born individual.

It is irrational to assume that the creative artist as a type would prove better as a leader than an elected delegate. It is irrational to assume that birth, background and wealth will necessarily produce better rulers. It is irrational to assume that a dictator with powers over life and death will act in the interests of society as a whole, or even in the interests of one group in society, or, indeed, that he will have anyone's interests at heart besides his own. It is irrational and disastrous to permit an individual or group of individuals to hold so much power that it is practically impossible to divest them of that power if they prove to be bad rulers. This, at least, democracy avoids.

The most convincing political argument against democracy as it exists today seems to me to be Pound's; that the men who possess the real power are not the elected delegates, but the men who control the purse strings, the financiers and the controllers of big business. We should not, however, accept this as an unsurmountable obstacle and reject democracy. A sincere, determined democratic government can solve this problem. As Pound himself said, democracy run by clean, decent, honest men should attain *Kraft durch Freude* as well as a dictatorship. In fact, it should attain it infinitely better than a dictatorship.

These writers, then, can be opposed on the following grounds. First, social, political or economic stability is not a necessary condition for great literature, nor is democracy inimical to the arts. Second, authoritarianism of the kind they advocated does not encourage the arts; it destroys them, because the ruling party has to destroy and prohibit any views and beliefs which are contrary to its own dogma. The artist's work must become political propaganda, with the form and content determined not by himself, but by politicians. Third, their position is not self-consistent. Nietzsche's was, in that he advocated the tyrannical rule of the strong for the benefit of the strong few. The mass was of no consideration. These writers, however, professed to advocate fascism for the benefit of the mass of people. They wanted great literature, one might almost say, at any price, and concluded, in general, that authoritarianism was necessary for this. But they also professed concern for the condition of society as a whole. A desire for fascism cannot go hand in hand with concern for the masses; it led Lewis, for example, into saying that the good, strong, autocratic ruler ought to treat the people like dogs for their own good. Once you have accepted the principle that the mass of the people deserves as much consideration as the well-born or wealthy minority, it is useless to try to cling to the kind of government which existed before that principle was established, or to try to set up a new government which is of a corresponding type, but suited to the changed conditions. It is useless to expect a small group invested with immense powers to act in the interests of the mass of the people for any length of time.

The ultimate argument is one of sympathy. It is impossible to prove scientifically that it is right to respect other people and treat them humanely, and wrong to hate and terrorise them. To have sympathy for one's fellow human beings, whether individually or in the mass, seems to me to be an eminently desirable human quality. There is little doubt that the writers here discussed were lacking in this quality.

V

Too much emphasis has been placed on the democratic system of government in relation to the decline of literature. What is more relevant is the effect that the First World War had on the artist and the conditions necessary for art. Yeats's experience of the Irish Rebellion made him greatly aware of the effects of mass-violence and mass-murder. Lawrence was driven almost mad by the war, although he did not take part in it. Many people would consider these two as the last of the indisputably great writers, and both reached maturity before the first war. My generation, brought up in the midst of war, and with total war always a possibility, if not a probability, finds it difficult to appreciate the great effect which this war had on those brought up in Victorian and Edwardian days. Those who thought that the likelihood of mass-violence and war was diminishing had their ideas rapidly disproved. Yet good literature continued to be produced.

The Second World War, however, really does seem to have caused a decline. The atom bomb, which put an end to the war, also appears to have put an end to first-rate literature, for a time at least. Wyndham Lewis, who complained more than anyone about the democratic tradition and the decline of the arts, came to think, after 1945, that talking about it was trivial compared with the threat of universal destruction. Before the existence of this threat, the poet or novelist could, if he wanted to dissociate himself from society and its predominant ideals, argue that the problems facing society were unimportant compared with his art. But now the position seems to have been reversed. The insecurities of a mass society—the constant threat of immediate and universal destruction and of world famine through over-population, for instance—are more likely to make the potential poet see poetry itself as trivial in comparison.

Thirty years ago Yeats managed to make good poetry out of the violence and horror of war. But his last poems are poems of bitterness and rejection. Lawrence's last book, *Apocalypse*, is a bitter attack on modern society. Eliot published no poetry written since the last war, and the *Pisan Cantos*, though written after the fall of Italy, are the result of Pound's experiences before and during the war, and immediately following Mussolini's defeat. Those *Cantos* which have appeared since are difficult to assess, but one may suspect that they are merely a continuation of a poetic technique without any real poetic inspiration. Pound certainly appears to have discarded many of the interests which had formed his poetic inspiration after the 1914–18 war.

Stephen Spender has said, "the greatest modern poet would be the poet most capable of accepting the most anti-poetic and brutal phenomena . . . and revealing them as expressions of man's spirit even in being denials of man's spirit".[28] Perhaps these phenomena have become too brutal and too anti-poetic to permit the writing of first-rate, sane literature. The second and third books of *The Human Age*, which Lewis wrote after the Second World War, contain passages of maniac violence and horror. It would be foolish to suggest that Lewis did not write as well after the war as he had done before it, simply because he saw that universal destruction was a probability. Lewis's imagination and language still had great force when he wrote *Monstre Gai* and *Malign Fiesta*. Yet there seems to be a complete absence of human values in these books; the sympathy with the human predicament which showed itself in *Childermass* is entirely lacking. Many men in the past have been in black despair about the future of civilisation, often believing that it could not last much longer. Today, however, man himself possesses the means to bring it to a swift conclusion. In the past he did not. There lies the difference. The advance of science, not democracy, has created the mass society, and also the means to destroy it. This is the real problem; whether the kind of sensibility necessary to the writing of good literature can survive the pressures exerted on the individual by the continual threat of mass destruction, together with other insecurities which seem inherent in the new mass society.

Index of References

INDEX OF REFERENCES

Introduction

1. Menon, *The Development of W. B. Yeats*, p. 1.
2. Williams, *Culture and Society*, p. 250.
3. Leavis, *For Continuity*, p. 119.
4. Orwell, *Critical Essays*, p. 119.
5. See Butler, *The Roots of National Socialism*, to which I am largely indebted for this account. For other discussions of the intellectual origins of national socialism see: Jethro Bithell, *Modern German Literature*, London, first published 1939; Carl Mayer, "On the Intellectual Origins of National Socialism", in *Social Research*, vol. IX, 1942, pp. 225-47; Ralph F. Bischoff, *Nazi Conquest through German Culture*, Cambridge, 1942.
6. See E. Wiskemann, *The Rome–Berlin Axis*, Oxford, 1949.
7. Butler, *Roots of National Socialism*, p. 78.
8. Ibid., p. 240.
9. Pinson, *Modern Germany*, p. 463.
10. See Albrecht-Carrié, *Italy from Napoleon to Mussolini*.
11. Artz, *Reaction and Revolution*, p. 54.
12. See Braune, *Edmund Burke in Deutschland*.
13. Routh, *Towards the Twentieth Century*, p. 120.
14. For an account of the superman doctrines of Carlyle and Nietzsche see E. R. Bentley, *The Cult of the Superman*, Robert Hale, London, 1947.
15. *Times Literary Supplement*, March 19th and April 2nd, 1914.
16. Powys, *The Meaning of Culture*, p. 298.
17. For a discussion of élite theories see Bottomore, *Elites and Society*, to which I am indebted.
18. Ibid., p. 10.
19. See Curtis, *Three Against the Third Republic*, to which I am indebted for this account.
20. Ibid., p. 216.
21. Orwell, *Critical Essays*, p. 114.
22. Pound, *Letters*, p. 389.
23. Ellmann, *James Joyce*, p. 361.
24. Graves and Hodge, *The Long Weekend*, p. 248.

25. Wood, *Communism and British Intellectuals*, p. 69.
26. See Ivan Maisky, *Who Helped Hitler?*
27. Atkins, *George Orwell*, p. 208.

Chapter I

1. Yeats, *Letters*, p. 837.
2. Ibid., p. 714.
3. Hough, *The Last Romantics*, p. 218.
4. Yeats, *Letters*, p. 831.
5. Menon, *The Development of W. B. Yeats*, p. 1.
6. Gibbon, *The Masterpiece and the Man*, p. 45.
7. Yeats, *Autobiographies*, p. 225.
8. Yeats, *Letters*, p. 876.
9. Moore, *Ave*, p. 217.
10. Yeats, *Letters*, pp. 850–51.
11. Ibid., p. 881.
12. Ibid., p. 219.
13. Yeats, *Autobiographies*, p. 171.
14. Ibid., p. 474.
15. Ibid., p. 456.
16. Ibid., p. 462.
17. Quoted by Hone, *Life of Yeats*, p. 365.
18. Hough, *The Last Romantics*, p. 230.
19. Yeats, *Autobiographies*, p. 465.
20. Moore, *Ave*, p. 217.
21. Menon, *The Development of W. B. Yeats*, p. 67.
22. Yeats, *A Vision*, p. 279.
23. Yeats, *Letters*, p. 661.
24. Ibid., p. 695.
25. Yeats, *On the Boiler*, p. 26.
26. Yeats, *Letters*, p. 656.
27. Ibid., p. 808.
28. Ibid., p. 837.
29. Ibid., p. 805.
30. Menon, *The Development of W. B. Yeats*, p. 91.
31. Yeats, *On the Boiler*, p. 20.
32. Yeats, *A Vision*, p. 290.
33. Yeats, *Letters*, p. 812.
34. Yeats, *A Vision*, p. 263.
35. Ibid., p. 277.
36. Yeats, *Letters*, p. 693.
37. Ibid., p. 812.
38. Yeats, *Letters*, p. 667.
39. Ibid., p. 534.

40. Yeats, *Autobiographies,* p. 514.
41. Raymond Williams, *Observer,* May 21st, 1961.

Chapter II

1. Lewis, *Rude Assignment,* p. 10.
2. Lewis, *Time and Western Man,* p. 42.
3. Lewis, *Art of Being Ruled,* p. 180.
4. Lewis, *Monstre Gai,* p. 17.
5. Lewis, *One Way Song,* p. 75.
6. Lewis, *Apes of God,* p. 285.
7. Ibid., p. 261.
8. Lewis, *Time and Western Man,* p. 365.
9. Lewis, *Rude Assignment,* p. 64.
10. Lewis, *Time and Western Man,* p. 42.
11. Ibid., p. 135.
12. Lewis, *The Demon of Progress in the Arts,* p. 54.
13. Lewis, *One Way Song,* p. 72.
14. Ibid., p. 41.
15. Ibid., p. 62.
16. Lewis, *Rude Assignment,* p. 101.
17. Lewis, *The Diabolical Principle,* p. 163.
18. Lewis, *Time and Western Man,* p. 26.
19. Lewis, *Rude Assignment,* p. 40.
20. Lewis, *Art of Being Ruled,* p. 391.
21. Lewis, *Time and Western Man,* p. 164.
22. Ibid., p. 292.
23. Lewis, *Art of Being Ruled,* p. 260.
24. Ibid., p. 406.
25. Lewis, *The Demon of Progress in the Arts,* p. 22.
26. Lewis, *Time and Western Man,* p. 456.
27. Lewis, *America and Cosmic Man,* p. 50.
28. Lewis, *Time and Western Man,* p. 132.
29. Lewis, *Rude Assignment,* p. 170.
30. Lewis, *Art of Being Ruled,* p. 63.
31. Ibid., p. 180.
32. Lewis, *Monstre Gai,* p. 18.
33. Ibid., p. 34.
34. Ibid., pp. 142–43.
35. Lewis, *Rude Assignment,* p. 188.
36. Lewis, *Time and Western Man,* p. 226.
37. Lewis, *Rude Assignment,* p. 221.
38. Lewis, *Time and Western Man,* p. 129.
39. Ibid., p. 352.
40. Lewis, *Art of Being Ruled,* p. 386.

41. Lewis, *The Demon of Progress in the Arts*, p. 23.
42. Lewis, *Art of Being Ruled*, p. 403.
43. Lewis, *Time and Western Man*, p. 186.
44. Ibid., p. 156.
45. Lewis, *Art of Being Ruled*, p. 168.
46. Ibid., p. 135.
47. Lewis, *Rude Assignment*, p. 53.
48. Lewis, *Art of Being Ruled*, p. 39.
49. Lewis, *Time and Western Man*, p. 366.
50. Lewis, *Childermass*, p. 283.
51. Lewis, *Time and Western Man*, p. 365.
52. Lewis, *Paleface*, p. 77.
53. Lewis, *Art of Being Ruled*, p. 421.
54. Lewis, *The Lion and the Fox*, p. 288.
55. Lewis, *Art of Being Ruled*, p. 421.
56. Ibid., p. 434.
57. Ibid., p. 73.
58. Ibid., p. 97.
59. Ibid., p. 99.
60. Ibid., p. 180.
61. Ibid., p. 228.
62. Ibid., pp. 370–71.
63. Ibid., p. 374.
64. Ibid., p. 230.
65. Lewis, *Time and Western Man*, p. 382.
66. Lewis, *Art of Being Ruled*, p. 49.
67. Lewis, *Time and Western Man*, p. 231.
68. Lewis, *Art of Being Ruled*, p. 177.
69. Ibid., p. 423.
70. Lewis, *Monstre Gai*, p. 166.
71. Lewis, *Art of Being Ruled*, p. 420.
72. Ibid., p. 432.
73. Lewis, *The Demon of Progress in the Arts*, p. 80.
74. Lewis, *Art of Being Ruled*, p. 399.
75. Lewis, *The Demon of Progress in the Arts*, p. 83.
76. Ibid., p. 97.

Chapter III

1. Pound, *Letters*, pp. 342–43.
2. Pound, *ABC of Economics*, p. 41.
3. Pound, *Letters*, p. 343.
4. Pound, *Jefferson and/or Mussolini*, p. 22.
5. Pound, *Letters*, p. 346.
6. Ibid., p. 332.

7. Pound, *Letters*, p. 330.
8. Pound, *ABC of Economics*, p. 69.
9. Pound, *Letters*, p. 371.
10. Ibid., p. 90.
11. Pound, *ABC of Economics*, p. 121.
12. Pound, *Letters*, p. 394.
13. Van Gogh, *Further Letters to his Brother. 1886–1889.* Letter 543.
14. Pound, *Patria Mia*, p. 24.
15. Pound, *Jefferson and/or Mussolini*, p. 270.
16. Pound, *Guide to Kulchur*, p. 157.
17. Pound, *Jefferson and/or Mussolini*, p. 103.
18. Pound, *ABC of Economics*, p. 16.
19. Pound, *Jefferson and/or Mussolini*, p. 104.
20. Ibid., p. 110.
21. Ibid., p. 126.
22. Pound, *Guide to Kulchur*, p. 144.
23. Ibid., p. 249.
24. Pound, *Patria Mia*, p. 62.
25. Pound, *Polite Essays*, p. 55.
26. Pound, *Make it New*, p. 19.
27. Pound, *Guide to Kulchur*, p. 109.
28. Ibid., p. 243.
29. Pound, *ABC of Economics*, p. 62.
30. Pound, *Letters*, p. 317.

Chapter IV

1. Fraser, *Vision and Rhetoric*, p. 111.
2. Eliot, *After Strange Gods*, p. 19.
3. Eliot, *Notes towards the Definition of Culture*, p. 19.
4. Williams, *Culture and Society*, p. 147.
5. Eliot, *Notes towards the Definition of Culture*, p. 18.
6. Ibid., p. 23.
7. Ibid., p. 48.
8. Ibid., pp. 106–107.
9. Ibid., p. 107.
10. Ibid., p. 16.

Chapter V

1. Lawrence, *Fantasia of the Unconscious*, p. 11.
2. Murry, *Son of Woman*, p. 172.
3. Lawrence, *Letters*, p. 233.
4. Lawrence, *Fantasia of the Unconscious*, p. 10.
5. Lawrence, *Letters*, p. 250.

6. Lawrence, *Letters*, p. 582.
7. Ibid., p. 319.
8. Ibid., p. 325.
9. Lawrence, *Kangaroo*, p. 216.
10. Lawrence, *Apocalypse*, p. 83.
11. Lawrence, *Psychoanalysis and the Unconscious*, p. 31.
12. Lawrence, *The Plumed Serpent*, p. 270.
13. Lawrence, *Letters*, p. 836.
14. Ibid., p. 327.
15. Lawrence, *Fantasia of the Unconscious*, p. 98.
16. Ibid., p. 99.
17. Lawrence, *Apocalypse*, p. 24.
18. Lawrence, *Psychoanalysis and the Unconscious*, pp. 115–16.
19. Lawrence, *The Rainbow*, p. 351.
20. Lawrence, *Psychoanalysis and the Unconscious*, p. 32.
21. Lawrence, *Fantasia of the Unconscious*, pp. 154–55.
22. Ibid., p. 121.
23. Ibid., p. 99.
24. Lawrence, *Sex, Literature and Censorship*, p. 215.
25. Lawrence, *Fantasia of the Unconscious*, p. 98.
26. Lawrence, *A Propos of "Lady Chatterley's Lover"*, pp. 260–61.
27. Lawrence, *Fantasia of the Unconscious*, p. 84.
28. Lawrence, *Apocalypse*, pp. 26–27.
29. Lawrence, *Selected Literary Criticism*, pp. 312–13.
30. Ibid., p. 313.
31. Ibid., p. 105.
32. Lawrence, *The Plumed Serpent*, p. 244.
33. Lawrence, *Fantasia of the Unconscious*, p. 68.
34. Ibid., p. 78.
35. Ibid., p. 68.
36. Ibid., p. 165.
37. Lawrence, *Letters*, pp. 361–62.
38. Ibid., p. 237.
39. Lawrence, *Selected Literary Criticism*, p. 120.
40. Ibid., p. 86.
41. Lawrence, *Letters*, p. 319.
42. Lawrence, *Selected Literary Criticism*, p. 236.
43. Lawrence, *Apocalypse*, p. 27.
44. Ibid., p. 34.
45. Russell, *Portraits from Memory*, p. 105.

Summing Up

1. P. Viereck, in *The Intellectuals* (de Huszar, ed.), p. 499.
2. G. Mann, in *The Intellectuals*, p. 466.

3. Pinson, *Modern Germany*, p. 502.
4. Ludwig, *The Germans*, p. 366.
5. Gilbert and Gott, *The Appeasers*, p. 46.
6. Taylor, *Origins of the Second World War*, p. 112.
7. Gollancz, *The Betrayal of the Left*, p. 26.
8. Seton-Watson, *Neither War Nor Peace*, p. 181.
9. Gilbert and Gott, *The Appeasers*, p. 23.
10. Pinson, *Modern Germany*, p. 493.
11. Gilbert and Gott, *The Appeasers*, p. 48.
12. M. Ascoli, in *The Intellectuals*, pp. 299–300.
13. Quoted by Williams in *Culture and Society*, p. 143.
14. Lawrence, *Fantasia of the Unconscious*, p. 104.
15. Butler, *Roots of National Socialism*, p. 289.
16. Myers, *England in the Late Middle Ages*, p. xi.
17. Ibid., p. 17.
18. Ibid., p. xiv.
19. Ibid., p. 73.
20. Russell, *History of Western Philosophy*, p. 100.
21. Trevelyan, *English Social History*, pp. 463–64.
22. Myers, *England in the Late Middle Ages*, p. xii.
23. Russell, *History of Western Philosophy*, p. 513.
24. Lewis, *Time and Western Man*, p. 42.
25. Bottomore, *Elites and Society*, p. 140.
26. Churchill, *Disagreements*, p. 256.
27. Russell, *History of Western Philosophy*, p. 819.
28. Spender, *Life and the Poet*, p. 51.

SELECTED BIBLIOGRAPHY

Albrecht-Carrié, R., *Italy from Napoleon to Mussolini*, Columbia U.P. (first published 1950), paperback ed., 1962.

Aldington, R., *Portrait of a Genius, but . . .*, Heinemann, London, 1950.

Artz, F. B., *Reaction and Revolution*, Harper and Row, New York, 1934.

Atkins, J., *George Orwell*, Calder, London, 1954.

Benda, J., *Belphégor*, Faber, London, 1929.

—— *La Trahison des Clercs* (tr. Aldington), Routledge, London, 1928.

Butler, R. D'Olier, *Roots of National Socialism*, Faber, London, 1941.

Carr, E. H., *The Twenty Years Crisis*, Macmillan, London, 1939.

Churchill, R. C., *Disagreements*, Secker and Warburg, London, 1950.

Cross, C., *Fascists in Britain*, Barrie and Rockliff, London, 1961.

Curtis, M., *Three Against the Third Republic*, Princeton U.P., 1959.

Daiches, D., *Critical Approaches to Literature*, Longmans, London, 1956.

—— *The Present Age*, Cresset Press, London, 1958.

Eliot, T. S., *After Strange Gods*, Faber, London, 1934.

—— *Collected Poems*, Faber, London, 1936.

—— *Four Quartets*, Faber, London, 1944.

—— *Idea of a Christian Society*, Faber, London, 1939.

—— *Murder in the Cathedral*, Faber, London, 1935.

—— *Notes Towards the Definition of Culture*, Faber, London, 1948.

—— *On Poetry and Poets*, Faber, London, 1957.

—— *The Family Reunion*, Faber, London, 1939.

—— *The Cocktail Party*, Faber, London, 1950.

—— *The Confidential Clerk*, Faber, London, 1954.

—— *The Elder Statesman*, Faber, London, 1959.

—— *Points of View*, Faber, London, 1941.

—— *Selected Essays*, Faber, London, 1951.

—— *The Use of Poetry and the Use of Criticism*, Faber, London, 1933.

—— Periodical—*The Criterion*, Editorial articles, 1922–38.

Ellmann, R., *The Identity of Yeats*, Macmillan, London, 1954.
—— *James Joyce*, O.U.P., New York, 1959.
Fraser, G. S., *Vision and Rhetoric*, Faber, London, 1959.
—— *Ezra Pound*. Oliver and Boyd, London, 1960.
Gardner, H., *The Art of T. S. Eliot*, Cresset Press, London, 1949.
Gibbon, M., *The Masterpiece and the Man*, Hart-Davis, London, 1959.
Gilbert, M. and Gott, R., *The Appeasers*, Weidenfeld and Nicolson, London, 1963.
Gollancz, V. (ed.), *The Betrayal of the Left*, Gollancz, London, 1941.
Graves, R. and Hodge, A., *The Long Weekend*, Faber, London, 1950 (first published 1940).
Hone, J., *The Life of W. B. Yeats*, Macmillan, London, 1942.
Hough, G., *The Dark Sun*, Duckworth, London, 1949.
—— *The Last Romantics*, Duckworth, London, 1949.
Hulme, T. E., *Speculations*, Routledge and Kegan Paul, London, 1924.
de Huszar, G. B. (ed.), *The Intellectuals*, Allen and Unwin, London, 1960.
James, H., "The Younger Generation," *Times Literary Supplement*, March 19th and April 2nd, 1914.
Keynes, J. M., *The Economic Consequences of the Peace*, Macmillan, London, 1919.
Knights, L. C., *Explorations*, Chatto and Windus, London, 1946.
Lawrence, D. H., *Aaron's Rod*, Heinemann, London, 1948 (first published 1922).
—— *A Propos of "Lady Chatterley's Lover"*, Secker and Warburg, London, 1941.
—— *Complete Poems*, Secker and Warburg, London, 1928.
—— *Complete Short Stories*, Heinemann, London, 1955.
—— *Apocalypse*, Martin Secker, London, 1932.
—— *England, My England*, Heinemann, London, 1924.
—— *Fantasia of the Unconscious*, Martin Secker, London, 1923.
—— *Kangaroo*, Heinemann, London, 1955 (first published 1923).
—— *Lady Chatterley's Lover*, Heinemann, London, 1958.
—— *Letters*, Heinemann, London, 1932.
—— *Movements in European History*, Oxford, 1925.
—— *The Plumed Serpent*, Heinemann, London, 1955 (first published 1926).
—— *Psychoanalysis and the Unconscious*, Heinemann, London, 1923.
—— *The Rainbow*, Heinemann, London, 1955 (first published 1915).
—— *Selected Literary Criticism*, Heinemann, London, 1955.
—— *Sons and Lovers*, Heinemann, London, 1955 (first published 1913).

Lawrence, D. H., *Studies in Classical American Literature*, Martin Secker, London, 1933.

—— *Women in Love*, Heinemann, London, 1955 (first published 1921).

Leavis, F. R., *For Continuity*, Minority Press, Cambridge, 1933.

—— *D. H. Lawrence*, Chatto and Windus, London, 1955.

Lewis, P. W., *America and Cosmic Man*, Nicholson and Watson, London, 1948.

—— *Apes of God*, Nash and Grayson, London, 1931.

—— *The Art of Being Ruled*, Harper, London, 1926.

—— *Childermass*, Methuen, London (first published 1928), 1956 ed.

—— *The Demon of Progress in the Arts*, Methuen, London, 1954.

—— *The Diabolical Principle and the Dithyrambic Spectator*, Chatto and Windus, London, 1931.

—— *Hitler*, Chatto and Windus, London, 1931.

—— *The Hitler Cult*, Dent, London, 1939.

—— *The Human Age*, Books 2 and 3 : *Monstre Gai* and *Malign Fiesta*, Methuen, London, 1955.

—— *Jews—Are they Human?*, Allen and Unwin, London, 1939.

—— *Left Wings Over Europe*, Cape, London, 1936.

—— *The Lion and the Fox*, Grant Richards, London, 1927.

—— *Men Without Art*, Cassell, London, 1934.

—— *One Way Song*, (first published Methuen, London, 1933), Faber, London, 1960 ed.

—— *Paleface*, Chatto and Windus, London, 1929.

—— *Revenge for Love*, Methuen, London (first published 1937), 1952 ed.

—— *Rotting Hill*, Methuen, London, 1951.

—— *Rude Assignment*, Hutchinson, London, 1950.

—— *Time and Western Man*, Chatto and Windus, London, 1927.

Ludwig, E., *The Germans*, Hamish Hamilton, London, 1942.

Maisky, I., *Who Helped Hitler?*, Hutchinson, London, 1964.

Menon, N., *The Development of W. B. Yeats*, Oliver and Boyd, Edinburgh, 1942.

Moore, G., *Ave, Salve, Vale* (3 vols.), Heinemann, London, 1937.

Mosca, G., *The Ruling Class*, McGraw-Hill, New York, 1939.

Mowat, C. L., *Britain Between the Wars*, Methuen, London, 1955.

Myers, A. R., *England in the Late Middle Ages*, Penguin, London, 1952.

Orwell, G., *Critical Essays*, Secker and Warburg, London, 1946.

Pareto, V., *The Mind and Society*, Cape, London, 1935.

Pinson, K. S., *Modern Germany*, Macmillan, New York, 1954.

Pound, E., *ABC of Economics*, Faber, London, 1938.

—— *Cantos*, Faber, London, 1954.

—— *Guide to Kulchur*, Faber, London, 1938.

Pound, E., *Letters* (ed. Paige), Faber, London, 1951.

—— *Make It New*, Faber, London, 1934.

—— *Patria Mia*, Seymour, Chicago, 1950.

—— *Pavannes and Divagations*, Owen, London, 1960.

—— *Polite Essays*, Faber, London, 1937.

—— *Rock Drill*, Faber, London, 1957.

—— *Thrones*, Faber, London, 1960.

Powys, J. C., *The Meaning of Culture*, Cape, London, 1930.

Routh, H. V., *Towards the Twentieth Century*, Cambridge, 1937.

Rowse, A. L., *The End of an Epoch*, Macmillan, London, 1948.

Russell, B., *History of Western Philosophy*, Allen and Unwin, London, 1955 (first published 1946).

—— *Portraits from Memory*, Allen and Unwin, London, 1956.

—— *Power: A New Social Analysis*, Allen and Unwin, London, 1938.

Seton-Watson, H., *Britain and the Dictators*, Cambridge, 1938.

—— *Neither War nor Peace*, Methuen, London, 1960.

Spender, S., *Life and the Poet*, Secker and Warburg, London, 1942.

Smith, D. M., *Italy*, University of Michigan Press, 1959.

Taylor, A. J. P., *From Napoleon to Stalin*, Hamish Hamilton, London, 1950.

—— *Origins of the Second World War*, Hamish Hamilton, London, 1961.

Trevelyan, G. M., *English Social History*, Longmans, London, 1946.

Williams, R., *Culture and Society*, Chatto and Windus, London, 1958.

Wood, N., *Communism and British Intellectuals*, Gollancz, London, 1959.

Yeats, W. B., *Autobiographies*, Macmillan, London, 1955.

—— *A Vision*, Macmillan, London, 1937.

—— *Collected Plays*, Macmillan, London, 1952.

—— *Collected Poems*, Macmillan, London, 1958.

—— *Essays and Introductions*, Macmillan, London, 1961.

—— *Letters* (ed. Wade), Hart-Davis, London, 1954.

—— *On the Boiler*, Cuala Press, Dublin, 1938.